Teaching About the Violent Past
Opportunities and Challenges for Teachers
in Conflict-Affected African Societies

Teaching About the Violent Past

Opportunities and Challenges for Teachers in Conflict-Affected African Societies

Line Kuppens and Justin Sheria Nfundiko

With additional contributions by
Louis-Gervais Adomon Anoma and Mary Kang'ethe

LEUVEN UNIVERSITY PRESS

Published with the support of the KU Leuven Fund for Fair Open Access, VLIR-UOS (2014-001-147), and UKRI Arts and Humanities Research Council, Justice and Memory Network (EdJAM) (project ref: AH/T007842/1, CFPSG0038)

Published in 2025 by Leuven University Press / Presses Universitaires de Louvain / Universitaire Pers Leuven. Minderbroedersstraat 4, B3000-Leuven (Belgium).

© Line Kuppens and Justin Sheria Nfundiko, 2025.
© chapter 7.1.1 (Kenya), Mary Wanjiru Kang'ethe, 2025.
© chapter 7.1.2 (Côte d'Ivoire), Louis-Gervais Adomon Anoma, 2025.

This book is published under a Creative Commons Attribution Non-Commercial Non-Derivative 4.0 International Licence. Further details about Creative Commons licenses are available at http://creativecommons.org/licenses/

Further details about Creative Commons licenses are available at http://creativecommons.org/licenses/
Attribution should include the following information:
Line Kuppens and Justin Sheria Nfundiko, *Teaching About the Violent Past: Opportunities and Challenges for Teachers in Conflict-Affected African Societies*. Leuven, Leuven University Press. (CC BY-NC-ND 4.0)

All figures are expressly excluded from the CC BY-NC-ND 4.0 licence covering the rest of this publication. Permission for reuse should be sought from the copyright holders.

All TDM (Text and Data Mining) rights are reserved.

ISBN 978 94 6270 472 5 (Paperback)
ISBN 978 94 6166 668 0 (ePDF)
ISBN 978 94 6166 669 7 (ePUB)
https://doi.org/10.11116/9789461666680
D/2025/1869/37
NUR: 847

Layout: Crius Group
Cover design: Daniel Benneworth-Gray
Cover illustration: Photo taken by Line Kuppens in Côte d'Ivoire.

To all teachers who lent their voices to this book and help building peace in and through their classrooms one day at a time

Contents

Preface	11
List of Abbreviations	15
Introduction	**17**
I.1. Research gaps and objectives	18
I.2. Case study contexts	21
I.3. Methodology	23
I.4. Outline of this book	27
Part 1. Theory & Concepts	**29**
Chapter 1. Reconciliation, memory and (peace) education	**31**
1.1. Conflict narratives	32
1.2. Challenging conflict narratives through transitional justice	34
1.3. Education as a subject & instrument of transitional justice	35
1.4. Direct peace education	37
1.5. Sociological time & societal 'ripeness'	39
1.6. Alternatives to direct peace education	41
1.7. Theory of change of direct peace education	43
Chapter 2. The risk-taking continuum 2.0	**47**
2.1. Curricular-instructional gatekeeping	48
2.2. The risk-taking continuum	50
2.3. Limitations of the risk-taking continuum	52
2.4. Alternative frameworks	55
2.5. Towards a risk-taking continuum 2.0: the conflict-history education framework	60
2.6. Using the conflict-history education framework	62

Part 2. Empirical evidence — 65

Chapter 3. Teaching about ethnic tensions in Kenya — 67
- 3.1. Ethnic tensions and violence in Kenya — 68
- 3.2. Education, conflict & peace — 72
  - *3.2.1. Kenya's education system* — 72
  - *3.2.2. Education & conflict* — 73
  - *3.2.3. Education & peace* — 74
- 3.3. Survey data — 76
- 3.4. Support for (in)direct peace education — 78
  - *3.4.1. Support for multicultural education* — 79
  - *3.4.2. Support for direct peace education* — 86
- 3.5. (Dis)comfort — 89
- 3.6. (In)competence: Stereotyping and ethnic favouritism in the classroom — 94
  - *3.6.1. Stereotyping in the classroom* — 94
  - *3.6.2. Ethnic favouritism in the classroom* — 99
- 3.7. Situating Kenyan teachers within the framework of conflict-history education — 102

Chapter 4. Teaching about the violent past in Côte d'Ivoire — 103
- 4.1. Conflict dynamics — 104
- 4.2. Education, conflict & peace — 107
  - *4.2.1. Côte d'Ivoire's educational system* — 107
  - *4.2.2. Education & conflict* — 108
  - *4.2.3. Education & peace* — 109
- 4.3. Survey data — 111
- 4.4. Support for (in)direct peace education — 114
  - *4.4.1. Support for indirect peace education* — 114
  - *4.4.2. Support for direct peace education* — 118
- 4.5. (Dis)comfort — 123
- 4.6. (In)competence — 129
  - *4.6.1. Focus on competing narratives of conflict* — 129
  - *4.6.2. Support for teacher training* — 137
- 4.7. Situating Ivorian teachers within the framework of conflict-history education — 137

Chapter 5. Teaching about ongoing violence in the eastern Democratic Republic of Congo   139
  5.1. Conflict dynamics   140
  5.2. Education, conflict & peace   142
      5.2.1. The Congolese education system   142
      5.2.2. Education & conflict   143
      5.2.3. Education & peace   144
  5.3. Survey data   147
  5.4. Support for (in)direct peace education   150
      5.4.1. Support for indirect peace education   150
      5.4.2. Support for direct peace education   154
  5.5. (Dis)comfort   157
  5.6. (In)competence   162
  5.7. Uprooted   165
      5.7.1. Background on 'Uprooted'   165
      5.7.2. Fostering critical design experts through 'Uprooted'   167
  5.8. Situating Congolese teachers within the framework of conflict-history education   170

Part 3. Conclusions & Policy recommendations   173

Chapter 6. Main findings and conclusions   175
  6.1. Situating teachers in terms of their support for direct peace education   176
  6.2. Explaining differences   182
  6.3. Teachers' professional development needs   183
  6.4. Limitations & future research directions   185

Chapter 7. Promoting critical design experts? Policy recommendations   191
  7.1. Reflections from the field   192
      7.1.1. Kenya: Mary Wanjiru Kang'ethe   193
      7.1.2. Côte d'Ivoire: Louis-Gervais Adomon Anoma   195
  7.2. Policy recommendations   198
  7.3. Teaching strategies   201
      7.3.1. Silent conversations   201
      7.3.2. Exploring the unknown   204
      7.3.3. Forum theatre   206

Appendix	209
Notes	213
References	215
Index	233

Preface

Reflecting on the fundamental question of whether to teach about the history of the post-election violence in Kenya, one of the teachers we interviewed shared the following metaphor: "When you drive a car, you have to use the side mirror, right? To look back and see where you are going (…) You have to look back and see if you are progressing" (history & government and KiSwahili teacher, 2016). In this book, we look back at violent conflicts in Kenya, Côte d'Ivoire, and the eastern provinces of the Democratic Republic of Congo (DR Congo) and reflect on teachers' openness to addressing those histories of violence and the aftermath in the classroom. Doing so, as the literature on peace education and related fields suggests, would promote reconciliation and intergroup understanding among future generations. Importantly, the following vignette from a Congolese teacher shows that young people growing up in these societies appear to be eager to learn more about their country's past:

> As I was about to begin my lesson on the history of conflicts in Europe from 1789 to 1945, I was surprised to find that the pupils had deleted the title from the blackboard [while I left an instant] and they replaced it with "The ongoing conflicts in the provinces of North and South Kivu in the DRC." (history teacher, Bukavu, 2024)

Other than presenting and interpreting the views of secondary school teachers on looking back on their respective countries' violent pasts in the classroom – what we call 'conflict-history education' or 'direct peace education'– writing this manuscript was an exercise in looking back on our own trajectories as researchers. Although we come from markedly different backgrounds, both of our journeys started as aspiring PhD candidates at the Centre for Research on Peace and Development (CRPD) of the University of Leuven (KU Leuven), Belgium, about ten years ago. At that time, Line, a freshly graduated student in International Relations, had not yet been to Kenya, Côte d'Ivoire, or DR Congo; nor did she have any background in educational sciences or experience as a teacher. Justin, for his part, grew up amidst Congo's insecurity and had been working as a lecturer in sociology at the Official University of Bukavu (UOB – *Université Officielle de Bukavu*) prior to starting his PhD. Neither had children.

By the time we completed this book, the countries we studied had changed, and so had we. To start, the research we conducted changed us. The many interactions we had with secondary school teachers, but also teacher trainers and secondary school students in Nairobi, Abidjan, Bouaké, Bukavu, Goma and beyond opened our eyes to the challenges teachers face almost daily in their classrooms, not only when it comes to teaching about sensitive issues, but also in ensuring learning in societies that are resource-constrained and poverty-stricken where a salary cannot be taken for granted and having a job on the side is not exceptional. Precisely against this backdrop, our respect for the role of teachers never faltered, if anything it deepened, because of their clear commitment to educating the youth of Kenya, Côte d'Ivoire, and DR Congo. Day in and day out, teachers showed up and prepared their lessons to the best of their abilities. Many, our results show, were even willing to go the extra mile to unlock the reconciliatory potential of education. While the post-conflict environment became and remained stable in Côte d'Ivoire and Kenya ever since large-scale fighting ended, eastern DR Congo remained mired in insecurity throughout our research to the point that open fighting resumed as we finalized this book, threatening the safety not only of the teachers we had been working with and their students, but also of Justin.

At the individual level, we completed our PhDs and became teachers ourselves. Although teaching at university rather than at secondary school, we are both teaching about peace and conflict now. For Justin this includes teaching about the history of conflict in his own society in courses such as 'Peace Processes and Conflict Management in the DR Congo' and the 'Politics of Education in the DR Congo'. This is not the case for Line. However, amidst violently repressed student demonstrations in support of Gaza and a university policy that *de facto* promoted silence in the name of social safety (Lopes Cardozo et al., forthcoming), she experienced the difficulties many of the teachers in this book described when considering whether, and if so how, to teach about violence as it unfolded in the early months after October 7, 2023. Last but definitely not least, we both became parents. Our children not only deepened our commitment to reconciling societies and a more peaceful world more generally, but also changed our expectations regarding the role of education and our idea of the teachers we want our children to have. So, instead of observers, we became implicated subjects in our field of research. We hope for the better of the results we present.

While drafting this manuscript, we never managed to shed the tension we felt between the realities of being a teacher in Kenya, Côte d'Ivoire, or DR Congo and "the teachers we want". Particularly in the aftermath of violent conflict, we continuously pondered: are we asking too much of too few, too soon? For readers hoping for a clear response, this book does not provide it. We suspect that there is no straightforward answer. Yes, it's a lot to ask of secondary school teachers to teach about their own history of conflict. But, no, many teachers appeared not to think of it as "too much". No, teachers cannot be expected to tackle societal challenges such as reconciliation on their own. But they do constitute a relatively large pool with a great reach in society, beyond that of many other initiatives of transitional justice such as truth commissions. Yes, it may be too soon to teach about the past while the wounds are still fresh, but similarly, it may be too late once the wounds have started to fester. Because of its inherent complexities, we stand by the book's main premise that the time for teaching about the history of conflict is 'ripe' when the teachers in conflict-affected societies are ready for it.

Finally, as we look back to how this book came into being and to the road we travelled as researchers, teachers and parents, we cannot but be grateful to all of those around us who helped us along the way. The seeds for this book were sown and carefully given room to grow by our joint supervisor and CRPD director, Prof. Arnim Langer. Our growth was further spurred by our other colleagues at CRPD, Dr. Leila Demarest, Dr. Tarila Marclint Ebiede, Dr. Maarten Schroyens, Ms. Alliance Kubota Mango, Dr. Anton Abdul Fatah and Dr. Amélie Godefroidt. Special thanks go to Dr. Sulley Ibrahim, who jointly conducted research in Kenya, the members of our respective doctoral commissions, in particular Prof. Germano Mwabu and Prof. Paul Kadundu, as well as to Ingrid De Wachter without whom conducting our research would have been an administrative nightmare. In Côte d'Ivoire, the assistance of Dr. Pulchérie Doffou was exceptional. Line is also grateful for the support of Dr. Alexis Koffi, Mr. Lars Vanreppellen, and Las, Clé, and Yacou. In Kenya, our thanks go to James and in DR Congo, we could count on the stellar support of Mr. Emmanuel Akonkwa Nfizi. Further along the academic career path, we are grateful to our colleagues at the Catholic University of Bukavu, the UOB, and at the University of Amsterdam for their trust in us and for the space they gave us to write this manuscript. A book cannot be published without a publisher. We are indebted to Mirjam Truwant, Anne Vandezande, and Beatrice Van Eeghem of the Leuven University Press for their trust and patience, to Isobel Robson for language editing, as well as to the reviewers of our manuscript for their excellent feedback. For giving our visuals a new look, we give a shout-out to Stefano Quadrini, and for backing our project financially, we want to thank VLIR-UOS, the KU Leuven Open Access Fund and the AHRC and GCRF-funded Education, Justice and Memory (EdJAM) Network. Nonetheless, our most heartfelt thanks go to all the secondary school teachers, teacher trainers and secondary school students who took part in our research. It extends to Louis-Gervais Adomon Anoma and Mary Wanjiru Kang'ethe who lent our manuscript their critical eye and added a much-needed practitioners' view. We dedicate this book to everyone who gave their voice to this book. Finally, we want to thank our families for standing with us along the way, and our children for making us see the world, and our research, in new ways.

List of Abbreviations

AFDL	*Alliance des Forces Démocratiques pour la Libération du Congo-Zaïre* (Alliance of Democratic Forces for the Liberation of Congo-Zaire)
CDVR	*Commission de Dialogue, Vérité et Reconciliation* (Dialogue, Truth and Reconciliation Commission)
CoP	Community of Practice
CRPD	Centre for Research on Peace and Development
DR Congo	Democratic Republic of Congo
ECM	*Education Civique et Morale* (Civic and Moral Education)
EDHC	*Education aux Droits de l'Homme et à la Citoyenneté* (Human Rights and Civic Education)
EdJAM	Education, Justice and Memory Network
EEPCT	Education in Emergencies and Post-Crisis Transition
FESCI	*Fédération Estudiantine et Scolaire de Côte d'Ivoire* (Student Federation of Côte d'Ivoire)
FGD	Focus group discussion
FHB	Felix Houphouët-Boigny
FPI	*Front populaire ivoirien* (Ivorian popular front)
ISP	*Institut Supérieur Pédagogique* (Higher Pedagogical Institute)
KANU	Kenyan African National Union
KICD	Kenya Institute for Curriculum Development
KCPE	Kenyan Certificate of Primary Education
KCSE	Kenyan Certificate of Secondary Education
M23	*Mouvement du 23 Mars* (March 23rd movement)
NARC	National Rainbow Coalition
NGO	Non-Governmental Organisation
PDCI	*Parti démocratique de Côte d'Ivoire* (Democratic party of Côte d'Ivoire)
PEP	Peace Education Programme
PEPT	Education for Peace and Tolerance
RDR	*Rassemblement des républicains* (Republican rassembly)
SEM	Structural Equation Model

TPD	Teacher Professional Development
TSC	Teacher Service Commission
UN	United Nations
UNHCR	United Nations High Commissioner for Refugees
UNICEF	United Nations Children's Fund
UOB	*Université Officielle de Bukavu* (Official University of Bukavu)

Introduction

> If education is to have a sustainable peacebuilding impact, then it will have to be driven by those individuals and groups within war-torn, war-born, and war-threatened societies themselves. (Bush & Saltarelli, 2000, p. 27)

Although education alone cannot fulfil the promise of a sustainable peace, "it can lay some foundations for future change" (Davies, 2017, p. 336). Being compulsory and endowed with the legitimacy and resources to instruct future generations, the school system constitutes a major avenue for teaching 'peace' at a crucial moment in the political socialization process of children and youth (Bar-Tal & Rosen, 2009; see also Bar-Tal, 2002; Bar-Tal et al., 2010; Galston, 2001; Sapiro, 2004). In conflict-affected societies in particular, 'peace education' can help to promote rapprochement between groups (previously) in conflict (Bellino et al., 2017; Cole, 2007; Cole & Barsalou, 2006; Gellmann, 2015; Ramírez-Barat & Duthie, 2015). Whereas peace education is oftentimes used as a catchall term for educational programmes oriented towards creating a peaceful and non-violent society, in this book we focus on peace education that takes place in conflict-affected societies and aims at addressing the core of a conflict, including the history of a conflict and the representation of the rival(s), to replace the fear and hatred felt towards 'the other' while hoping for a better, shared future (Bar-Tal et al., 2010, p. 32). Critically, this would require current and future generations to look back on their country's past conflict and human rights abuses to prevent their future recurrence (Davies, 2017; see also Salomon & Nevo, 2005; Yogev, 2012). Teaching conflict history would help to mediate and contextualize the selective and uncritical knowledge about past conflict that young people have or are at risk of developing in the absence of such teaching (Barton & McCully, 2005; Paulson, 2015). For "it is only in a didactically prepared setting and in rational exchange that young people gain the capacity to critically reflect on, and perhaps question prevalent interpretations of history" (Lässig, 2013, p. 13; see also Pingel, 2008).

Notably, truth commission reports can provide a useful and important lens to teach about conflict history, as the cases of Guatemala (Oglesby, 2004), South Africa (Bentrovato & Wassermann, 2018; Tibbitts & Weldon,

2017) and Sierra Leone (Paulson, 2006) prove. Yet most educational curricula from post-conflict countries still exclude any significant reference to the country's histories of collective violence (Bentrovato, 2017; De Baets, 2015; Paulson, 2015). Whether or not any violent pasts are integrated in school curricula tends to be decided 'from above' or 'from outside' (Horner et al., 2015; Kuppens & Langer, 2018). Driven by a desire to achieve results as quickly as possible, non-governmental organizations (NGOs) and foreign donors typically set up projects with national ministries of education to implement peace education programmes whose intervention approaches do not (sufficiently) take into account the local context and its actors (Barakat et al., 2013; Higgins & Novelli, 2018; Pingel, 2008; Wessels, 2013). Teachers, in particular, are rarely genuinely consulted as stakeholders in conflict-educational curricular reforms. Research from Israel (Goldberg, 2017) to Sierra Leone and Liberia (Shepler & Williams, 2017), and from Ukraine (Korostelina, 2015) to Estonia (Kello & Wagner, 2017) nonetheless shows that teachers have diverging opinions when it comes to teaching about violent pasts, which inform their teaching practices in the classroom. At one end of the spectrum, there are teachers who may oppose the integration of their country's conflict history by resisting the implementation of new curricula or by subverting its message in contexts in which such content is integrated. Their reasons may vary from outward opposition because of political beliefs, to fears of raking up sociopolitical tensions or of reviving students' painful and traumatic experiences. At the other end, there are teachers who may experience the need to promote reconciliation and learn from the past, even when it is not officially included in the curriculum. Between these two ends, there are teachers who have different preferences and practices regarding teaching about violent pasts. To paraphrase Bush and Saltarelli (2000), if teaching conflict history is to have a sustainable impact on reconciliation, it will have to be supported by *teachers* within war-torn, war-born, and war-threatened societies themselves. In other words, besides support 'from above' and 'from outside', support 'from below' is crucial.

I.1. Research gaps and objectives

In this book, we are interested in secondary school teachers' support for teaching conflict history; secondary schooling constituting a crucial period in adolescents' sociopolitical socialization (Neundorf & Smets, 2017;

Sapiro, 2004). In addition, we aim to deepen our understanding of the realities, needs and capacities of teachers and their confidence and competence to take on the responsibility of moving reconciliation forward in their own classrooms. While our book is not the first to ponder these issues, we identify three important shortcomings in the existing research.

First, the academic field of peace education is characterized by a dearth of systematic empirical research that looks at teacher populations *at large*. Most recent studies tend to be qualitative in nature (for exceptions, see Zembylas et al., 2016; Fatah et al., 2023). While these qualitative studies have greatly advanced our understanding of the challenges and opportunities related to teaching about the history of conflict in post-conflict societies from the perspective of secondary school teachers, qualitative case studies only use small sample sizes and do not allow the exploration of the traits and circumstances that influence the position of teachers. Consequently, many aspects like the differences in the position of teachers, and the factors that explain these differences, remain unexplored. To the best of our knowledge, existing studies also don't use standardized measures to examine the position of teachers. Without common measures, it is difficult to assess how the support for teaching about violent pasts varies across contexts and over time.

Second, and in a related manner, few studies on the perceptions and practices of teachers dealing with violent pasts use a common theoretical framework. By way of illustration, we present the 'risk-taking continuum' of Kitson and McCully (2005) in chapter two, which categorizes the various strategies teachers may adopt when addressing the history of conflict. The continuum ranges from complete avoidance of the relevant sections of the curriculum to dealing constructively with that past. Despite its analytical value, this framework has been underutilized as an analytical lens in subsequent research on teaching about violent pasts (for an exception, see Fatah et al., 2023). In this book, we use their framework as a starting point and adapt it based on other models and insights from both older and more recent studies. We hope it can guide future studies and enable more comparative perspectives. In addition to an analytical heuristic, we also propose to use the adapted framework in the professional development of teachers who want to teach about past conflicts to encourage self-reflection and capacity building.

Third, research on teaching conflict history and on peace education more generally, has been largely concentrated on selected conflict-affected geographical contexts, which include Israel (e.g. Bar-Tal et al., 2010; Bekerman, 2007; 2009; Salomon, 2004), Northern Ireland (e.g. Gallagher, 2010; Niens, 2009), Bosnia and Herzegovina (Danesh, 2007; 2010; Hromadzic, 2009) and Sri Lanka (Davies, 2004; 2017). So far, sub-Saharan Africa remains largely underexposed, apart from Rwanda (e.g. Bentravato, 2016; Freedman et al., 2008; Rubagiza et al., 2016; Russell, 2019) and South Africa (e.g., Christie, 2009; Dryden-Peterson & Robinson, 2023; Weldon, 2010). Nearly 75% of African countries have nonetheless been marked by violent internal conflict since gaining independence in the 1960s or 1970s (Demarest & Langer, 2018, p. 344). While anticolonial liberation wars were the dominant type of conflict in the aftermath of World War II, nowadays it is internal conflict that wreaks havoc in multiple African countries, resulting from flawed democratic transitions, widespread poverty, corruption and poor governance, and/or the presence of severe group-based inequalities (Demarest & Langer, 2018). Still, many countries in the sub-Saharan African region have experimented with peace education programmes (see Robiolle-Moul, 2013). It is therefore highly interesting to concentrate more on sub-Saharan Africa in peace education research, and specifically on teaching conflict history.

To address these research gaps, this book will explore:
1. Secondary school teachers' positions and strategies in African post-conflict societies towards critically and constructively engaging with the history of conflict in their own country with their students from multiple perspectives, using an adapted version of Kitson and McCully's (2005) risk-taking continuum as an analytical framework;
2. Individual traits, beliefs and experiences that explain differences in teachers' attitudes regarding teaching conflict history, and;
3. The perceived needs of secondary school teachers' to gain the confidence and acquire the skills required to take on the responsibility of promoting reconciliation in their own classrooms.

By examining the role of secondary school teachers and the circumstances and preconditions in which they can pursue reconciliation, we not only aim to fill the above-mentioned academic voids, but we also aim to develop and formulate a range of actionable policy recommendations for international and local policymakers, as well as propose teaching strategies that can support teachers in the classrooms of conflict-affected countries within and beyond sub-Saharan Africa in dealing with the legacies of violence. To this end, we collaborated with two experienced practitioners of peace education in Africa, who share their critical reflections in the final chapter. We will also offer a set of teaching strategies that will allow interested teachers to teach about violent pasts from multiple perspectives. We therefore hope that our readership will not only include students and scholars but also education officials, teachers and other relevant parties with an interest in the role of education in the process of reconciliation and in peacebuilding generally.

I.2.   Case study contexts

To gain original insights into the role of teachers in societies transitioning from war to peace, this book presents a comprehensive and comparative analysis of the support that secondary school teachers in Kenya, Côte d'Ivoire, and the Kivu provinces (North and South Kivu) of the Democratic Republic of Congo (DR Congo) offer to address their country's conflict histories and legacies in the classroom.

These three fundamental case studies are characterized by a history of tensions and violence between opposing ethnic and/or religious groups, even though other conflict dynamics play at the local and global level.

In Kenya, where ethnicity is heavily politicized, ethnic clashes in the aftermath of the disputed 2007-2008 presidential elections caused the death of at least 1,000 people. Since the mid-1990s, political elites in Côte d'Ivoire have frequently used ethnicity and religion to mobilize political support; at times this has led to severe tensions as well as a violent intrastate conflict from September 2002 to March 2007 and the post-electoral crisis of 2010-2011 (e.g. Langer, 2005; McGovern, 2011; Bouquet, 2007; 2011). In eastern DR Congo, large-scale violence erupted in the aftermath of the Rwandan genocide when large numbers of Hutu genocidaires took refuge in the country. The fighting first involved Hutu refugees against Tutsi living in the DR Congo, but soon gained in magnitude and complexity turning into what came to be known as Africa's World War (Verweijen, 2015).

While all three countries have faced severe violence between identity-based groups, there are important differences in the degree of violence experienced, the duration of the conflict, the number of actors involved, and the nature of peacetime stability. Since their episodes of post-electoral violence ended, conflict did not re-emerge neither in Kenya, nor in Côte d'Ivoire. But the degree of post-electoral violence and its antecedents differed fundamentally in both contexts. In contrast to Côte d'Ivoire, for instance, past violence in Kenya has been less widespread and mainly clustered around election times (Branch, 2011; Hornsby, 2013). Of these three countries, however, the exposure to violence has been the highest and longest in the Kivu provinces. In the relatively less violent periods between the official end of hostilities in 2003 and upsurges in violence due to advances of the rebel movement M23 in 2012 and 2022, inter-ethnic conflicts persisted and armed groups proliferated as they competed over the region's vast mineral resources. Conflict thus became an end in itself, blurring the distinction between self-defence and self-enrichment (Stearns, 2022). It follows that the extent and degree to which teachers (and students) have been exposed to conflict ideologies and have experienced violence varies significantly from case study to case study and could explain some important differences in the attitudes of teachers towards teaching conflict history. Another reason these countries were selected for case studies, was that the teachers of those countries are temporally more or less removed from their respective histories of conflict. Amidst ongoing tensions, the attitudes of Congolese teachers might differ significantly from those of teachers in Côte d'Ivoire and Kenya who have experienced relative tranquillity in the last decade. Whereas the mere passage of time could have some impact, we argue that *sociological* time vitally shapes teachers' support. Sociological time revolves around the everyday interactions of non-elites within cultural, social, and economic settings, and helps us to understand how groups, as a collective, need time to grieve before they are ready to forgive, if ever (MacGinty, 2016; 2022). It is influenced by political time (i.e., election dates, truth commissions, etc.), which can promote an environment conducive to societal change by 'ripening' the individual's, in this case the teacher's, willingness to address and confront the violent past.

Finally, because of their roots in colonial-era structures, there are important differences between the case study contexts when it comes to the governance and structure of education. For instance, while confessional schools constitute the majority in DR Congo, they are few in Kenya and Côte d'Ivoire (André & Poncelet, 2013). Despite these differences, there are also such common features as the shared experience of schooling as a disciplinary institution – one that continues to shape school discipline and student-teacher relationships (Harber, 2019; Kalolo & Kapinga, 2023; Ocobock, 2012). Most importantly, in relation to the focus of this book, the selected countries are of interest because each has taken decidedly different approaches regarding the integration of the individual country's violent past and legacies within the respective school systems. While textbooks in Côte d'Ivoire generally have little or nothing on their violent history, the Congolese curriculum has incorporated key historical events, dates, and figures of conflict – although only up to 2006 (Nfundiko, 2020). Ten schools in Bukavu (South Kivu) are even experimenting with dedicated pedagogical materials to instruct students about the history of conflict in the Kivu provinces, a pilot project that we will reflect on in this book.

I.3. Methodology

This book employs a decidedly mixed-methods approach, combining the results of three large-N surveys with rich insights from in-depth interviews, focus group discussions (FGDs), curriculum analysis, and classroom observations. The main rationale behind the choice of a mixed-methods approach was to take an extensive approach to exploring teachers' positions and strategies and explaining differences in positions, while nonetheless providing room for teachers to elaborate upon their positions and motivations, and seek nuance. In all three research contexts, research permits were obtained from the relevant authorities at national and sub-national levels. All data has been collected in accordance with research ethics, ensuring informed consent on behalf of all participants, guaranteeing confidentiality, and minimizing harm. These issues are even more important in contexts of political and social instability, where teachers may fear that their expressed opinions could lead to repercussions from both administrative and political authorities.

The survey data was collected by a team of three principal investigators, who, at the time of data collection, were doctoral researchers, in secondary schools in the respective countries' and provinces' main cities, i.e., Nairobi (Kenya), Abidjan (Côte d'Ivoire), Bukavu (South Kivu, DR Congo), and Goma (North Kivu, DR Congo). By focussing on the respectively de-jure and de-facto capitals of Kenya, Côte d'Ivoire, and the Kivu provinces, we aimed to maximise ethnic and religious diversity at school. Nairobi and Abidjan were, moreover, the hotbeds of violence during the post-electoral crises, whereas Bukavu was the first major city in eastern DR Congo to come under rebel control in 1996, followed by Goma, from which the rebels operated between 1998 and 2004. Rebels from the M23 movement also assumed control of the city in 2012, and have recently closed in on both Goma and Bukavu again (IPIS, 2024; Mukwemulere, 2024).

The Ivorian survey was paper-based and administered between February and April 2015. The Kenyan and Congolese surveys were conducted on tablets using Qualtrics (Qualtrics LLC, Provo, UT) from May to June 2016 and from April to July 2018, respectively. In each context, schools were selected using randomized stratified sampling based upon a list of secondary schools obtained from the relevant educational authorities: after stratification by municipality or neighbourhood (accounting for population size), we sorted the list by type of school (government-funded, privately-funded, denominational where relevant), and by number of pupils and teachers per school. In total, we systematically selected 114 secondary schools in Bukavu and Goma, 77 schools in Abidjan, and 64 in Nairobi (see Table I.1). Although all teachers at the selected schools were invited to participate, only teachers who were present on the day of the school visit ultimately did so. If fewer than one-third of the teachers were available, the school was visited a second time. In total, 1,642 Congolese, 984 Ivorian and 925 Kenyan teachers participated in our surveys. Teachers who agreed to participate were surveyed on a wide range of topics including the place of peace and conflict in education, and their personal experiences with and views on conflict in their region. While the surveys bore similarities across contexts, the questionnaires were amended to reflect country-specific circumstances. To thank teachers for their participation and compensate them for their time, participating teachers received school supplies and beverages during the interviews or FGDs, or airtime once the survey had been completed. While these tokens were not questioned in the Ivorian and Kenyan contexts, some Congolese teachers – particularly in Goma – expected financial compensation. These expectations need to be understood in the context of the institutionalization of the humanitarian aid sector in eastern DR Congo (Mendenhall et al., 2022; Treveon, 2013).

Table I.1. School characteristics by survey

	Côte d'Ivoire (N=77)		Kenya (N=64)		DR Congo (N = 114)	
Type of school						
Public	4		24		6	
Private	71		40		78	
Confessional	2				30	
Neighbourhood	Abobo	21	Dagoretti	13	*Bukavu*	
	Adjamé	5	Embakasi	11	Ibanda	35
	Attécoubé	2	Lang'ata	8	Kadutu	16
	Cocody	8	Makadara	3	Bagira	15
	Koumasi	4	Kamukunji	3	*Goma*	16
	Marcory	4	Kasarani	8	Goma	32
	Plateau	1	Njiru	4	Karisimimbi	
	Port Bouët	4	Starehe	8		
	Treichville	1	Westlands	6		
	Yopougon	27				
Number of pupils	Min.= 14, Max.= 4990 M= 763.81 (SD = 774.25)		Min.= 21, Max.= 1500 M= 384.86 (SD = 390.23)		*Unknown*	
Number of teachers	Min. = 9, Max. = 145 M = 31.49 (SD = 21.44)		Min. = 5, Max. = 80 M = 21 (SD = 18.44)		M_{Bukavu} = 12.7 M_{Goma} = 19	
Notes	*The proportion of public schools is representative of the number of publicly-funded schools in Abidjan, which – though fewer – tend to be much larger than privately-funded schools.*		*Among the selected public schools, there are 5 national, 1 extra-county, 12 county, and 6 sub-county schools.*		*Due to the legacy of Belgian colonialism, confessional (denominational) schools are much more common in DR Congo than the other two case studies (see André & Poncelet, 2013).*	

In each context, the researchers also gathered qualitative data. In Côte d'Ivoire and DR Congo, a detailed qualitative analysis of the educational content and practices in secondary schools was conducted *prior* to the survey, comprising a thorough document and content analysis of the curriculum and classroom observations. In Abidjan and Bouaké – Côte d'Ivoire's second largest city and headquarters of the rebellion at the time of the civil war – secondary school classes were observed, focusing especially on human rights and citizenship education, history-geography, and French. In Bukavu, the second author attended courses at the Higher Pedagogical Institute for a period of 46 full days. In addition to the curriculum analysis and observations, FGDs were conducted with Ivorian and Congolese teachers. In the context of eastern DR Congo, this data was further complemented with insights from in-depth interviews of 90 secondary school teachers and 25 teacher trainers. The resulting insights were used to familiarise with and gain in-depth understanding of the Ivorian and Congolese contexts and to improve questionnaire design and survey conduct. In Kenya, by contrast, 68 in-depth interviews were conducted after the surveys to gain a deeper understanding of the answers provided. As in Côte d'Ivoire, secondary school classes were also observed and followed up by in-depth interviews. In addition to the data from the doctoral studies, we also include more recent qualitative data for the case study of the DR Congo. From June 2023 to July 2024, the authors were involved in a pilot study developing and testing educational materials on the history of conflict in the Kivu provinces. Throughout this process, we conducted four FGDs with a group of 20 history and civic education teachers.

Before proceeding it is important to acknowledge several limitations inherent in our methodology. First, the survey data was collected in the cities of Goma, Bukavu, Abidjan and Nairobi. While across all three country contexts, much of the violence was concentrated in these cities, and members of all ethnic and religious groups are still living together in these spaces, our data does not account for all spatial variations within each country. Illustratively, it may not be possible to apply the findings among teachers from Abidjan to teachers from Bouaké, whose experiences of the 2002-2007 civil war and 2010-2011 post-electoral crisis vary substantially. Also, until recently, insecurity in the Kivu provinces was predominantly a rural rather than an urban problem. The positions and strategies adopted by the teachers who participated in our study to deal with the violent past in Goma and Bukavu could therefore be different from those of their peers in the rural areas.

Second, our data are only a snapshot. Not only have the country contexts changed since the data was collected, more generally a considerable amount of time has passed (with the exception of the latest data from the DR Congo, which was collected during the re-emergence of the M23, but prior to the movement taking control of the Kivu provinces in early 2025). Our findings should therefore be interpreted in their historical context, and it is important to be aware that the readiness of teachers to deal with the violent past in the classroom may have changed since our data was collected – in either direction.

Third, all data had already been described, presented and interpreted in the context of doctoral research and published in various research outlets (e.g. Fatah et al., 2023; Kuppens, 2018; Kuppens & Langer, 2016a; 2016b; 2018; 2019; 2020; 2022; 2023; Kuppens et al., 2018; Nfundiko, 2020; Nfundiko et al., 2025). Although some ideas had been introduced earlier, we nonetheless reinterpret the data using a new framework that was developed specifically for this book. A downside is that measures and interview questions were not designed in full accordance with this framework, which is why we evaluate our measures in the final chapters and put forward new ones to facilitate future research.

I.4. Outline of this book

The book is divided into three main parts. The first part lays the theoretical foundation, the second part examines empirical case studies, and the third part discusses implications and future directions for research, and furthermore formulates policy recommendations and suggests teaching strategies.

The first part consists of two chapters. Chapter 1 'Reconciliation, memory and (peace) education' sets the scene for the book. We discuss how different interpretations about past events present a challenge to reconciliation in conflict-affected countries and we describe how meaningful linkages can be created between transitional justice and education. Next, chapter 2 'The risk-taking continuum 2.0' outlines the theoretical framework and conceptual tools necessary for interpreting the empirical data presented in part two.

The case study chapters of part two are organized by country and the data is presented in order of the degree of violence that was experienced, starting with Kenya and ending with eastern DR Congo. Each country chapter starts by outlining the particular conflict dynamics and current conditions, the structure of the education system, and the nature of the data that was collected. Subsequently, we examine teachers' support for addressing the violent past in their classrooms in each of these contexts. Then, the focus varies depending on the chapter. In chapter 3 'Teaching about ethnic tensions in Kenya', we examine teachers' intergroup attitudes because of the legacies of the politicization of ethnicity. In the context of Côte d'Ivoire (chapter 4 'Teaching about the violent past in Côte d'Ivoire'), we zoom in on teachers' own reading of the past, and discuss how this affects their readiness to teach conflict history. Chapter 5 deals with the pedagogical skills and attitudes of teachers towards corporal punishment in 'Teaching about ongoing conflict in the Democratic Republic of Congo'. This chapter also includes an additional section on the experiences of teachers with the teaching materials of the 'Uprooted' project, dedicated to assist teachers in teaching about the violent past and piloted in ten schools in and around Bukavu.

In the final part, we start by synthesizing the findings from the case studies, identifying patterns and differences (Chapter 6). We also discuss how these findings might relate to other conflict-affected societies in Africa and beyond, and reflect on the analytical value of our theoretical framework. We also present new measures that future studies could use to implement the framework. And finally, two experienced practitioners from Kenya and Côte d'Ivoire were so kind to critically reflect on our findings (Chapter 7), and share their main takeaways for policymaking on the role of education in promoting reconciliation in Africa. We conclude this final chapter with a set of policy recommendations for teaching conflict history in (post-)conflict societies, and suggest a number of teaching strategies that teachers could experiment with if they want to engage constructively with the reconciliatory potential of education.

PART 1
Theory & Concepts

CHAPTER 1

Reconciliation, memory and (peace) education

> ... all wars are fought twice, the first time on the battlefield, the second time in memory. (Viet Thanh Nguyen, Nothing Ever Dies, 2016, p. 4)

> ...unless young people can analyse the roots of conflict and prevent these roots from regrowing into branches later on, any peace will be fragile. (Davies, 2011, p. 45, in Lopes Cardozo & Hoeks, 2014, p. 68)

Creating a shared future out of a divided past is perhaps the most challenging of all post-conflict issues (Bloomfield et al., 2003). The impact of conflict is long-lasting and deeply intertwined with emotions and identity-related attitudes. Understanding what caused division and how it was exacerbated by conflict is crucial in this respect. However, individuals and communities previously in conflict with each other typically interpret their joint past in markedly different ways (see also Barkan, 2015; Bar-Tal et al., 2014; Ross, 2001; Sanchez-Meertens, 2013). Even though rival groups may to some extent agree on 'objective' facts and events that led to and/or occurred during the conflict, they tend to disagree on its main causes, culprits, and on the suffering caused (Bilali & Volhardt, 2019; Bloomfield et al., 2003). The divisive nature of these conflict narratives is further amplified by the concomitant negative attitudes, prejudices, and stereotypes about the "enemy" that group members developed in the run-up to and throughout the course of the conflict. These enduring collective memories of violence and related emotions stand in the way of promoting reconciliation. In the first sections of this chapter, we discuss why and how these narratives of conflict are created, and how they are transmitted across generations. We also briefly describe the role of transitional justice in transforming these divisive conflict memories into something that can bring about peaceful co-existence.

Formal education is both a subject and instrument of transitional justice (Keynes, 2019). On the one hand, schooling may reinforce conflict dynamics by denying some groups access to education in their mother tongue or by spreading stereotypical content. On the other hand, it can be a powerful tool in the reconciliation process of opposing groups. It can encourage emerging generations from all communities formerly in conflict to

> [accept] as legitimate the other's narrative and its specific implications; [be] willing to critically examine one's own group's actions toward the other group; [be] ready to experience and show empathy and trust toward the other; and [be] disposed to engage in nonviolent activities. (Salomon, 2002, p. 9; see also Salomon, 2004; 2006)

These objectives can arguably be achieved through what is commonly referred to as direct peace education (Bar-Tal & Rosen, 2009) or education *for* peace (Salomon, 2002). Throughout this book, we also refer to it as conflict-history education. It differs from indirect peace education, or education *about* peace, which does not address the core of conflict and aims at promoting peaceful attitudes and non-violent behaviours more generally. We elaborate on this distinction in the third section of this chapter, followed by a reflection on society's readiness to introduce one or the other in the aftermath of mass violence. As part of this process, we also reflect on the potential of citizenship, human rights, and multicultural education. And finally, we critically examine the fundamental assumption that the teaching practice of exploring multiple perspectives to shed light on past conflict dynamics will bring about intergroup empathy and contribute to the reconciliation process of formerly opposing groups.

1.1. Conflict narratives

To justify and sustain animosity and violence between identity-based groups, group elites construct so-called conflict narratives. Typically, these narratives trace back to the origins of a conflict and its course of development. In doing so, they indicate who is to be held accountable for the violence, which is (are) usually 'the other(s)'. At the same time, these narratives legitimize the actions of the ingroup, depicting themselves favourably, and deplore the group's suffering at the hands of 'the other(s)' (Bar-Tal & Salomon, 2006; Bilali & Ross, 2012; Kuppens & Langer, 2023). Conflict narratives can thus be understood as a form of collective memory of conflict, or the collectively shared social representations of the violent past (Bilali & Ross, 2012; Licata et al., 2007; Wertsch & Roediger, 2008). Throughout this book, we therefore use interchangeably the terms conflict narratives and collective memories of conflict. At times, we also simply use memories of conflict, thus referring to collective constructions of the past, rather than first-hand recollections of experiences during conflict. In doing so, we do not deny individual meaning-making, lived experiences and identity, but emphasize the importance of internalizing circulating discourses about the violent past and group identities which add social relevance to personal experiences and beliefs, and empower group members to translate private motivations into commitment for a collective cause (Sanchez-Meertens, 2013).

To fulfil its functions, each side's "historical" account tends to be biased and selective: ingroup victimization is magnified and outgroup suffering neglected; ingroup actors are heroes and outgroup actors are perpetrators. In this way, group narratives cultivate a culture of victimhood by the "enemy" (c.f., Bar-Tal et al., 2014; Ron & Maoz, 2013; Staub et al., 2010). Whether suffering took place in the recent or the distant past is often of secondary importance (Barkan, 2015). In South Africa, for instance, stories of victimhood experienced during the frontier wars of the 1800s and the Anglo-Boer war of 1899–1902, as well as black "terror acts" between 1961 and 1994, justified the Afrikaner hegemony under Apartheid. While, conversely, the discrimination of the Apartheid regime legitimized black and coloured South Africans' liberation struggle (Ahonen, 2013). Such narratives can extend to the field of education, whereby formerly advantaged groups tend to ignore pre-war inequalities that benefitted their group, in contrast to formerly disadvantaged groups. This is the case of the Tutsis and the Hutus in Burundi (Dunlop, 2024). By claiming the past in different and sometimes opposing ways, conflict narratives, or, more generally, a group's collective memories seem mutually incompatible and give rise to negative attitudes, prejudices, and stereotypes about the (former) "enemy". These enemy images usually encompass all members of a rival group, notwithstanding individual members' role and level of involvement in political, ethnic or religious violence.

No violence can be sustained without the reproduction of these collective memories of conflict over time and across generations. First, collective memories are transmitted through institutional settings – or so-called vertical transmission (Licata et al., 2007). State-controlled channels include national media, cultural institutions and events (e.g., commemoration ceremonies, museums, or monuments), and, most importantly, the formal education system. School curricula are inherently political and potentially divisive, especially in the so-called national subjects of citizenship education, history, geography, literature, and religion (e.g., Smith & Vaux, 2003; Tawil & Harley, 2004). While multiple memories and narratives can gain public articulation and recognition, school curricula and textbooks usually tend to convey a single, dominant interpretation of the past. This 'official' memory serves to legitimize the authority of the ruling group(s). National subjects, as Shanks (2016) aptly observed, are therefore more invested in preserving identity than in promoting pedagogy. Second, collective memory is shared through storytelling within family networks and wider social and cultural circles, known as horizontal transmission (Licata et al., 2007). Rather than the official memory, these networks may also convey 'unofficial' or dissenting narratives of the conflict, depending on the group to which their members belong. Horizontally transmitted conflict histories can moreover include significant historical inaccuracies or lack essential political and social context, such as personal experiences of violence (Kuppens & Langer, 2023).

Even after open fighting has ended, conflict narratives typically persist in popular memory – challenging the notion that time alone will heal wounds and soften resentment between enemies (Jelin, in Cole & Barsalou, 2006; Cole, 2012; Kuppens & Langer, 2023). While many post-conflict governments repress the past, narratives are still likely to be passed down through families and social networks to make sense of the past. These lingering memories of conflict are particularly likely to threaten peacetime stability if the group-based inequalities and divisions that underpinned past conflict have not been addressed in its aftermath (Kuppens & Langer, 2023). An official culture of silence would therefore "not produce a common history – it serves only to reinforce the social identities of those who fought against each other" (Weinstein et al., 2007, p. 66; see also Cole, 2012). In the aftermath of mass violence and to promote reconciliation, therefore, it is crucial to challenge selective or exaggerated accounts of the past and reject the notion that entire communities bear inherent or collective culpability.

1.2. Challenging conflict narratives through transitional justice

Transitional justice efforts are essential for bridging past divisions and promoting new forms of coexistence, in short, for reconciling society (Bloomfield et al., 2003; Brett & Malagon, 2022; Rosoux, 2017). These efforts encompass both judicial (retributive) and non-judicial (restorative) approaches. While the former approach – like criminal trials and special courts – prioritizes accountability, the latter focuses on uncovering historical truth and promoting healing through mechanisms like truth commissions, inquiries, reparations, and official apologies (Keynes et al., 2021). Truth-telling commissions in particular create opportunities for critical and empathetic engagement with competing historical narratives. They provide a platform for acknowledging grievances and understanding the suffering of everyone affected by conflict (Dinur, 2018; Licata et al., 2007). From South Africa to Guatemala, experience has shown that exposing the realities of past atrocities not only reveals entrenched systems of repression that require dismantling, but also has profound emotional and psychological effects on both victims and perpetrators (Bloomfield et al., 2003). By re-examining the past from multiple perspectives, these mechanisms can challenge rigid, one-sided narratives – where one group sees itself as entirely "right" – and promote a more nuanced understanding that acknowledges atrocities committed by multiple parties, while recognizing that groups may have had, to varying degrees, "understandable" motivations (Rosoux, 2018; see also Pham et al., 2019); without necessarily implying moral equivalence between the historical narratives of opposing groups (Teeger, 2015).

Rethinking and reframing relationships requires not only acknowledging past injustices but also recognizing their contemporary effects, that is, on social status, economic opportunities, and political power. Failure to address these historical legacies risks keeping tensions alive. This is especially true when political debates or policies in the present are interpreted through groups' different interpretations of what happened in the past (Keynes, 2019; Kuppens & Langer, 2023; Miles, 2019; Teeger, 2015).

1.3. Education as a subject & instrument of transitional justice

As a subject of transitional justice, in recent decades, truth commissions have increasingly focused on 'telling the truth about education' (Paulson & Bellino, 2017). Accordingly, subsequent reports have identified education as a site in need of considerable reform to address past injustices, like guaranteeing equal access to education, education in their native language, but also the removal of stigmatizing and dehumanizing content and practices. The Arusha Peace and Reconciliation Agreement (2000) that ushered in the ending of nearly 15 years of civil war in Burundi, for instance, recommended education redistribution towards marginalized groups (Dunlop & King, 2021). More generally, it is now widely accepted within the field of 'education, peace, and conflict' that education is not merely a victim of conflict but can also exacerbate conflict dynamics in the realms of redistribution, recognition, and representation (Novelli et al., 2017; see also Bush & Saltarelli, 2000; Davies, 2004; 2010). Schooling can fuel conflict dynamics by, among other things, providing unequal access to quality education or disproportionately allocating resources; failing to accommodate cultural and religious diversity in curricula and textbooks or misrepresenting or stigmatizing certain groups; and excluding marginalized communities from educational decision-making at school, regional, or national levels (Brown, 2011; King, 2015). In post-independence Rwanda, for instance, the Hutu-led governments implemented quotas that restricted post-primary education access for Tutsis, reversing the colonial-era advantage Tutsis had in schooling (King, 2015); while in South Africa, white students received twelve times more education funding per capita than black students at the peak of Apartheid (Christie, 2009, pp. 80-81). Beyond resource disparities, the curricula in both countries reinforced dominant power structures: Apartheid-era textbooks promoted white superiority and black inferiority (Weldon, 2010), while colonial Rwandan textbooks described the Bahutu as possessing "atavistic stupidity" in contrast to the "sage and prudent" Tutsi (King, 2015, p. 66). In addition, peace education scholars further draw attention to the more subtle effects of the 'hidden curriculum', which refers to "those unstated norms, values, and beliefs embedded in and transmitted to students through the underlying rules that structure the routines and social relationships in schools and classroom life" (Giroux, 1983, p. 47). Schools can normalize the use of violence by resorting to corporal punishment, glorifying nationalism and war, or encouraging competition through high-stakes testing (Bush & Saltarelli, 2000; Davies, 2004; Harber, 2019; Harris & Morrison, 2003; Korostelina & Lässig, 2013; for a more extensive discussion, see Kuppens, 2018). These patterns illustrate what Bush & Saltarelli (2000) termed the 'negative face' of education in which education deepens societal divisions and perpetuates conflict.

Education can, however, also serve as an instrument of transitional justice (Keynes, 2019). Such 'forward-looking' reforms include the integration, or educationalization (Keynes et al., 2021), of lessons learned from truth commissions.[1] It also includes the development of such new courses as peace and human rights education (Paulson & Bellino, 2017; see also Russell, 2019). These initiatives represent what Bush & Saltarelli (2000) described as the 'positive face' of education. Following the conclusion of the Truth and Reconciliation Commission in South Africa, for example, new history textbooks were developed that included the history as documented by the Commission, including testimonies and first-person stories about the behaviour of victims, resisters, and bystanders (Ahonen, 2013; Tibbitts, 2006; Tibbits & Weldon, 2017). In particular, the South-African Truth and Reconciliation Commission report (1998) suggested that the study of violence and conflict should not be about condoning it, but rather about "recognising the potential for evil in each one of us so that we can take full responsibility for ensuring that such evil will never be repeated" (in Christie, 2012, p. 42). More generally, the idea is that integrating content from the truth and reconciliation processes can contribute to consolidating, documenting, and strengthening transitional justice and peacebuilding efforts (Bellino et al., 2017). Davies (2017) refers to this as 'justice-sensitive education', which aims to give learners the tools to identify and understand large-scale human rights violations after the violence has ended; to search for "truth" or multiple truths about the past conflict; and to use a backward- and forward-looking perspective to work out how to create and be part of a better future where rights matter (Davies, 2017, p. 335). However, most truth commissions do not initially prioritize education in their efforts, and often leave the educationalization of the historical knowledge they collect to education policymakers and individual teachers (Keynes et al., 2021).

1.4. Direct peace education

Teaching and learning through transitional justice (Bellino et al., 2017) or justice-sensitive education (Davies, 2017) are thus proposed as essential mechanisms for the foundational assumption that underpins the fields of peace education and transitional justice: that learning *about* the violent past is key to learning *from* it (Manning & Paulson, 2024; see also Evrard & Destrooper, 2021). They are similar to what Bar-Tal and Rosen (2009) coined as 'direct peace education'. Direct peace education addresses the core of a conflict, including the history of conflict and the image of the "enemy", and seeks to replace fear and hatred of the 'other' with hope for a better future together based on a pedagogy of multiple perspectives (Bar-Tal et al., 2010, p. 32). It includes at least four key elements: (1) studying the history of the conflict, describing the atrocities committed by all sides in the conflict with an emphasis on the consequences and costs; (2) focusing on reducing mistrust and hatred between (formerly) opposing groups; (3) critically analysing the grievances and motivations of the (former) opponents to challenge the perception of them as uniformly hostile and instead see them as potential partners for positive relations; and (4) teaching about the peace process (see also Kuppens et al., forthcoming). The authors distinguish direct peace education from indirect peace education, which provides general knowledge about conflicts and war, their causes and the resulting suffering; and cultivates non-violent behaviour and conflict-resolution skills of individuals. It involves not only the inclusion of peace and tolerance content in the school curriculum, but also the creation of a school climate that supports these notions, including the way in which content is taught, relationships between and among staff and students based on tolerance and respect, and a rejection of corporal punishment and bullying (see also Davies, 2004; Harber, 2019; Harris & Morrison, 2003). Like direct peace education, the aim of indirect peace is to promote reconciliation, but in a less explicit and therefore probably less threatening manner than direct peace education. Similarly, Salomon (2002) distinguishes between education *for* peace and education *about* peace. While the former could bring about change at the collective level, the latter is more likely to encourage individual changes in mentality and behaviour (Salomon, 2002).

Engaging with multiple perspectives on the violent past is key to direct peace education. Importantly, the study of multiple perspectives helps students to acknowledge that the past is negotiated and constructed (for a discussion, see Kuppens & Langer, 2016a; see also Ahonen, 2013; Cole, 2007; 2012; Cole & Barsalou, 2006; McCully, 2012). It also invites students to be open to and understand the views, emotions, and motivations of other individuals and groups (Korostelina & Lässig, 2013), thus promoting ethno-empathy (i.e., the ability to take the perspective of the other group). Manning and Paulson (2024), for example, report how students in a peace education programme in Cambodia who were exposed to multiple perspectives came to understand lower-level perpetrators as 'complex' victims of the Khmer Rouge regime. Similarly, Zembylas (2009) argues for peace pedagogies that encourage learners "to see the Other as a human being who has also been traumatized by past events and who has similar needs for security, rights, and homeland" (Zembylas, 2009, p. 191; see also Zembylas, 2012). At the very least, we argue, it should encourage 'political generosity', which is "the ability to legitimise the cultural and political identity of those with opposing views, primarily on the basis of their right to hold them" (Emerson, 2012, p. 290); or 'historical perspective-taking', which Bilali and Vollhardt (2013) define as the "willingness to consider (former) adversary groups' perspectives regarding the history of the conflict" (p. 144).

To effectively engage in multiple-perspective pedagogy and cultivate critical, deliberative, and more peaceful citizens, teachers are advised to use deliberative classroom didactics that focus on student agency, debate, and critical thinking (Bush & Saltarelli, 2000; Davies, 2010; Freedman et al., 2008; Lopes Cardozo & Hoeks, 2014; Ramírez-Barat & Duthie, 2015); thus sparking 'academic controversy' (Johnson, 2007). In doing so, they should avoid false equivalence, equivocation and, in extreme cases, revisionism by critically addressing issues of responsibility, rather than simply presenting multiple narratives (Manning & Paulson, 2024). This is particularly true in contexts of past and present power asymmetries. Teachers should also draw attention to the ways in which different interpretations of history shape how we understand the present (Miles, 2019; Robinson, 2022; Teeger, 2015). Finally, by examining not only the content but also the role of conflict narratives, multiperspectivity can also help students understand how political and social actors, including the media, tactically construct and/or perpetuate these narratives to broaden support or influence public perceptions of conflict (Kello, 2016; see also Keynes et al., 2021).

1.5. Sociological time & societal 'ripeness'

In countries emerging from conflict, the complexity of the socio-political context can hinder efforts to integrate multiple perspectives on the past, or to provide direct peace education (Barakat et al., 2013). Political elites may, for example, disagree about the content of what should be taught and, more fundamentally about what actually happened in the past. For example, the introduction of history textbooks documenting the history of conflict in Rwanda was stopped by the post-conflict regime in an alleged effort to preserve 'Rwandan unity' (Freedman et al., 2008). Accordingly, teachers are forbidden from teaching about atrocities committed before or after the genocide, or from answering questions regarding the role of moderate Hutus (Russell, 2019). Similarly, in the direct aftermath of the Cambodian civil war, Cambodian teachers were instructed not to mention the Khmer Rouge era in their classrooms 'for the sake of national reconciliation'. And after the Khmer Rouge period was briefly included in the revised curriculum in the early 2000s, renewed tensions led to ongoing revisions and omissions (Dy, 2009).

Apart from not being politically 'ripe', the sociological time might not be 'right' either. Teachers might be reluctant to teach about the violent past for fear of triggering traumatic experiences among students and reigniting (ethnic) tensions in schools (e.g. Bellino, 2014; Kello, 2016; Weinstein et al., 2007). For example, a Rwandan genocide survivor and teacher explained that when teaching about the causes of the genocide, "we must pay attention to avoid hurting the souls of others, because the hearts of certain people were hurt" (Russell, 2019, p. 1), while a peer recounted how a student told him "what I should say and shouldn't say" (Russell, 2019, p. 147). Teachers may also be reluctant because they lack confidence in their ability to address such sensitive issues in the classroom (e.g. Bar-Tal, 2004, in Zembylas et al., 2012, p. 1073; Davies, 2016, p. 13). Even successful initiatives have therefore taken decades to overcome protests and rejection of textbooks that include multiple perspectives (Pingel, 2008). This is not unlike other transitional justice efforts, such as reparations, which have also often taken many decades (Neumann & Thompson, 2015).

It is important to note in this respect that sociological time is not teleological (see also Manning et al., 2024). On the contrary, societal support for direct peace education may wax and wane over time as conditions change. Significantly, although South African teachers used the past to explain the present just four years after Apartheid ended, they no longer causally linked black students' poverty to historical injustice twenty years later (Dryden-Peterson & Robinson, 2023), as they had begun to fear classroom divisions over historical accountability and reparations (Teeger, 2015).

Harber (2019), for his part, ponders whether the time can ever be 'ripe' as long as people accept and share the traditional assumptions and practices of the conventional model of mass schooling. Indeed, he highlights the contradiction between the system's hierarchical and authoritarian student-teacher relationships, school discipline, and rote learning pedagogies focused on preparing students for high-stakes examinations, on the one hand, and peace education's egalitarian relationships, positive discipline, and participatory pedagogies aimed at promoting critical thinking, non-violence and tolerance, on the other. Similarly, Lopes Cardozo (2008) argues that the goals of peace education cannot be achieved without addressing not only direct, but also structural and cultural violence within and outside of schools. While we agree that there is potentially a strong dissonance between what peace education is expected to achieve and what it can actually achieve (see also section 1.7. for an assessment of the theory of change and the empirical evidence supporting it), we see value in the signalling function of curricular peace education in addition to its transformative potential at the individual, school, and – step by step – societal levels.

1.6. Alternatives to direct peace education

Where direct peace education is not permitted in the classroom, some post-conflict countries have chosen to integrate conflict histories or experiences of violence from other countries, like the Holocaust (Murphy, 2010; Tibbitts, 2006). This offers opportunities for teachers to relate 'cold' cases to their country's 'hot' context and draw parallels to promote knowledge about the root causes of conflict and how to overcome them (Bellino, 2014, p. 131; Cole, 2012, p. 241; McCully, 2012, p. 146; Ramírez-Barat & Duthie, 2015, p. 16). Although there is not much research on the use of analogies in history education in particular, analogical reasoning would be an effective and motivating way of learning in general (van Straaten et al., 2016).

Other alternative approaches include indirect peace education, human rights education, citizenship education, and multicultural education (Bar-Tal & Rosen, 2009; Bar-Tal et al., 2010). While citizenship education is seen as essential for establishing a robust democracy (e.g., Almond & Verba, 1963; Torney-Purta, 2002; Dassonville et al., 2012), multicultural education aims to provide equal learning opportunities for all groups and promote inclusive classrooms (Banks & Banks, 2001; Stephan & Stephan, 2001); and human rights education focuses on promoting a culture of respect, equality, and dignity for all people by promoting awareness and understanding of human rights principles (e.g., Russell & Tiplic, 2014; Tibbitts, 2006). Textbooks and curricula therefore oftentimes contain elements of

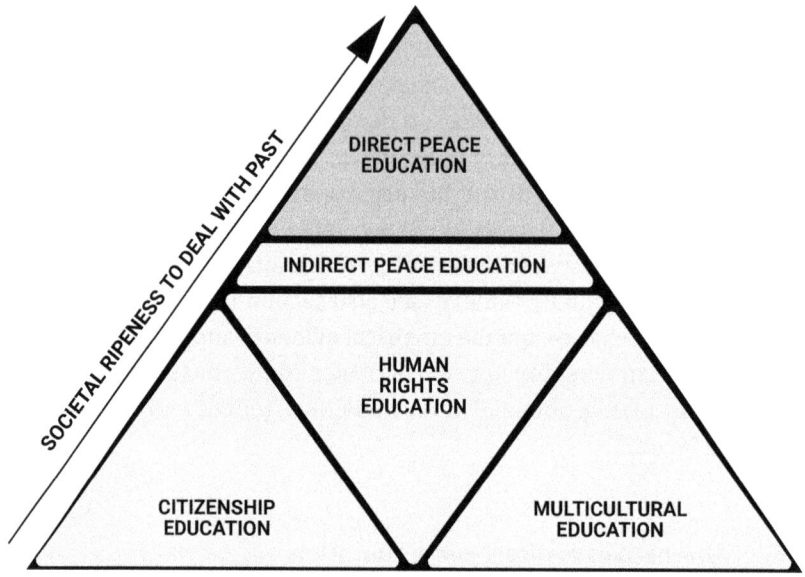

Figure 1.1. Typology of peace education interventions by degree of societal ripeness required. Adapted from Kuppens (2018)

all three educational approaches. More fundamentally, scholars acknowledge that they are interrelated and mutually reinforcing (Kuppens & Langer, 2019; see also Fountain, 1999). In the words of Salomon and Cairns (2010): "Education for democracy [or multiculturalism / human rights] could easily be regarded as a variant of the prototype of peace education and at the same time the prototype of the category of civil [multicultural/ human rights] education" (Salomon & Cairns 2010, p. 6). Human rights, citizenship and multicultural education are all linked to indirect peace education. While they share the goal of cultivating non-violent behaviours and peaceful attitudes, each emphasizes different dimensions. In terms of pedagogies, these educational approaches share a commitment to democratic and non-violent teaching practices that encourage interaction, participation, cooperation, and critical thinking (Kuppens, 2018; see also Russell & Tiplic, 2014).

Ideally, students in (post-)conflict societies will engage with their own history of conflict and its legacies in the present to promote reconciliation. However, when the political and/or sociological time is not conducive to addressing competing memories of violence openly, types of indirect peace education can be valuable, at least in the short term (see figure 1.1.). Having said that, these indirect approaches should also address notions of peace, civics, human rights, or multiculturalism in a way that is *relevant* to students in post-conflict societies, thereby aligning with critical scholarship in peace education (see Bajaj, 2008; Bekerman & Zembylas, 2011). Without examining how war and human rights abuses have affected and continue to affect students' living conditions, the theoretical study of and respect for human and civil rights, for instance, may ring hollow (Cole, 2012, p. 232; Davies, 2016, p. 3). This implies that, although less controversial, indirect peace education and variations thereof may still require the 'right' political and sociological timing to be accepted. Notably, it took nearly thirty years for educational policies in Botswana to shift away from assimilationist towards multicultural education (Mulimbi & Dryden-Peterson, 2018b), while countries emerging from intrastate conflicts generally prefer discussing nationalism and abstract civics over past and current human rights violations, because it could allegedly threaten the legitimacy of the state (Russell & Tiplic, 2014).

From here on in, we will consider the preference of teachers for one or the other form of education – and direct peace education in particular – as an indicator of the readiness of their respective countries to engage in conflict-history education. After all, teachers represent an interesting cross-section of society and have their fingers on its pulse. Before we examine their role further in the second chapter, we will conclude this chapter with some brief reflections on the underlying theory of change of direct peace education.

1.7. Theory of change of direct peace education

Learning *about* the violent past to learn *from* it is the key aspiration of both the academic research and the practice of peace education and transitional justice. Beyond the assumption that *more* knowledge about conflict fosters peace, research on direct peace education is informed by the belief that preventing future conflict crucially depends on young generations being able to assume the perspective of the 'other' to revisit their understanding of the violent past and thereby changing their attitudes towards that 'other'. Theoretically, the confrontation with the information, experiences, and perspectives of other group members would evoke uncertainty and push students with one-sided views to accommodate other perspectives by adjusting their own reasoning, thereby arriving at a new reconceptualized conclusion – Johnson and Johnson (2010) framed this as the 'Constructive Controversy Theory' (p. 229) and Kucukaydin and Cranton (2012) called it 'transformative learning'. Zembylas (2009) similarly argued that ambivalent feelings constitute an opportunity to recognise the trauma and suffering of the 'other'. These theories of change are reminiscent of cognitive dissonance theory (Festinger, 1957). The theory's basic idea is that conflicting cognitions – i.e., narratives of conflict – cause discomfort if they don't make sense when juxtaposed. Because dissonance is an unpleasant state (Festinger, 1957), the theory can explain how, in our context, students' attitudes would change after engaging with views on the past that differ from theirs. Although most peace education studies to date adopt a normative, aspirational or prescriptive attitude instead of empirically and systematically examining how direct peace education transforms conflict narratives and improves intergroup attitudes (see Harber, 2019 for a review of empirical evidence), studies in social psychology have established that taking the perspective of the 'other' – as well as voicing one's own perspective – in post-conflict settings contributes to intergroup forgiveness and positive changes in intergroup dynamics (Bilali & Vollhardt 2013; Bruneau & Saxe 2012; Casas et al. 2020). Also in contexts of relative tranquillity, approaches of cognitive dissonance can reduce prejudice (Heitland & Bohner, 2010).

However, there are also situations in which students may reject perspectives on the violent past that are inconsistent with their own interpretations. Teachers and students are no tabula rasa, they have been exposed to conflict narratives for a long time. The discrepant information may therefore threaten their sense of group identity, and lead them to reject it and to hold on to their own entrenched beliefs and attitudes (Bar-Tal & Hameiri, 2020). For instance, when a talk show which encouraged discussion about intergroup conflict and cooperation was aired in eastern DR Congo, instead of improving intergroup attitudes, it consolidated group identities (Paluck, 2010). Similarly, feelings of guilt can evoke defensiveness and contribute to the persistence of identity-based reasoning (Miles, 2022; Vollhardt, 2020). Pingel (2008) thus cautions that "laying bare possible reasons for the conflict is painful and controversial and may divide rather than unite society" (p. 185).

More fundamentally, critical research in peace education has criticized these mechanisms for being overly 'psychologized' (Zembylas & Bekerman, 2013; see also, Higgins & Novelli, 2018; Teeger, 2015; Zuma, 2014). They raise questions about the assumption in transitional justice and peace education that empathy will bring about peace. Such reasoning is said to obfuscate the role of structural and historical factors in creating conflict and maintaining inequality. In their view, peace education should focus on analysing the root causes of contemporary inequalities and power imbalances, and empower learners to challenge oppressive systems thereby driving social change (Bajaj, 2009, p. 552; see also Williams, 2017; Zembylas, 2018). On a related note, Manning and Paulson (2024) caution that multiperspectivity, as a type of affective learning, risks detracting and distracting from questions of responsibility (see also Miles, 2022). However, we believe that instead of rebutting the use of 'psychologized' perspectives, peace education needs to approach that which is psychological from a social perspective because "what individuals believe, and how individuals think and act is always shaped by cultural, historical, and social structures"; or in short that "which is psychological, is first social" (Lasky, 2005, p. 900). Accordingly, we posit that questioning when and how group identities and intergroup attitudes and relations came into being and how they persist, is a necessary step towards promoting new attitudes and relations. We nonetheless conclude that more research is needed to refine the theoretical and pedagogical frameworks of direct peace education, notwithstanding the fact that empirical evidence from the field of social psychology suggests positive effects under specific circumstances.

CHAPTER 2

The risk-taking continuum 2.0

> Teachers rather than students should represent a starting point for any theory of peace [citizenship in original] education. Most students exercise very little power over defining the education experiences in which they find themselves. It is more appropriate to begin with those educators who both mediate and define the educational process. (Giroux, 1983, p. 194)

In this chapter, we contest the notion that the introduction of a direct peace education curriculum by the ministry of education, once moved through the educational bureaucracy to teachers, automatically means its intended content is conveyed to the students it targets. Like Giroux (1983), we acknowledge instead that teachers have agency to 'mediate and define' how a direct peace education curriculum is implemented (or not) in the classroom; hence the importance of acquiring their support. Drawing on existing case studies from across the globe, we demonstrate how the introduction of direct peace education involves negotiation and discussion to overcome resistance. This is also true, moreover, for the null curriculum (i.e., what is *not* taught). In contexts where authorities have abstained from integrating the violent past in the curriculum, teachers may decide to dedicate a lesson to the subject, or bring in sources of information that are not included in the official curriculum.

Crucially, when it comes to teaching about the violent past, teachers vary in their preferences and practices. Scholars have therefore attempted to identify different strategies for dealing with conflict-related knowledge in the classroom. Kitson and McCully (2005), most notably, identified three positions along a continuum: avoiders, containers, and risk-takers. The first category refers to teachers who avoid teaching about the violent past, silencing any discussion; containers teach sensitive issues, but try to take the sting out of it; and risk-takers consciously seek to link past and present as they teach about the history of conflict (see Kitson & McCully, 2005). We critically engage with their continuum and use it as a basis for introducing a new heuristic for analysing teachers' attitudes towards direct peace education. In doing so, we draw from research on peace, civic and multicultural education, as well as on memory studies. The resulting risk-taking continuum 2.0, coined as the conflict-history education framework, positions teachers along two axes that represent their epistemological beliefs and their perceived constraints to teaching conflict-history education, respectively.

2.1. Curricular-instructional gatekeeping

Up until 2008, conflict-history education in Cyprus was premised on the educational policy of '*I don't forget*'. This policy focused one-sidedly on the trauma that the Greek-Cypriot community suffered. As a new government came into power, the policy was replaced with a new policy of '*Peaceful Coexistence*' in an attempt to foster a rapprochement between Greek and Turkish Cypriots. Some teachers felt uncomfortable with the idea of reconciliation however, and refused to apply the policy in the classroom (Zembylas et al., 2016). In post-Apartheid South Africa, all students learn about their country's history of segregation in their ninth-grade history classes. To mitigate race-based conflict in the classroom and assuage students' potential feelings of guilt and anger, teachers have been found to teach "both sides of the story", emphasizing that not all whites were perpetrators and not all blacks victims, rather than teaching about the systemic violence of Apartheid (Teeger, 2015; see also Robinson, 2022).

These examples clearly show how teachers actively shape policy initiatives, rather than merely implement them. Since outsiders rarely observe teaching practices and classrooms hence resemble a 'black box' (Faden, 2014, p. 191), teachers determine how and to what extent they adhere to the curricular content and pedagogical approaches (Cole, 2012, p. 239; Faden, 2014, p. 191). Thornton (1989) refers to this as 'curricular-instructional gatekeeping'. Gatekeeping can take several forms, ranging from agreement to, submission to, adaptation of, defiance of, resistance to and selection of textbook content (Horner et al., 2015, p. 41; see also Faden, 2014; Lässig, 2013). More generally, scholars increasingly recognize that institutions and classrooms take original and creative ways to interpret policies (Ball et al., 2011, p. 3), or that policy and the practice thereof are 'decoupled', if not because of a lack of capacity then because of a lack of will (Bromley & Powell, 2012 in Russell, 2019). While teachers may consciously rework or challenge the official curriculum, it is important to note that they may also do so unconsciously, for instance by expressing their personal views or interpreting social reality for their students (Ichilov, 2003, p. 221; Murphy et al., 2016, p. 45). Even minor cues can be consequential in this respect since teachers are often perceived as reliable and trustworthy sources of information and are important agents of socialization (Bar-Tal & Harel, 2002).

It is important to know how instructional-curricular gatekeeping occurs, but knowing why is equally important. While teachers may deviate from established policies or curricula if they consider them unjust for their students, school and profession – a phenomenon Levinson (2015) labels 'loyal subversion' – it is more probable that the process of gatekeeping in conflict-affected societies is shaped by teachers' lived experiences, and the emotional significance they ascribe to them (Horner et al., 2015; Staeheli & Hammett, 2010, p. 669). Teachers have been found to resist the incorporation of conflict-history education into the curriculum, as this forces them to confront and discuss their own, and their students', distressing and traumatic experiences (Bar-Tal, 2004, in Zembylas et al., 2012, p. 1073; Barton & McCully, 2005, p. 108; Davies, 2016, p. 13; Ichilov, 2003, p. 232; Kello, 2016, p. 35; McCully, 2012, p. 148; Tawil & Harley, 2004). Teachers may even have played an active role during conflict, as was the case in Rwanda (African Rights, 1995, in Njoroge, 2007). Furthermore, gatekeeping depends on teachers' social identity and political views. Hadjivaplou (2002) describes how Cypriot educators who participated in a conflict resolution workshop gave very different accounts of the history of Cyprus depending on their group affiliation (i.e., Greek or Turkish Cypriot). Their intergroup attitudes are equally important: to preserve national unity against the former common enemy, which is to say 'North Sudan', teachers in South Sudan avoided discussing the internal ethnic conflicts the 'new Republic' had been experiencing since its independence in 2011 (Skårås & Breidlid, 2016). These observations raise important questions regarding the ability of teachers to talk about the causes, consequences and costs of conflict and warfare, especially when it relates to their own (history of) conflict (see e.g., Freedman et al., 2008; Weldon, 2010).

It is nonetheless important to acknowledge the influence of societal and socio-political structures on teachers' agency in adapting, defying, or resisting official textbook content. Teachers in high-stakes testing contexts, for instance, often have limited instructional discretion, as they are expected to prepare students for national exams. Consequently, they may feel compelled to prioritize examinable subjects over those not included in the exam curriculum, such as peace education, thereby limiting the impact of the latter (Bellino, 2014, p. 140; Burde et al., 2017; Shepler & Williams, 2017). In contrast, teachers in print-poor societies tend to have more freedom to engage in gatekeeping, for example, by selecting which content to bring into the classroom. Other external factors influencing teachers' instructional discretion include their relationship with the state and school administration. In Botswana, for instance, teachers feel a strong sense of gratitude towards the government for their education and livelihoods and demonstrate a high level of respect for the school's authority structures (Mulimbi & Dryden-Peterson, 2018b). It thus seems unlikely that they would deviate from of resist the formal (peace) curriculum. Finally, curricular-instructional gatekeeping, where it has been attempted, may also soon dwindle if it is penalized. In Northern Cyprus, for example, Turkish-Cypriot teachers' calls for a more Cypriocentric curriculum quickly diminished after several educators lost their jobs or were forced into early retirement (Hadjivaplou, 2002, p. 200). While it is important to acknowledge the influence of societal and socio-political structures on teachers' agency, it is equally crucial to recognize that these structures do not fully determine teachers' actions in this regard (Ball et al., 2011, Biesta et al., 2015; Lasky, 2005).

2.2. The risk-taking continuum

In 1991, seven years before the signing of the Good Friday Agreement, a revision of the Northern Irish curriculum recommended that history teachers consider ways to connect past and present when teaching about the country's history up until 1922. Subsequent observations by two researchers, Kitson and McCully, revealed significant differences in the way teachers implemented this recommendation in their classrooms. On the one hand, they observed teachers who entirely dismissed the recommendation. However, on the other hand, they also observed teachers making many valuable connections between the past and present. Positioning teachers' strategies on a continuum, they then created the so-called risk-taking continuum, ranging from 'avoiders' to 'risk-takers' (see Figure 2.1.; Kitson & McCully, 2005). Avoiders, they explained, steer clear of teaching about the violent past. They view critical enquiry into conflict as outside of the scope of history education and instead focus on helping students become

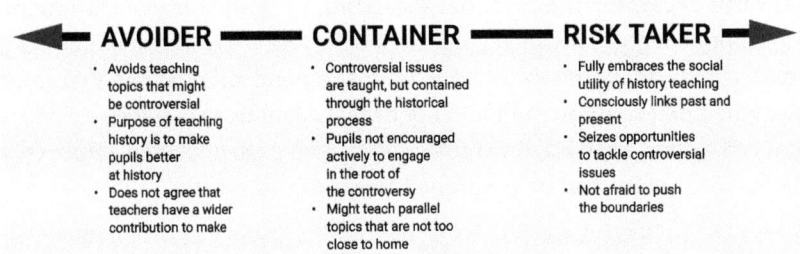

Figure 2.1. Risk-taking continuum. Adapted from Kitson & McCully (2005, p. 35)

more proficient in the discipline of history. A student teacher who participated in a Northern Irish study captured this position succinctly: he wanted to teach history because of a personal passion for the subject, rather than pursuing it as a means of conflict resolution (see Bellino et al., 2017). In contrast, risk-takers endeavour to actively engage students in exploring multiple perspectives on the violent past. They are motivated by a commitment to contribute to peacebuilding beyond the mere transmission of knowledge and skills, which is conventionally considered the principal function of schooling (Harber, 2019). Consequently, the perceived social utility of history education distinguishes between those who avoid making connections between past and present and those who seek them out (Kitson & McCully, 2005). Nonetheless, it should not be forgotten that not all teachers conform to these extremes. Concurrently, Kitson and McCully (2005) identified 'containers'. While these teachers do not reject conflict-history education, they are fearful of potential emotional repercussions. Therefore, they demonstrate a preference for abstaining from the particularities of their own country's internal conflict, while at the same time exploring multiple perspectives on conflicts that are politically and emotionally remote. Alternatively, when addressing one's own history of conflict, teachers may engage in a process of "closing off" the past to downplay the salience of contemporary inequities rooted in the past. This phenomenon has been observed among South African teachers (Dryden-Peterson & Robinson, 2023). It is evident that containers generally favour teacher-led over student-led activities, like role-play, to avoid any escalation in the classroom. It is important to note that containers do not oppose conflict-history education out of principle, rather, they are motivated by concerns regarding the potential escalation of conflict in the classroom. This unique feature distinguishes them from risk-takers, with whom they share beliefs about the social utility of history education. It can therefore be argued that containers should not be placed midway between avoiders and risk-takers, as in Kitson and McCully's (2005) original continuum (see figure 2.1.), but instead be positioned closer to risk-takers.

2.3. Limitations of the risk-taking continuum

The risk-taking continuum is both self-explanatory and simple in nature, thus demonstrating a key heuristic quality. Nonetheless, there are some important limitations to be considered. Harris and Clarke (2011) used the model to examine multicultural education in the United Kingdom and they persuasively identified two main limitations that also relate to conflict-history education. First, it is argued that the continuum construes teachers' positions as fixed, rather than context- and content-specific. Yet the position adopted by teachers depends on the relationship between their own identity and that of their students' backgrounds. In classrooms where one group is dominant, for instance, teachers who belong to that group may not discern the need for reconciliation. This may result in them abstaining from taking risks. For example, consider the following example taken from multicultural education: Teachers in Botswana who presumed their classes were ethnically homogenous did not discuss students' ethnic backgrounds nor did they consider how these backgrounds were relevant to their schooling experiences (Mulimbi & Dryden-Peterson, 2018a). However, it should be noted that minority group teachers may also be less inclined to 'take risks' in majority group classrooms, albeit for different reasons. The reasons include, amongst others, increased fears for negative student reactions. Research carried out on the island of Ambon shows that Indonesian teachers who do not share the religious background of their students are less inclined to teach about the causes of the religious conflict on the island than their peers who share their students' religious background (Fatah et al., 2023). Teeger's (2015) research suggests that the broader school environment also influences this issue: black South African teachers working in diverse schools were as conflict averse as their white colleagues, even in classrooms that had only black African students. As regards content, the teaching of events that took place in a relatively distant past might be less distressing than the teaching of more recent events. Notably, South African teachers have over time started to approach Apartheid history as a remote past (Dryden-Peterson & Robinson, 2023). Nevertheless, events which occurred further back in time, like the partition of British India and the Civil War in Spain, remain controversial [see respectively Chabra, 2016, and Magill, 2016 in Bentrovato et al. (Eds.), 2016]. Conversely, the positioning of teachers along the continuum may not be as straightforward as initially anticipated. In conflict-affected societies, teachers may encounter a "double bind" situation. As Bekerman and Zemblyas (2016) argue, while some teachers in Israel and Cyprus expressed a genuine desire to contribute to a peaceful and multicultural society, they did not want to weaken their pupils' sense of group belonging. This is indicative of two opposing forces of the social utility of education.

Second, Harris and Clarke (2011) challenge the positive framing of risk-taking, in contrast to avoiding, which is taken to be inherently negative. However, a teacher may feel comfortable and confident to take risks, but appear naïve in her/his abilities to do so, which may be harmful. In Cyprus, Zembylas, Charalambous and Charalambous (2016) observed how a teacher, who was usually very inclusive, reverted to the categories of "us" versus "them" when addressing the violent past (Zembylas et al., 2016). Thus, in spite of well-meaning intentions, risk-taking could (partially) yield a negative, rather than a positive outcome. It should be noted that teachers may also want to 'take risks' for the wrong reasons. Of particular concern are teachers who view *their* perspective as the truth who may want to take the risk of teaching it, excluding or misrepresenting other perspectives on the violent past. These teachers may or may not be aware of other perspectives on that same past, or they may consider the other perspectives to be prejudiced. Ultimately, a significant number of teachers have firsthand experience of violent conflict and exposure to violent ideologies that have been used to legitimise violence (Bellino et al., 2017; Johnson, 2007, p. 29; McCully, 2010, p. 215). What is more, "it might well be very difficult to identify teachers who did not have some political involvement and carry the burden of hostility to the enemy" (Davies, 2004, p. 168). Therefore, teachers must first understand their role in shaping or subverting conflict dynamics (Gur-Ze-ev, 2001, p. 316; Njoroge, 2007; Weldon 2010). Otherwise, avoidance may be the better option (see also Kuppens & Langer, 2016a). This also applies to teachers' competences to deal with students' trauma and its impact on students' attitudes and behaviour. A study conducted among young people in Northern Uganda, for instance, demonstrated that affected learners exhibited more aggression, were less disciplined and lacked motivation (Akulluezati et al., 2011). The emotional issues surrounding the past conflict pose a challenge to teachers' traditionally technical expertise (Harber, 2019). Notably, by 2000, Bosnian teachers had still not received training on how to address children's war traumas (Aguilar & Retamal, 2009, p. 6). In the absence of training or support in trauma counselling, why discourage teachers from shielding students against the risk of reviving traumatic experiences, as was the approach taken in Sierra Leone and Liberia (Shepler & Williams, 2017)? In sum, there is consensus that imposing lessons on the violent past on those who have not been subject to the requisite processes of acknowledgement, reconciliation, and emotional processing is both unethical and ineffective. This principle applies to teachers who have been affected by bias, anger, or trauma in addition to teachers who lack the necessary expertise in pedagogy and skills needed to deal with the emotional impact of conflict.

Adding to Harris and Clarke's (2011) limitations, we contend that researchers and policymakers should be careful to recommend direct peace education on teachers' own initiative in contexts where there is a significant risk of severe disciplinary penalties and potential job loss for teaching conflict history. Notably, under the Ba'ath party, Iraqi teachers were subjected to ideological testing and surveillance (Shanks, 2016). Rwandan teachers too must be careful to adhere to the official account of the past in keeping with the Genocide Ideology Law (Russell, 2019). Generally, shedding light on conflict narratives that are not accepted by the surrounding communities may give cause for targeted attacks against teachers. Teachers have become victims of violence in the past merely for the group they belonged to, quite apart from speaking out about conflict (Pherali, 2013). They may also be targeted because of their affiliation with the state. Notably, local militia in the DR Congo commonly suspect teachers of being state informants because of their profession: being literate, having mobile phones and traveling regularly to collect salaries, they are perceived to have the ideal "capacity to inform" superiors and other state actors (Brandt, 2021, p. 554). If teachers' fears for community reprisals are warranted, their wellbeing and safety should undoubtedly be prioritized. And even when conflict-history education is officially approved, it risks overburdening teachers who typically work under poor material conditions and may consequently lack motivation and morale, quite aside from the stresses and pains of the conflict (Dy, 2009; see also Pingel, 2008). This is particularly likely where conflict has depleted teaching resources, and/or exacerbated teacher shortages (Harber, 2019). So overall, it seems that direct peace education comes with real dilemmas depending on the context. While there may be better and worse approaches, it is unclear whether any one of them is ideal.

2.4. Alternative frameworks

The above identified limitations could help explain why the continuum has not been used more as an analytical lens. Before introducing our adapted framework, we would like to discuss alternative frameworks that have been used in the literature and their relation to the risk-taking continuum. We did not only review frameworks in the field of peace education and transitional justice, but also got inspiration from citizenship and multicultural education, as well as from memory studies. While there are clear parallels, these frameworks vary in the number of positions or strategies they identify, and fundamentally in their criteria for categorization. Although we already referred to Levinson's (2015) strategy of 'loyal subversion', our overview no longer includes her work because it's too one-sided in that it only theorizes about the coping strategies of teachers who acknowledge a moral wrong (or the need for a moral "right" in our case, that is, the teaching of the history of conflict from multiple perspectives), thereby excluding teachers who do not acknowledge this.[2]

First, in the process of mapping the attitudes and practices of Estonian and Latvian history teachers, Kello (2016) identified five teacher strategies for or attitudes towards dealing with the history of conflict. Rather than using teachers' epistemological beliefs regarding the purpose of history education, as Kitson and McCully (2005) did, she differentiated between teachers based on their actual classroom practices. On the one end, she identified teachers just 'doing the job', which we equate with Kitson and McCully's (2005) avoiders. These are teachers who think that encouraging multiple perspectives is unnecessary, or even counterproductive. Instead, they faithfully stick to the curriculum as outlined by the government (which in the Latvian context did not include multiple perspectives). On the other end, she observed teachers who 'enhanced heterogeneity' and others who 'left the truth open', much like the risk-takers. Both strategies expose students to a wide range of contrasting viewpoints to promote their ability to listen to and deal with different interpretations. The difference is that teachers who 'leave the truth open' adopt a more exploratory approach which does not necessarily confront students' existing beliefs, in contrast to teachers who want to 'enhance heterogeneity' who deliberately encourage them to engage with perspectives that challenge their own (Kello, 2016). In between, she identified teachers who attempted to 'smooth the edges' by emphasizing the common ground between (formerly) opposing groups, or speak of conflict through allegory – not unlike containers. With the risk-taking continuum in mind, the fifth strategy she identified is somewhat confusingly termed 'hiding, avoiding'. Instead of thinking of conflict-history education as outside of the purview of education – as avoiders on Kitson and McCully's continuum do – these are teachers who do not wish to address the violent past out of time constraints or because of potentially divisive student reactions (Kello, 2016); reasons that closely correspond to the motives of Kitson and McCully's (2005) containers.

Teachers' personal perspectives on contentious issues are also key to Kelly's classification (1986). Kelly had previously analysed four teacher attitudes regarding the teaching of contentious topics in the field of citizenship education. In particular, he used the degree of neutrality or commitment to an issue as the distinguishing feature to differentiate between teachers' practices and stances. Teachers who adopt an exclusive neutral stance do so with the intention of avoiding problematic issues, which is very similar to that of avoiders. These teachers generally subscribe to the idea that schools should maintain a nonpartisan or neutral stance, and treat knowledge as being devoid of value-laden influences. In contrast, the category of exclusive partiality includes teachers who provide their personal views on the issue without discussing any other perspectives, which could be due either to the belief that they are providing an accurate representation of the subject, or because they are personally committed to the values or views they are promoting (Kelly, 1986, p. 117). These illustrations underscore the potential repercussions of undertaking risk-taking actions for suboptimal motives (see the discussion on the limitations of the risk-taking continuum). Impartial teachers are motivated to enter into discussions with their students to explore different viewpoints and strive to ensure that students consider all relevant positions on an issue – much like risk-takers (Kitson & McCully, 2005) and teachers who enhance heterogeneity or who leave the truth open (Kello, 2016). Within

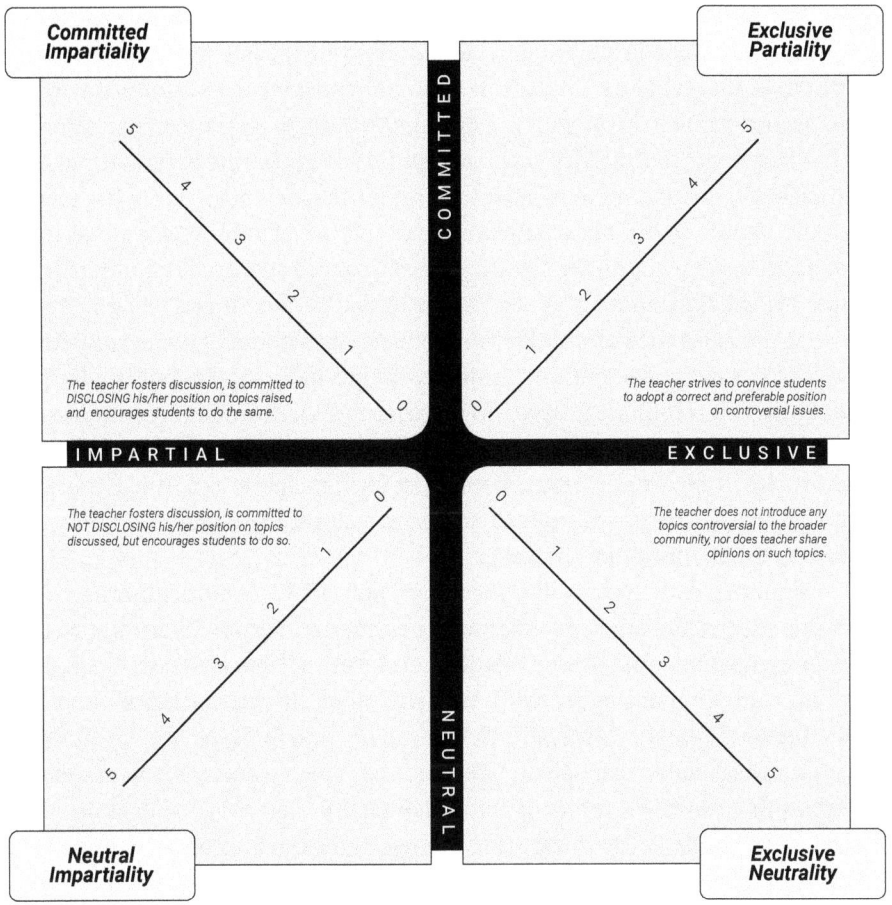

Figure 2.2. Four stances on discussing sensitive issues of Kelly (1986). Adapted from Miller-Lane et al. (2006, p. 33)

this group, teachers can either express ('committed impartiality') or not express ('neutral partiality') their own point of view (Kelly, 1986; see also Castro et al., 2021). According to Kelly (1986), 'committed partiality' would represent the ideal, whereby teacher disclosure does not serve to sway student opinion but to model a thinking process and foster sharing. Miller-Lane, Denton and May (2006) later compiled the various stances into a useful graphic organizer, which included Likert scales to illustrate the complex positions that teachers might hold (see figure 2.2.).

In the field of multicultural education, Cockrell et al. (1999) distinguished between transmitters, mediators and transformers (see also Harris & Clarke, 2011). Transmitters do not consider the social utility of education and focus only on the dominant culture, with the expectation that minority group students will accept this. We liken the assimilationist stance of transmitters to avoiders, or rather teachers just 'doing the job' (Kello, 2016). Mediators acknowledge the value of multiculturalism in education, yet focus on the significance of a shared cultural foundation. In this regard, they adopt a stance similar to that of containers, recognizing the social relevance of multicultural education without actively contributing to its advancement. For example, studies have shown that teachers in Botswana (Mulimbi & Dryden-Peterson, 2018b), Rwanda (Freedman et al., 2008) and South Sudan (Skårås & Breidlid, 2016) have been found to prioritize unity over diversity in their professional practices. Third, transformers seek to prepare students to live in a culturally diverse world and foster equity, much like risk-takers.

Similarly, Banks (1993) identified four approaches to multicultural education that increasingly de-essentialize culture and group identities, and explore how unequal power relations underpin society (see also Agirdag et al., 2016; Kuppens et al., 2018). While none of the approaches involves a complete denial of diversity, the so-called contributions and additive approaches enable teachers to "contain" the topic respectively by merely presenting the "safe" topics of cultural diversity (Gay, 2013), such as dress and food habits, or by integrating themes and examples about minority groups. The transformative approach emphasizes perspective-taking and critical analysis of the socio-political context, while the social action approach motivates students to address structural inequalities through social action. The latter two approaches, which teachers have been observed implementing only rarely (Agirdag et al., 2016; Sleeter, 2011), resemble risk-taking, and align closely with the principles of critical peace education. Critical peace education scholars Bekerman and Zembylas (2009) would consider teachers who put these approaches in place to be 'critical design experts', that is, teachers who analyse socio-political structures with their students, with the goal of understanding and transforming violence and oppression.

In addition to criticizing the existing continuum, Harris and Clarke (2011) also developed a new continuum for the field of multicultural education, which they named the confident-uncertain-uncomfortable

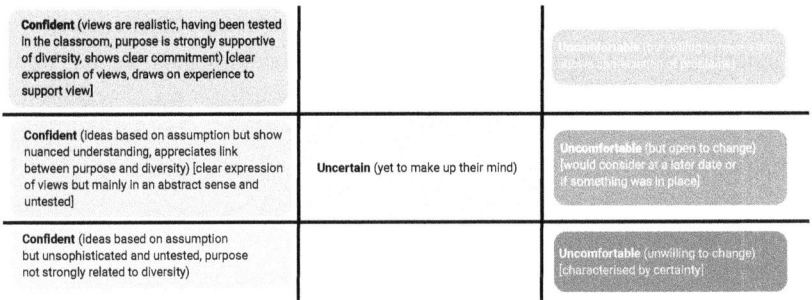

Figure 2.3. Confident-uncertain-uncomfortable continuum. Adapted from Harris and Clarke (2011, p. 167)

continuum. As an extension of the risk-taking continuum, it acknowledges that not only do teachers need to value the social utility of education, but they must also possess the necessary subject knowledge and pedagogical skills to effectively implement multicultural education. In doing so, as a starting point, it takes the (dis)comfort experienced by teachers, distinguishing seven positions that vary in teachers' level of confidence to teach about issues related to multiculturalism, and their actual ability to do so (see figure 2.3.). The responses range from 'uncomfortable and unwilling to change' (a combination of avoiding and containing) to 'confident with realistic views, tested skills, and clear commitment' (an ideal type of risk-taking).

Finally, although not directly related to teaching practices, the work of David Mwambari (2023) is illuminating when it comes to dealing with multiple interpretations of the violent past. As an anthropologist specializing in memory studies, he examined how Rwandans deal with the regime's master narrative of the 1994 Genocide Against the Tutsi, which silences the memory of Hutus killed during the civil war and genocide. First, the author identifies the champions, that is, Rwandans who publicly endorse the government's master narrative and contribute to the propagation of the state's single interpretation of the past via commemorative practices. Second, there are the antagonists, who privately and/or publicly resist the official memory and acknowledge the memory of the Hutus killed during the civil war and genocide too. Finally, the fatalists must be considered. These Rwandans do not necessarily oppose the master narrative, but question the need to remember publicly when personal wounds already serve as a daily reminder of the personal trauma. Classifying Rwandan teachers is challenging. While most teachers may appear to act as champions in the classroom, research shows that a significant number does not consider the master narrative to be the "real history", and could, thus, be antagonists (or fatalists) in disguise (Russell, 2019).

2.5. Towards a risk-taking continuum 2.0: the conflict-history education framework

Inspired by the work of the above authors, we will revisit the original risk-taking continuum. To enable use for the purposes of both research and teacher self-reflection, we have deliberately sought to keep it simple for interpretation and application. In doing so, we propose that two continua be intersected and that scales be integrated, in a manner analogous to that illustrated in the graphic organizer developed by Miller-Lane et al. (2006). However, rather than use the positions established by Kelly (1986), we have opted to intersect the adaptations of Kitson and McCully's (2005) risk-taking continuum with Harris and Clarke's (2011) confident-uncertain-uncomfortable continuum (see Figure 2.4.). To a lesser extent, we have also drawn upon the categories proposed by Kello (2016).

Thus, the horizontal continuum of the new conflict-history education framework under consideration represents teachers' epistemological beliefs regarding direct peace education – i.e., the social utility of teaching conflict history. The vertical continuum reflects teachers' competence with respect to their knowledge of the causes and consequences of their country's past conflict and their pedagogical skills, as well as their experienced levels of (dis)comfort in terms of trauma and/or fears over community backlash and reprisal. Ideally, a distinction would be made between these two dimensions. Notably, teachers may harbour reservations regarding both their subject knowledge and pedagogical skills, as well as fear in-classroom and/or societal opposition. However, incorporating a third axis would make the framework excessively complex and difficult to use. Instead, teachers need to be positioned (or position themselves) on the part of the vertical axis that is most relevant to them. Should experienced discomfort prove to be more decisive in explaining teachers' potential reluctance to teach conflict history than their subject knowledge or pedagogical skills, teachers are positioned (or position themselves) in the lower

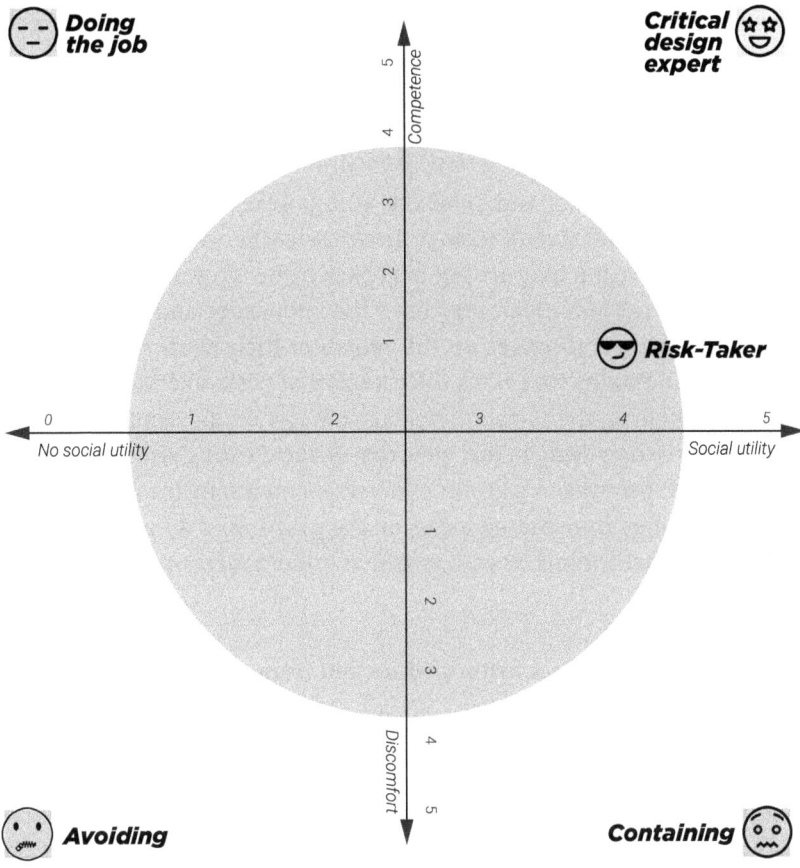

Figure 2.4. Conflict-history education framework (by authors)

half of the framework. Conversely, where discomfort is not a significant concern, at least not when compared to their subject knowledge and pedagogical skills, they are positioned (or adopt a position) in the upper half.

At the extremes, four ideal types are identified. As posited by this framework, anyone designated as an 'avoider' not only disregards the reconciliatory potential of conflict-history education, but would also feel uncomfortable implementing direct peace education if it were to be integrated in the official curriculum. Similarly, teachers just 'doing the job' are not convinced of the social utility of direct peace education. However, they would not experience any particular discomfort if it were to be integrated into the curriculum. Moreover, they would possess the requisite knowledge and skills to implement it. While 'containers' are in principle committed to contributing to peacebuilding through conflict-history education, they are reluctant to do so because of potential classroom or societal backlash and any distress it may cause. Next, instead of 'risk-takers', we define a fourth ideal type of 'critical design experts', inspired by the work of Bekerman and Zembylas (2009). Like the risk-takers in the model of Kitson and McCully (2005), these are teachers who are committed to peacebuilding, but they are not held back by the prospect of discomfort (like containers). Moreover, they have the knowledge and skills to teach about multiple perspectives on the causes of their country's history of conflict. And finally, we retain the category of 'risk-takers' for teachers who score high on the social utility axis, but low on the competence one. These are teachers who, in our view, are de facto taking risks in teaching multiple perspectives to a group of diverse, potentially traumatized students when they have biased views on the past and/or do not know how to deal with that trauma or with negative student reactions.

2.6. Using the conflict-history education framework

From this point onward, we will use this framework as an analytical tool to examine teachers' position vis-à-vis direct peace education in the conflict-affected societies of Kenya, Côte d'Ivoire, and the Kivu provinces of the DR Congo. Note that this framework was developed after all the data was collected, meaning that the survey items we used to establish the position of teachers were somewhat limited, as it did not fully capture all dimensions. Three additional points are worth making here. First, we will apply this framework to the full teacher corps. Although the original continuum of Kitson and McCully (2005) focuses on history teachers in particular, dealing with the violent past is not limited to history education. Other subjects, including citizenship education, social studies, geography, languages and religion, also lend themselves to shaping conflict narratives (Tawil & Harley, 2004). What is more, all teachers, including those teaching mathematics or science, can convey negative stereotypes and prejudices about other groups, or criticize colleagues for addressing content they deem inappropriate. When teachers experience backlash from peers, they may prefer to avoid teaching about the history of conflict, even if they agree with it in principle.

Second, we consider and examine individual traits and skills that could explain teachers' position on the intersecting continua. Whereas Kitson and McCully (2005) already hypothesized that teachers' positions are informed by their social identities, lived experiences, and training, as well as by their larger school environment, systematic empirical evidence remains thin. In turn, we will consider the intergroup attitudes and stereotypes of teachers (Chapter 3), their interpretation of what caused conflict and who is to blame (Chapter 4), and their pedagogical skills (Chapter 5) in particular. The ensuing results could yield important insights for studies on reconciliation more generally, as many questions about the characteristics of proponents and opponents of rapprochement within communities affected by violent conflict, remain unanswered (Rosoux, 2015).

Third, we acknowledge that teachers' positions are time- and context-sensitive. Because we make use of cross-sectional data (i.e., collected at one point in time), the positions we identify in this book are representative of the sociological time at the moment of data collection. Since that time, changes may have occurred in either direction – towards or away from more openness – due to political or personal events, the re-emergence of conflict dynamics, or the mere passage of time.

PART 2
Empirical evidence

CHAPTER 3

Teaching about ethnic tensions in Kenya

One of the proverbs in this country says that you bend a fish when it is still fresh but when it is dried, it breaks. So, we have to bend the learners as they are still young. Let us teachers (...) preach about togetherness and embrace one another. (English teacher, Starehe, 2016)

Tribalism in Kenya is so deep-rooted that it cannot be wiped out by one generation. When I was in college in the years from 1991 to 1994 tribalism was there (...) I have come out with bitterness and now I am expected to be dealing with a crowd [of students]. The only difference is that, before I was a subordinate. Here [in school] I have [an] authoritative position. I can guide my students. But, at the end of the day tribalism is still there. (History & government teacher, Kasarani, 2016)

Kenya is a multi-ethnic country. Although there is "no original sin in ethnicity", over time it has become an instrument of power (Lonsdale, 2019). The ensuing socio-economic and political inequalities between ethnic groups have led to political grievances and, at times, ethnic violence, particularly around election times. In the first section of this chapter, we discuss the emergence and increasing salience of ethnic identities during the colonial period, and how the politicization of ethnicity led to the marginalization of some ethnic groups at the expense of others. Notably, "a feeling among certain ethnic groups of historical marginalization, arising from perceived inequities concerning the allocation of land and other national resources, as well as access to public goods and services" was identified to be one of the main causes of the 2007-2008 post-electoral violence by the Commission of Inquiry into Post-Election Violence (2008, p. 23). To address these grievances and mitigate tensions, the country has since undergone constitutional reform and continues to promote social cohesion as a better way to manage ethnic diversity. Social cohesion is defined as the quality of relationships among individuals and groups within society. In cohesive societies, everyone feels a sense of belonging, perceives the society as a unified whole greater than the sum of its parts, and is able to resolve differences peacefully when they arise (Langer et al., 2017). Across Africa and beyond, countries at risk of splintering turn to public education to reduce that risk by promoting social cohesion through multicultural education, which provides learners from diverse groups equal learning opportunities, creates inclusive school and classroom climates, and develops a common sense of identity among pupils from diverse backgrounds and groups (Heyneman & Todoric-Bebic, 2000; Kuppens & Langer, 2019). Because of its focus on promoting social cohesion through inclusive classrooms, Kenyan teachers' attitudes and practices in multicultural education are the focus of the first part of this chapter. Next, we analyse teachers' support for teaching about the post-electoral violence of 2007-2008 keeping in mind that the intensity of violence in the country was low compared to other contexts on the continent.

Whereas ethnicity and interethnic relations are under scrutiny in this chapter, it is important to note that we do not aim to essentialize these identities. Even though we use ethnicity as a category of descent-based attributes, such as common origins, history, language and shared cultural beliefs (Chandra, 2006), we think of ethnicity as a subjective sense of group belonging, or an emotional bond, which is socially defined in terms of their meaning for the members of the group (Brown & Langer, 2010, p. 412; Quaynor & Borkorm, 2019; Rwengabo, 2016). Once socially constructed, however, ethnic groups are fairly persistent long after they have been created and labelled as such (Wimmer, 2013).

3.1. Ethnic tensions and violence in Kenya

Kenya is home to three main linguistic groups and at least 42 ethnic groups, but the largest five groups comprise more than 70% of the population (Battera, 2012, p. 118; Branch, 2011, p. 4). The Kikuyu (20.8%), Luhya (14.4%), and Kamba (11.4%) belong to the majority group of Bantu speakers, while the Luo (12.4%) and Kalenjin (11.8%) co-constitute the Nilotic linguistic groups. Speakers of Cushitic languages, the third group, are predominantly from the north of the country (e.g. Somalis, Borana, Oromo, Galla) and are generally much smaller in terms of population size (Mwakikagile, 2007).

Ethnicity gained prominence during colonization with the tentative creation of ethnically homogeneous districts. With the exception of three districts, a single ethnic group constituted the absolute majority in each district (Burgess et al., 2015; Mueller, 2020; for a more extensive overview, see Berman et al., 2009). The first indigenous political associations in Kenya largely followed these district lines, thereby largely shaping Kenyans' understanding of interests, rights and mobilization strategies in ethnic terms (Lynch, 2006; see also Ibrahim, 2021). When the country gained independence, these ethnically delineated administrative divisions were used to create parliamentary constituencies (e.g. Burgess et al., 2015; Li, 2018). As a result, politics have often followed an ethnic pattern, with elected representatives favouring the home region.

Also at the national level, politics followed ethnic patterns. Notably, President Jomo Kenyatta, Kenya's first post-independence leader, favoured his own ethnic group, the Kikuyu, by redistributing fertile land the colonists had alienated from the original Kalenjin inhabitants of the Rift Valley to them (ICG, 2008). The issue of unequal land distribution has significantly contributed to the recurring surges of violence in the country. Ethnic politics were further consolidated by the high degree of centralization of executive powers in the constitution of the newly independent country (Mkangi & Githaiga, 2012). Minority groups were wary of the Kikuyu-Luo dominance within Kenyatta's party, the Kenyan African National Union (KANU). They had advocated in vain for a federal system that granted autonomy to the regions, *'majimbo'* in KiSwahili (HRW, 2008, p. 15). However, the Luo wing within KANU would soon break away. In 1966, President Jomo Kenyatta and the popular Luo leader, Jaramogi Oginga Odinga, fell out, leaving the latter to create his own party. Soon after, Kenya turned into a *de facto* one-party state, which was formalized into a *de jure* one-party state in 1982 under President Daniel arap Moi, an ethnic Kalenjin – Kenyatta died in 1978.

Multi-party democracy was only reinstituted in 1991. Yet in the early years after the reinstatement, the political opposition was too fragmented to defeat Moi and he won the subsequent 1992 and 1997 elections. These elections were fraught with tension and small-scale violence however. In both elections combined, more than 1,500 people died and many more were internally displaced, particularly in the Rift Valley and to a lesser extent also in and around Mombasa (Harneit-Sievers & Peters, 2008, p. 134). Having managed to unite the opposition, the so-called National Rainbow Coalition (NARC) defeated Moi in the 2002 elections. Unfortunately, the multi-ethnic coalition was short-lived. The point of contention was the revision of the constitution, and more particularly political power sharing between ethnic groups and a solution to the historical problem of land rights. New discussions arose as well concerning the issue of decentralization (Dercon & Guitérrez-Romero, 2012, p. 732). Dissatisfied with the draft constitution (i.e., Wako Draft) proposed by the newly appointed president, Mwai Kibaki (Kikuyu), two of his cabinet ministers, Raila Odinga (Luo) and Kalonzo Musyoka (Kamba), left the coalition and formed their own party, the Orange Democratic Movement (ODM). They campaigned against the new constitution, which was rejected by 57% of the Kenyan population in a 2005 referendum (Lynch, 2006, p. 234).

On December 27, 2007, Kenyans returned to the ballot box to elect a new president, resulting in a face-off between incumbent president Kibaki and main opposition leader Odinga. The latter's campaign message subtly centred on the slogan of "forty-one tribes against one [i.e., the Kikuyu]" in an attempt to mobilise support across all groups. This went so far as to making violence against the Kikuyus "a deliberate electoral strategy" (Collier, 2009, p. 70-72). When Kibaki was declared the winner by a small margin of 232,000 votes, ODM party supporters spoke of a stolen election – which wasn't helped by the fact that the first results had indicated that Odinga was leading with more than one million votes (Dercon & Guitérrez-Romero, 2012, p. 734). Violence erupted in Nairobi, Nyanza, Western Province and throughout the Rift Valley between ethnic Kikuyu in support of Kibaki and Kalenjin warriors and ethnic Luo, in support of Odinga. Over the course of a few months, an estimated 1,113 people were killed and 3,561 wounded, with more than 350,000 Kenyans having fled their homes (e.g. Berman et al., 2009, p. 500; Dercon & Guitérrez-Romero, 2012, p. 735; Harneit-Sievers & Peters, 2008, p. 137; Horowitz, 2016, p. 335; HRW, 2008, p. 22; Stewart, 2010, p. 134). On 28 February 2008, a power-sharing agreement (i.e., the National Dialogue and Reconciliation Accord) put an end to the violence and accorded the presidency to Kibaki and the post of prime minister to Odinga. This time a new *majimbo*-inspired constitution was passed, which decentralized powers to the district level in an attempt to address the historic grievances of Kikuyu and Kalenjin political dominance (Mkangi & Githaiga, 2012). In other words, the devolution explicitly aimed at empowering ethnic minority communities "who have for too long stood outside of ethnic dominance not only in power but as well in development" (Steeves, 2015, p. 461).

There were no skirmishes during the subsequent 2013 presidential elections, which were won by Uhuru Kenyatta (son of the first president), and his opponent-turned-running-mate, William Ruto (Kalenjin).[3] Tensions did run high again in the run-up and aftermath of the August 2017 presidential elections in which Uhuru Kenyatta and Raila Odinga campaigned against each other. In a historical court decision, Kenyatta's win was overruled because of procedural irregularities. After Odinga boycotted the ensuing repeat elections of October 2017, claiming that the ordered electoral reforms had failed to materialise, Kenyatta was re-elected although only 38% of Kenyans voted. By way of contesting the legitimacy of the vote, Odinga proclaimed himself the "people's president". The ensuing political impasse lasted until the beginning of March 2018 (ICG, 2018). Although no large-scale violence erupted during this time, there were cases of unlawful and excessive police violence, killing at least 45 Kenyans after the first elections (Amnesty International & HRW, 2017).

This brief overview shows that divisive policies and the fear of political exclusion have characterized Kenya's politics in recent decades (Lonsdale, 2019). To this day, many Kenyans believe it remains in their best interest to elect a strong ethnic leader in order to get a share of the national cake, even if they themselves do not consider ethnicity central to their identity (Bratton & Kimenyi, 2008). By the same logic, politicians who seek office maximise their votes by "playing the ethnic card", mobilising support along ethnic lines in exchange for material benefits (Eifert et al., 2010; Horowitz, 2016). Supposedly, there wasn't as much ethno-nationalist rhetoric during Kenya's most recent elections in August 2022. Instead of ethnicity, the electoral campaign of the winner, former vice-president William Ruto, centred on playing out 'Hustlers' – a Kenyan class of low socio-economic status who allegedly hoist themselves up by their own bootstraps and of whom Ruto is allegedly part – against 'Dynasties' – in other words, the quasi-oligarchic Kenyatta and Odinga families, who have dominated the political sphere since independence. Yet Lockwood (2023) argues that Ruto's victory should not be interpreted as 'hustler populism', or a shift from ethnic to socio-economic voting, but as anti-Kenyatta "backlash" among the Kikuyu community who felt unhappy about their fellow Kikuyu's failure to give them prosperity.

3.2. Education, conflict & peace

3.2.1. Kenya's education system

By 2026, the 2-6-6-3 structure, which consists of 2 years of preschool, 6 years of primary, 6 years of secondary (divided in junior and senior levels) and 3 years of higher education, should have replaced Kenya's former 8-4-4 structure of education (8 years of primary, 4 years of secondary and 4 years of higher education). Because the older system was still in place at the time of research and writing, this section focuses on that. Under the 8-4-4 system, primary education starts at the age of 6 up until the age of 14, followed by secondary education until the age of 18. The language of instruction is English, although local languages are used during the three first years of education. Both primary and secondary education are free and compulsory – yet school costs remain an obstacle in practice (e.g. uniforms, textbooks, etc.; see Glennester et al., 2011; Lewin et al., 2011; Smith et al., 2016). Although corporal punishment has been prohibited in schools since 2010, it continues to be used (Chege et al., 2022; Ocobock, 2012).

The Kenyan education system is strongly examination-oriented. To progress from primary to secondary education, students have to pass the Kenyan Certificate of Primary Education (KCPE) examination, the score of which determines what type of secondary school pupils are allowed to attend. In terms of government-funded schools, the best-performing pupils from across the country attend the so-called national schools. These schools are perceived to be better equipped and offer a higher level of teaching (Makori & Onderi, 2014). By contrast, the poorest performers attend local sub-county schools. These schools are the most common (70% of government-funded schools). Finally, county and extra-county schools attract mid- to high-performing students from both within and outside their respective regions (Lewin et al., 2011; Makori & Onderi, 2014; Nyatuka & Bota, 2014). Typically, national and extra-county schools are boarding schools, while county and sub-county schools can be both. Upon completing secondary education, students sit the Kenyan Certificate of Secondary Education (KCSE) examination. To be allowed to enter public universities, pupils require an average score of C+ (Lattimer & Kelly, 2013).

Teachers in Kenya have to meet the minimum standards and requirements set out by the Teachers Service Commission (TSC). Teacher training is organized by level of education (early childhood development and education; primary education; general secondary education; technical education; and special needs education). Training for primary teachers takes two years, and is offered by 21 public and 70 private teacher-training institutes all over the country. Aspiring primary school teachers need to achieve a C average on the KCSE, including at least a D in mathematics and a C- in English (Nyankanga et al., 2013, p. 83). Secondary school teachers can either attend one of three teacher-training colleges who offer a diploma for secondary education, or enrol for a Bachelor of Education at university – thus requiring the university entry average of C+. The Kenya Institute of Special Education and the Kenya Technical Teachers College prepare teachers for special needs and technical education, respectively. Apart from certification, the TSC also handles other teacher affairs, such as recruitment and public school appointments. Notably, the TSC typically appoints teachers outside of their region of origin, for at least 5 years, to enhance national unity.

3.2.2. Education & conflict

The 2007-2008 violence had a significant toll on the education system in the most affected areas. In total, an estimated 158,000 pupils and 1,350 teachers had to flee their houses, and 65 and 40 schools were looted and burned down, respectively (DevEd, 2013, in Mendenhall & Chopra, 2016, p. 90). Ethnic hatred also entered the school compound. Studies have documented how pupils were asked sensitive ethnicity-related questions, such as why their community is so rebellious (cf. Luo) or why they are not going to school in Kisumu (the region of origin of the Luo community) (Yieke, 2008, p. 24).

Perceived inequalities in access to the education system and the distribution of educational funds may have aggravated the grievances of minority ethnic groups in the run-up to the violence (for an overview on ethnic favouritism in education, see Kuppens & Langer, 2022). Although the newly independent government sought to reduce widespread ethnic inequalities in access to quality schools in an effort to combat the sense of social injustices associated with the racially and ethnically segregated colonial education system (Wainaina, Arnot & Chege, 2011, p. 83), during Kenyatta's presidency, pupils identifying as Kikuyu completed on average 47% and 39% more years of primary education compared to Kalenjin and Luo students, respectively. When Moi ascended to power, there was a 54% increase in secondary school attainment among his ethnic group, the Kalenjin, relative to the national average (Kramon & Posner, 2016). Similarly, the Kikuyu showed the strongest increase in primary (and smallest decrease in secondary) attainment relative to the national average during the Kibaki administration (Kramon & Posner, 2016). As educational levels rapidly improved and became more comparable among major ethnic groups, Simson and Green (2020) argue that the small advantage of having a president from one's own ethnic group has lost significance. However, inequalities in educational resources, such as infrastructure and access to qualified teachers, can create significant disparities in how different ethnic groups benefit from education, affecting their future economic opportunities and social status (Brown, 2011).

Importantly, the final report of the Kenyan Truth, Justice and Reconciliation Commission (2013) recognized that since 2007-2008, regional differences continued to exist and therefore recommended to establish at least two national schools in each of the former provinces (Makori & Onderi, 2014; Nyatuka & Bota, 2014) – although the 2010 constitution replaced the system of eight provinces and 46 districts by counties, the provinces remain commonly used as geographic references. Despite this, by 2014, there was still only one national school in the area formerly known as Northeastern province, compared to 11 in the area formerly called the Rift Valley (Nyatuka & Bota, 2014). More generally, access to education remains highly precarious in the former Northeastern province, largely because of security threats in the region (Smith et al., 2016).

3.2.3. Education & peace

Although attempts to mainstream notions of peace in the curriculum predated the post-election violence, a peace education curriculum only materialized in its aftermath with the technical support of UNICEF as part of a multi-country programme on Education in Emergencies and Post-Crisis Transition (EEPCT; see Barakat et al., 2013; Lauritzen, 2016). At first, the so-called Peace Education Programme (PEP) was integrated at primary school level alone, and was based on a peace education curriculum developed by UNHCR in 1998 in the refugee camps of Dadaab and Kakuma (Mendenhall & Chopra, 2016; Obura, 2002). PEP was implemented incrementally, starting in those regions that were hit the hardest by the violence before being rolled out nationally. Teachers were trained using a cascade model whereby 8,500 teachers and education officials were trained as master trainers (Mendenhall & Chopra, 2016, p. 95; see also Barakat et al., 2013). Not all master trainers did effectively train their colleagues, as they were supposed to (Lauritzen, 2016). In 2012, the Kenyan Ministry of Education formulated an accompanying Education Sector Policy on peace education in order "to promote and nurture a culture of peace and appreciation for diversity in the Kenyan society through education and training" (Ministry of Education, Science, and Technology, 2014, p. 3). At that time, peace education was also extended to secondary education by integrating it transversally. Notions of peace were integrated in the subjects of religion, social studies, history and government, and, most notably, life skills education. The latter does not constitute an examinable subject on its own, and therefore often tends to get disregarded in the strict exam-oriented Kenyan system (Lauritzen, 2016; Mendenhall & Chopra, 2016; Smith et al., 2016).

While life skills education is currently taught one session per week in secondary school, it will no longer be a stand-alone subject in the proposed 2-6-6-3 education system. Instead, the core competencies will be included transversally. Apart from citizenship, these competencies (i.e., communication, collaboration, self-efficacy, critical thinking, problem-solving, creativity and imagination, digital literacy and learning to learn) are only indirectly connected to indirect peace, multicultural or human rights education (KICD, 2017, p 21). Still, notions that promote social cohesion are integrated in other subjects, such as 'history and government' (for a review, see Ibrahim, 2021). In the first grade of secondary school (form 1, expected school age of 14), students study the cultural practices of various ethnic groups in Kenya, which is extended to groups outside of Kenya in the second grade. They also look at the political organization of these groups, focussing particularly on the decentralized kingdoms of the Asante in Ghana, the Buganda in Uganda, and the Shona in Zimbabwe. The 'history and government' curriculum also addresses the political history of Kenya, starting with an analysis of ethnic associations' contributions to the struggle for independence in Kenya in the third grade. It even discusses the politicization of ethnicity. In the final year, students are encouraged to examine how "many of the political parties are ethnically inclined" and "lack a national outlook which has hindered the development of democratic ideals for national unity" (Form IV textbook: History & Government, 2015, p. 99). Finally, it also discusses the ways in which different social, political and economic inequalities can contribute to violent conflict. However, rather than looking inwards, students analyse the war-affected context of the DR Congo, which they compare with the relatively peaceful Republic of Tanzania (Form IV textbook: History & Government, 2015, p. 85). Other subjects integrate similar topics. The first-year English textbook, for instance, advises against electing leaders based on ethnicity:

> Most people do not know what to look for in a leader. Some base their choice on the gender of the person. For others, what matters is where somebody comes from ... This is unfortunate. Our choice should be determined by more worthwhile reasons. (Form I: Excelling in English: An Integrated Approach, 2016, p. 140)

It continues by outlining leadership qualities, such as promoting national unity within ethnic diversity, improving the welfare and wellbeing of citizens, and demonstrating a sense of responsibility, among others. While the curriculum does not explicitly discuss the 2007-2008 post-electoral violence, or any other episodes of violent outbursts, teaching about the political history of Kenya and its social inequalities does provide opportunities to address conflict history too.

3.3. Survey data

Eight years after the post-electoral violence (i.e., in 2016), we visited 64 government-funded and privately-funded secondary schools across the following neighbourhoods of Nairobi: Dagoretti, Embakasi, Lang'ata, Makadara, Kamukunji, Kasarani, Njiru, Starehe, and Westlands. In total, 925 secondary school teachers participated; an overview of teachers' background characteristics can be found in Table 3.1. The youngest teacher was 19 years old at the time of data collection, the oldest teacher 83. Slightly more than half of the participating teachers was male (52.2%). In terms of ethnicity, there was an overrepresentation of Luo (18.5%) and Luhya (19.1%) compared to their shares in the general population (12.4% and 14.4%, respectively), and relatively few Kalenjin (4.4%) compared to their share in the general population (11.8%). There were about as many Kikuyu (21.1%) and Kamba (10.4%) teachers as there were in the general population. Finally, 11.4% of teachers identified as Kisii, 4.2% as Meru and 10.9% identified as one of the many smaller ethnic groups in the country. Notably, the largest

Table 3.1. Teacher Characteristics of the Kenyan sample (N=925)

Variable	%	Mean (SD)	Min.	Max.
Age		33.04 (9.97)	19	83
Teaching experience (in years)		9.39 (9.21)	0	63
Gender				
Male	52.2%			
Female	47.8%			
Ethnicity				
Kikuyu	21.1%			
Luo	18.5%			
Luhya	19.1%			
Kalenjin	4.4%			
Kamba	10.4%			
Kisii	11.4%			
Meru	4.2%			
Other	10.9%			
Religion				
Christianity	95.5%			
Islam	0.8%			
Other	3.8%			
Education level				
MA degree or higher	18.8%			
BA degree	72.5%			
Diploma teacher college	8.4%			
Subjects taught (combinations possible)				
National subjects[a]	54.5%			
Other social sciences[b]	17.4%			
Math & natural sciences[c]	43.9%			
Other[d]	9.0%			

Notes: [a]includes national languages, history & government, geography, religious education, social studies and life skills education; [b]includes foreign languages, economics, business studies, ICT; [c]includes physics, chemistry, and biology; [d]includes physical education, technical education, arts group of teachers (39%) felt the epithet Kenyan fitted them as well as the one from their ethnic group, whereas 31.6% felt more Kenyan and 22.2% more or only Kenyan. Only 6.6% felt that they belonged more, or only to their ethnic group – six teachers did not have the Kenyan nationality (0.6%). In terms of religion, the sample was very homogenous (95.5% are Christian).

On average, teachers had been teaching for about 9.4 years (SD=9.2). Most teachers attended university, obtaining a Bachelor's (72.5%) or a Master's (18.8%) degree. 8.4% obtained a diploma from a teacher training college – only two teachers did not obtain any tertiary degree. In terms of subjects taught, the majority (54.5%) taught at least one of the so-called 'national' subjects, which include KiSwahili (17.8%), English (17.2%), history and government (14.7%), geography (11.7%), religious education (17.2%), and life skills education (4.3%). There was also a considerable group (43.9%) teaching mathematics, biology, physics and/or chemistry. Within the group of other social science subjects, teachers of economics and business studies constituted the large majority.

3.4. Support for (in)direct peace education

Whereas the official secondary school curriculum does not explicitly address the post-election violence of 2007-2008 or earlier episodes of ethnic tension and conflict, the subjects of 'history & government' and English do offer the possibility to discuss the politicization of ethnicity to some extent. Teachers of those subjects are therefore in a position that allows them to make connections to their country's past. But did the teachers in our sample do so? And to what extent did the participating teachers actually support discussing the country's ethnic tensions and episodic violence in the classroom? In this section, we will examine teachers' attitudes and views, focusing on their epistemological outlook on direct peace education ('social utility of teaching conflict history'), which enables us to position them on the horizontal axis of our new framework. After a brief examination of teachers' views on ethnic diversity in Kenya more generally, we will first look into their attitudes towards multicultural education as a variant of indirect peace education. After discussing teachers' support for multicultural education, we turn to direct peace education and teaching about the post-election violence of 2007-2008 in particular. We predominantly present descriptive survey data, complemented with interview data (see also Kuppens et al., 2020).

3.4.1. Support for multicultural education

To assess teachers' views on ethnic diversity in general, our survey included four statements rated on a seven-point Likert scale ranging from 1 'Strongly disagree' to 7 'Strongly agree'. Our results showed that, on the one hand, teachers (strongly) agreed (71.8%) that ethnic diversity enriches Kenya (see Table 3.2.). Similarly, an even greater number of teachers (90.3%) supported the idea that all Kenyans should be familiar with the customs and traditions of other ethnic and religious groups. On the other hand, ethnic diversity was also perceived as a threat to Kenya's political stability by many (65.9%). 83.9% of teachers therefore agreed (strongly) that ethnic loyalties should be broken down for the sake of national unity. Our interviews also revealed the challenge of balancing unity and diversity in a highly diverse society, especially where ethnic relations have sometimes turned violent. One teacher explained it as follows: "When you hear a politician in Kenya calling for unity it is never national unity; it is ethnic unity for their own gain" (KiSwahili teacher, Makadara, 2016).

To assess teachers' support for multicultural education, we used Banks' (1993) seminal five dimensions of multicultural education. The first dimension relates to the materials used for multicultural education, or the "extent to which teachers use examples, data and information from a variety of cultures and groups to illustrate key concepts, principles, generalizations and theories in their subject area or disciplines" (Banks, 1993, p. 5). The second dimension of 'knowledge creation' expects teachers to help their students understand that knowledge is culturally constructed and contested (see also Bennett, 2001, p. 176; Stephan & Stephan, 2001, p. 49). Third, multicultural education should contribute to developing positive attitudes toward different ethnic groups (dimension of 'prejudice reduction') and, fourth, facilitate academic achievement of *all* students, irrespective of (ethnic) background, through the use of inclusive teaching techniques and methods (dimension of 'equity pedagogy'). Finally, the school culture in its entirety should ensure equal learning opportunities and cultural empowerment for all students irrespective of their background (Banks, 1993, p. 7). We interviewed teachers and matched relevant survey items with the respective dimensions as outlined in Table 3.3. (for a more detailed discussion, see Kuppens et al., 2020).

Table 3.2. Percentage of secondary school teachers by extent of agreement with the survey statements on ethnic diversity in Kenya (N=925)

	Strongly disagree	Disagree	Rather disagree	Nor disagree, neither agree	Rather agree	Agree	Strongly agree
Ethnic diversity enriches Kenya.	15.2	6.6	3.7	2.6	12.1	19.1	40.6
Kenyans should be familiar with the customs and traditions of other ethnic and religious groups.	3.7	1.9	1.3	2.8	7.7	25.6	57.0
Ethnic diversity is a threat to Kenya's political stability.	18.1	8.6	3.8	3.7	6.6	12.9	46.4
For the sake of national unity, ethnic loyalties must be broken down.	5.6	5.0	2.5	2.9	5.8	16.4	61.7

Table 3.3. Operationalization of the five dimensional framework of multicultural education by Banks (1993)

Dimensions	Indicators (non-exhaustive)	Survey items
Content integration	• Teachers give and/or ask pupils for examples on the history, language, and traditions of diverse ethnic groups in society; • Curricula incorporate content on diverse ethnic groups in society; • Classroom materials reflect diverse cultural backgrounds (e.g. mandatory readings); • Minority groups are represented in curricula;	The curriculum needs to include the study of the customs and traditions of the main ethnic and religious groups in Kenya.
Knowledge construction	• Teaching practices stimulate critical thinking; • Teachers provide context to historical and current events discussed in the classroom; • Integration of multiple perspectives; • Critical analysis of the place of minority groups in society;	No survey items
Prejudice reduction	• Teachers debunk stereotypes; • Prevention of stereotyping in the classroom; • Discouragement of stereotyping and discrimination; • Promotion of cross-cultural interactions (intergroup contact);	Diversity at school contributes to the debunking of stereotypes. Schools are the ideal place for pupils to learn how to respect other ethnic groups.
Equity pedagogy	• Lessons tailored to the abilities and cultural background of pupils; • Use of cultural knowledge to make learning more relevant; • Culture-sensitive teaching practices; • Teachers have high expectations of all pupils; • Cooperative learning techniques;	To what extent do you take pupils' ethnic and/or religious background into account when you interact with them?

Dimensions	Indicators (non-exhaustive)	Survey items
Empowering school culture	• Accommodation of language policies; • Accommodation of dress regulations; • Diverse ethnic school composition; • Extra-curricular school events (e.g. sports, arts, drama) promoting multiculturalism; • Positive school-community relations.	Pupils should be allowed to speak their ethnic language on the playground; Pupils have the right to wear cultural or religious clothing and/or symbols at school.

Note: This table was first published in Kuppens, Ibrahim & Langer (2020) with the exception of item 2 of 'prejudice reduction' which has been added.

Our data shows that, in terms of content integration, a total of 70.8% of the teachers supported the inclusion of the customs and traditions of the main ethnic and religious groups in the curriculum (see Table 3.4.). One teacher explained that integrating such content "will enable the students or the children to appreciate other people's culture and respect it" (Music and Economics teacher, Westlands, 2016), even though there are "42 tribes in Kenya, we can't touch everything" (English teacher, Starehe, 2016). Many teachers also emphasized the importance of diverse examples, as this interview with a mathematics teacher shows:

> You make sure that when you are giving examples you give diverse examples. If you are using somebody's name, you can use from different tribes from all over Kenya. So that they do not see that everyday every time when you are giving examples, it is from only one tribe. When you use a Luo today, tomorrow you use a Kamba. They will see that you have no interest in any particular tribe. (Mathematics teacher, Kasarani, 2016)

Knowledge construction, the second dimension, was deemed more challenging. Some teachers nonetheless tried to help students understand how knowledge and beliefs about ethnic groups are created and sustained in Kenya. The third dimension of prejudice reduction again resonated strongly with teachers. Nearly all teachers (94.8%) agreed that schools are the ideal place for pupils to learn how to respect other ethnic groups. A great many teachers (75.6%) similarly believed that diversity at school contributes to the debunking of stereotypes. Besides intergroup groupwork and seating arrangements, teachers explained the way they used humour to actively challenge stereotypes when students express prejudice:

> For instance, you may be teaching, you ask for a response and then you will hear someone throw a stereotype from a corner. Ah, *mwalimu* [teacher] leave that one alone; she is a '*Kawoo*'. *Kawoo* is a short form for Kamba, but it has its own hidden meaning. The intention behind it is to dismiss that person (…) of course when the stereotype comes out the first thing is to laugh. But later on, when you discuss it and show how damaging it can be they tend to appear to understand that it can be damaging. (KiSwahili teacher, Dagoretti, 2016)

> I ask them: People say Luos are proud, they like living large, that is their assumption. But is it true? Don't we have Kikuyus who are also proud and live large? We have been saying Kikuyu women are brown; Luo women are [dark], is it true? We have dark Kikuyu women, very black! And yes, there are those who kept telling us [that] Kikuyus are thieves, that is not true. We have Luos who are thieves and very bad ones! [laughter] Yes, like that we can tease each other. (Geography and Christian Religious Education teacher, Makadara, 2016)

Turning to equity pedagogy, the fourth dimension, our data showed that 41.9% of teachers took the ethnic background of their pupils into account when teaching. Those who did explained, for instance, how they supported students who have difficulties in English pronunciation, like the Kikuyu who "have a problem with the pronunciation of 'r' and 'l' letters" (Mathematics and Biology teacher, Embakasi, 2016). Although the question aimed to assess how many teachers implement culturally sensitive teaching practices, some may have interpreted "taking the ethnic background of students into account" negatively – perhaps as providing favours to their kin, which many clearly disapproved of (see section 3.6.2.). As a result, the reported figure may underestimate the true proportion of teachers who apply equitable pedagogies.

Finally, when it comes to encouraging an empowering school culture, teachers liked organising multicultural extra-curricular activities: "We will continue with these interactions, games, sports, drama, and music festivals, where students from different schools, cultures interact. Then they will see themselves as Kenyans" (Christian Religious Education teacher, Westlands, 2016). Another teacher shared: "If we are proud of our cultural values, we can organize cultural shows in schools and different communities present something from their culture. It will make others to appreciate how each community has a very good unique practice" (Geography teacher, Makadara, 2016). However, teachers did oppose multicultural school policies that they deemed divisive. For instance, most teachers opposed pupils speaking their ethnic language on the playground (81.3%) and wearing cultural or religious clothing and/or symbols at school (75%) – it is important to note that wearing a school uniform is mandatory in Kenya and that speaking local languages is officially prohibited. One teacher explained in this respect that "having one common language, KiSwahili, these students interact more and regard themselves as uniform without considering their ethnic backgrounds" (History & government teacher, Kasarani, 2016). Exceptionally, a teacher spoke out in favour of local languages:

> I think in Africa we should be allowed to speak in our African languages and that is when we shall be able to realise the best things that we have. From a tender age someone shall be learning what he or she understands and that motivates because you do something that you really understand (...) While the language barrier will be a major challenge as interactions shall be really reduced, it is the best way to go. (Economics and Business teacher, Westlands, 2016)

Exceptions aside, most teachers seem to emphasize unity *over* diversity, rather than celebrating unity *in* diversity (Kuppens et al., 2020; see also Heyneman & Todoric-Bebic, 2000).

Before turning to direct peace education, we would like to examine whether there were any systematic differences among teachers in terms of support for multicultural education, considered from the perspective of the background variables of gender, age, teaching experience, and ethnicity, or of the subject matter taught. In evidence of the latter, for instance, national subjects are more amenable to multicultural education. To assess the existence and degree of any differences, we correlated the different statements and teachers' different background characteristics using Kendall's τ-b because of the ordinal nature of the variables – for ethnicity, we used the measure of association for nominal variables, Cramer's V (see Table A.1 in appendix). The few significant correlations

Table 3.4. Percentage of teachers by extent of agreement with the survey statements on multicultural education (N=925)

	Strongly disagree	Dis-agree	Rather disagree	Nor disagree, neither agree	Rather agree	Agree	Strongly agree
The curriculum needs to include the study of the customs & traditions of the main ethnic & religious groups in Kenya.	13.5	7.6	2.9	5.2	11.2	23.5	36.1
Schools are the ideal place for pupils to learn how to respect other ethnic groups.	1.8	1.2	1.1	1.1	5.5	24.2	65.1
Diversity at school contributes to the debunking of stereotypes.	6.3	8.4	3.2	6.4	13.4	25.8	36.4
Pupils should be allowed to speak their ethnic language in the playground.	57.3	20.1	3.9	4.2	4.9	4.5	5.1
Pupils have the right to wear cultural or religious clothing and/or symbols at school.	42.7	25.2	7.1	5.0	6.5	6.7	6.8

that emerged were weak[4], but suggest that women, as well as older and more experienced teachers emphasized unity slightly more than male, younger colleagues – please also note that female teachers tended to be somewhat older than their male peers.[5] Most notably, women appeared to be slightly more inclined than men to oppose the use of one's mother tongue on the playground and the wearing of cultural attires and/or symbols. Older and more experienced teachers also tended to be more opposed to the latter (but not necessarily to the former), while simultaneously they were more convinced that schools are the ideal place for pupils to learn how to respect other ethnic groups and to debunk stereotypes. Notably, teachers of the national subjects were slightly more inclined to support the inclusion of the customs and traditions of Kenya's main ethnic groups in in the curriculum. Yet like the female teachers, they were also somewhat more opposed to the use of one's mother tongue at school.

3.4.2. Support for direct peace education

To understand teachers' support for engaging with multiple perspectives on the violent past, the survey queried teachers at what levels of education they thought the political history of Kenya, and the causes and consequences of the post-electoral violence of 2007-2008 in particular, should be taught, if at all. Interestingly, the results showed that about 60% of teachers thought that the political history of Kenya, as well as the causes and consequences of the post-electoral violence should be taught at school, whether at primary or secondary level (see bar chart 3.1.). One teacher used the following allegory to explain his support – a view shared by other colleagues:

> A generation is being built by depending on what happened. For something not to repeat itself, the generation has to know whether the thing was wrong or right, and which direction we should follow. So that one [i.e., the post-election violence] should also be taught, and we should also teach the mechanism, the ways to follow, and the problems, the impacts that it brought upon the nation. (History & government teacher, Njiru, 2016).

> When you drive a car, you have to use the side-mirror, isn't it? To look back and see where you are going. I know you have those pictures where you are young. You say when you look at them: 'Am I the one?'. You have to look back and see

> if you are progressing or retrogressing. So the post-election violence, (...) we should at least remind them [i.e., students] and tell them the impact or effects, of fighting one another (...) So it should be emphasized so that in the future they don't repeat. (History & government, and KiSwahili teacher, Westlands, 2016)

> It is good to teach them about the political, ethnic and religious violence, because it makes them understand the reasons why there are such things and how they can avoid them, and the importance of having harmony in a community. (KiSwahili and English teacher, Kasarani, 2016)

These quotes suggest that these teachers shared the belief that underpins peace education and transitional justice scholarship and practice which is that learning *about* the violent past will engender learning *from* it. Some teachers had already experimented with integrating some elements of conflict-history education. Notably, the interviews suggested that this was particularly the case for teachers of the national subjects: "For teachers of history as a subject, or Christian religious education, where we promote unity, that [i.e., conflict-history education] is what we teach in class" (Christian religious education teacher, Westlands, 2016). Similarly, a KiSwahili teacher (Dagoretti, 2016) shared:

> We have these literature books where there are a lot of issues about tribalism and everything. So I tell them this writer knew we are in a certain country where tribalism is the order of the day and therefore the question of undoing these things comes up easily. Then I give them examples of what is happening in this country, 2007-2008, 1992, 1993, 2002; ethnic tensions, ethnic wars and all that.

Whereas teachers who supported the inclusion of Kenya's political history at the primary level were also more likely to support the teaching of the causes and consequences of the post-election violence at that level – the same was true for teachers at the secondary level – it is important to note that teachers who supported the inclusion of Kenya's post-election violence at the primary level were not more likely to support it at the secondary level, too.[6] This suggests that overall there was, in principle, strong support for direct peace education, but that teachers didn't always agree on which level of education was most appropriate for teaching about past ethnic clashes. One teacher in favour of starting at primary level argued:

88 EMPIRICAL EVIDENCE

> If you want to create a good foundation, then it should start early. So it would be better if it starts somewhere middle primary, somewhere there. Not, of course lower primary, it may not be very effective because at that time they have not known those differences [i.e., between ethnic groups]. But those differences come at around, before adolescence stage. That is around class 5, 6.[7] It would be very convenient to have it at that time. (Economics and Music teacher, Westlands, 2016)

However, other teachers considered this too young: "it is supposed to be only on secondary level because in secondary they are mature people" (KiSwahili teacher, Lang'ata, 2016). We also examined if there were individual traits that could explain differences in teachers' views on the required level for conflict-history education. In terms of support at the secondary level, neither sex, age, teaching experience or teaching one of the national subjects could explain the differences. At the primary level, however, there were significant but weak correlations between sex, age, and teaching experience.[8] These indicate that women and older, more experienced teachers were slightly more likely than younger, less experienced, male colleagues to support direct peace education in the earlier years of education – remember that on average, female teachers tended to be somewhat older than their male counterparts.

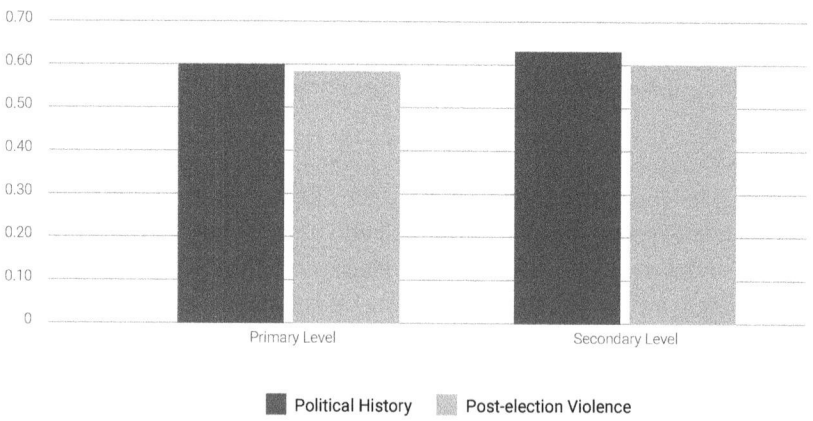

Bar chart 3.1. Support for direct peace education by level of education among Kenyan teachers (N=925)

3.5. (Dis)comfort

As an indicator of sociological time, the Kenyan teacher data thus suggests that there was significant 'support from below' for direct peace education at the time of our survey. In this section, we empirically examine teachers' position on the lower part of the framework's vertical axis, focussing on the discomfort teachers experienced with the idea of direct peace education. To do so, we primarily rely on the interviews we conducted with the teachers who participated in the survey. Two main areas of discomfort emerged: on the one hand the risk of retraumatization and on the other hand fears related to the politicization of ethnicity in the classroom and beyond.

One recurring concern in the literature about direct peace education is the potential for retraumatization. Many of the interviewed teachers did recount traumatic experiences from the post-election violence. They recounted a family shop was burned down (KiSwahili teacher, Kasarani, 2016), physical attacks (Geography and Kiswahili teacher, Kasarani, 2016) and one teacher had to change schools:

> Because of the violence that was going on, myself and a few colleagues were actually almost attacked on our way to school one morning. In fact, the vehicle was stopped and they ordered us to alight from the vehicle. And the order was; anyone who is from this part of the country [eastern or western as the incident happened at Kikuyu] alight from this vehicle. So we all sat back because you cannot make it so easy for them. But the driver looked back [inside the vehicle] and told them [the assaulters] that none of these people [the passengers] look like they are from that part of the country. So we proceeded to school. Yet, that was the last day I went to that school. I never went back. (KiSwahili teacher, Dagoretti, 2016)

For some teachers, these traumatic experiences did not change their attitude towards direct peace education:

> I think I personally can talk about it, because I was also affected and I tell them the effects. I cannot talk about another person, because I don't know how he will take it. Because maybe someone lost a close relative, are you getting it? So I don't know how he is feeling. But to me, I can talk about it freely. (History & government, and KiSwahili teacher, Westlands, 2016)

Others believed the student's perspective merited more consideration:

> I think it [i.e., conflict-history education] should not be emphasized too much, because in the end run, it will make people more hypersensitive than they are. They are already demarcated (…) So if you put it on a hypersensitive mode, and already they are still on the back, when you confront them they will feel much more worse than they are (Geography and Mathematics teacher, Dagoretti, 2016; see also box 3.1. for similar concerns)

For the same reasons, some teachers even wished to change the approach to discussing land issues in Kenya, which, unlike the post-election violence, are part of the official curriculum:

> When you say [that the] Mau Mau forest has been encroached by people from the Central province [Kikuyu] and people from the Rift Valley [Kalenjin], how will people from other areas think about them? (…) We have students who have been affected by tribal clashes because of land, what happened in 2007–2008 is evident. And we come and be talking about it in our syllabus. I wish we diverted it so that it creates a positive agenda to the pupils when you are handling the land issue. (Geography teacher, Kasarani, 2016)

While acknowledging the risk that it could cause students to relive the trauma they suffered, other teachers believed this risk had diminished over time (and would continue to diminish):

> Some of them are young, they were not there or they did not see these things. They only wonder, they just wonder what you are talking about. They feel very bad and sorry. But some of them, the senior ones, the ones that are maybe in form 4 [expected age of 17-18] may have seen these things practically. They could just get offended. Some of them may even cry if you remind them of what happened, they just cry. (…) Some of will tell you "my parents were mistreated by such and such". So, you may find a situation where some students not wanting to work with some students from a given area, but of course it is almost disappearing over the course of time. (Economics and Music teacher, Westlands, 2016)

The political climate, however, was still perceived as tense. No longer afraid of traumatizing students again, the teacher from the quote above continued:

> This area of ethnicity and cohesion is a very sensitive area and many people don't want to talk about it because they even don't know how to handle it; because somebody may think that you are talking about somebody else. There is a lot of suspicion. (Economics and Music teacher, Westlands, 2016)

Like him, there was a considerable number of teachers who did not feel comfortable to discuss the post-election violence, and ethnicity and ethnic politics in general, because of fears to stir up political animosities between students: "I do not want to lie, the Luos and the Kikuyus they are not in good terms politically. So the students will carry that, when they hear parents speak against the Luos they will also be against Luos" (Economics and Business teacher, Kasarani, 2016). His colleague teaching 'history and government' confirmed: "The students themselves have divisions in that there is one camp; there is another camp, depending on how maybe the politics are being done" (2016). This seemed to be the main reason for teachers to avoid discussing the post-election violence. And, whereas concerns over traumatizing students again were perceived to decrease with the passing of time, this was not the case for the politicization of ethnicity in the school environment. On the contrary, some teachers believed that the risk of politics entering the school environment was steadily increasing:

> You know, the students we have today are more informed than the students we [ever] had before. Because they have access to information; they google, they go to the internet, they listen to the radio, they go to the TV, they are able to watch what is happening and therefore I can say that in the long run if things are not scaled down, it might end up affecting us down there [here] in the school. So I think the tribal affair from the outside environment will soon start having an impact on the school if something is not done. (Economics teacher, Stahere, 2016)

Particularly around election times, ethnic affiliations would come to the fore to the extent that, as one teacher explained, parents are careful not to send children to schools dominated by the 'other' group: "when you hear that your son or your daughter has been admitted to a school very far from your ethnic community we fear because of what happened in

2007-2008" (Arts teacher, Kamukunji, 2016). So if "election time finds my child in school (...), I [teacher speaks as a Kikuyu] will not take my child to Kisumu [main city of the region where the Luo are dominant] even if he is admitted [to] the national school" (Chemistry teacher, Starehe, 2016). The same teacher also explained how tensions rise among staff at those times:

> You see the things that people will be posting [in the WhatsApp group] you can almost tell one is inclined on this and most of these political things are purely tribal, (...) even though we have been discouraging people from sending tribal sentiments. (Chemistry teacher, Starehe, 2016)

A minority of teachers was of the opinion that these 'micropolitics' were also at play outside of election times: "Politics affect teachers' interactions, especially between these big tribes which are predominant in politics" (Mathematics teacher, Westlands, 2016). Yet, he added, it "is a cold war; interactions between teachers, that negativity amongst teachers. It is a cold war. It does not explode." Most even considered statements like "talks about this tribe is bad; my tribe is good" as "normal" to the extent that Kenyan teachers would "not view it [tribalism] as a problem. It is just something that is in us" (English teacher, Kasarani, 2016).

Box 3.1. A 'critical design expert' in the making? Focus on Jonathan (pseudonym), Economics teacher in the neighbourhood of Embakasi (2016)

Researcher: Do you think that political values should be taught to students?

Teacher: Yes, I think life is made up of three main aspects: economic, social and political. So we cannot ignore the political when we are teaching. It is from there that we understand the structure of leadership, which is very important. I think students should also be taught that politics does not mean subdivision into ethnic cocoons.

Researcher: How can we teach students that politics should unite instead of divide, while at the same time students are confronted with hate speech and political division in the media?

Teacher: (...) when we go to class we can always tell them examples like currently we have got some of the leaders who are actually arrested and denied their freedom because of hate speech. (…) So, we should teach them that once they become leaders, they should know how to share the national cake, to distribute resources equally. That is what I think can really make us live peacefully. I think it is the bone of contention today.

Researcher: Do you also think that political history should be included, and if so, from what age on?

Teacher: Yes, political history is important because from there we can be able to judge whatever is coming for the future. When we want to say that we don't want to talk about the political history, then we don't know where we are heading to. I think people who are in class 1, 2, up until 3, most of them won't understand about the structure of leadership, so from class 4 is okay.

Researcher: What about the specific episode of 2007-2008?

Teacher: It should also be included, but carefully. I think it will help us to learn about the negative effects of violence. When we tell something about how people are burned in a particular church, we discourage the students to engage in such activities. So, when you talk about the political violence that we had in 2007, it is just necessary to learn about the negative effects of war.

Researcher: When you discuss such a topic, are the students interested?

Teacher: They are so interested. Particularly they want to know how events unfolded. When you reach the point on which you explain that people are killed, you see that they are emotionally touched. So that's a sign that they are learning that this thing has got big negative effects.

Researcher: Is it difficult for a teacher to teach such a topic?

Teacher: Yes, it could be difficult, particularly if you have a student whose parent was killed. So, that time obviously, the child will have some emotional feelings that are not easy to control.

Researcher: Do you think that teachers are sufficiently trained to handle such situations?

Teacher: All the teachers from our university have been trained on guidance and counselling. The moment you realize that a student has got such kind of trauma, then it is necessary that we call them in a separate environment and then start talking about this issue and ensure them that life will still continue. So, through guidance and counselling, all teachers are ready to handle that.

3.6. (In)competence: Stereotyping and ethnic favouritism in the classroom

Research has shown that people inevitably think in groups or categories to simplify and navigate complex social environments (e.g. Allport, 1954, p.19; Devine & Sharp, 2009, p.61; Reyna, 2000, p.92). Teachers can nevertheless 'correct' the stereotypes they hold, but only if they are aware of their existence and consciously decide not to act on them (e.g. Devine, 1989; Fazio, 1990; Wegener & Petty, 1995 in Olson & Kendrick, 2008, p. 120). Whereas large-scale research on teachers' stereotypes in a Western context has shown that the intergroup attitudes of teachers generally affect their teaching (see e.g. Chang & Demyan, 2007; Tenenbaum & Ruck, 2007), similar studies have so far not been conducted in post-conflict and divided societies, even though teachers in these contexts are significantly more prone to negative intergroup attitudes due to their increased exposure to intergroup tensions and possibly violence (e.g. Bentrovato et al., 2016; Zembylas et al., 2016). For the Kenya case study, we therefore focus particularly on the stereotypes teachers hold to establish their position along the upper part of our framework's vertical axis (see also Kuppens, Langer & Ibrahim, 2018). After examining stereotyping, we turn to ethnic favouritism in the classroom. In a context such as this, where ethnic loyalties, stereotyping and favouritism appear deeply engrained in the political system, teachers who favour pupils who belong to their own ethnic group or benefit pupils who do not necessarily merit this treatment, imply that ethnic favouritism is normal and socially acceptable within, but by extension also outside, of a school context; thereby potentially exacerbating the politicization of ethnicity (see also Kuppens & Langer, 2022). In the following sections, we will once again combine survey data with interview data to examine these issues.

3.6.1. Stereotyping in the classroom

Stereotypes may be considered as overgeneralizations of character traits to members of a specific group (Hamilton et al., 2009, p. 179). Ethnic stereotyping is highly prevalent in Kenya. Common stereotypes include the Kikuyu being exploitative and money-loving; the Luo intelligent, yet violent; and the Maasai valuing cattle and grass above all else (Hornsby, 2013, p. 788; Ndonye et al., 2015, pp. 47-48; see also Ibrahim, 2021). Although

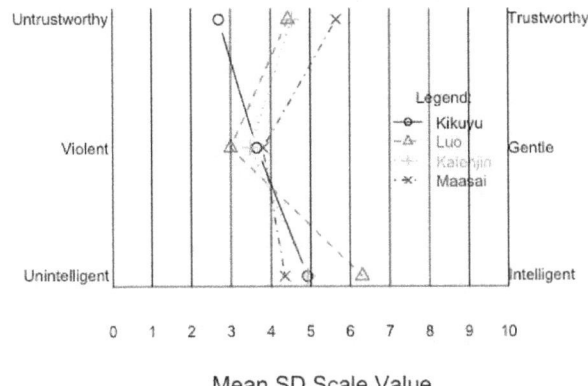

Figure 3.1. Kenyan teachers' attitudes on three semantic-differential scales assessing the extent of stereotypic ascription of characteristics to ethnic groups (from Kuppens et al., 2018)

stereotypes can be random and meaningless (and often used jokingly), they can lead to, or justify, social exclusion and discrimination, or even violence (e.g. Beelmann & Heinemann, 2014, p. 10; Brown & Bigler, 2002, p. 79; Reyna, 2000, p. 86). This was evident during the 2007-2008 post-election violence, when common stereotypes were used to incite ethnic hatred (HRW, 2008; Ndonye et al., 2015; Yieke, 2008). On local radio stations and in text messaging (Abdi Ismail & Deane, 2008; Makinen & Kuira, 2008, p. 331), Kibaki was represented as "a snake we have to get rid of" (HRW, 2008, p. 36) – exploiting mistrust towards the cunning, money loving Kikuyu (Hornsby, 2013, p. 748) – while Odinga was described as "the beast from the West" (Yieke, 2008, p. 16), hinting at the idea that the Luo, who are originally from Western Kenya, are violent. It was also said that Odinga was unable to lead given that he is a "child" (HRW, 2008, p. 4; see also Nyairo, 2015). Note in this respect that contrary to most other ethnic groups in Kenya, the Luo do not practise circumcision to symbolise the transition from child- to manhood.

To assess their stereotypes, we asked teachers to rate the Kikuyu, Luo, Kalenjin, and Maasai on three semantic-differential scales (ranging from

–5 to 5 with 0 indicating a neutral position) with respect to the following stereotype-congruent traits: trustworthiness, intelligence and aggression. Teachers prone to stereotyping were expected to rate the Kikuyu as more untrustworthy; the Luo as more intelligent and violent; and the Maasai as less intelligent than other groups. We also assessed whether teachers exhibited an ingroup bias, in other words a more positive assessment of their own group (note that these results were first published in Kuppens et al., 2018).

Figure 3.1. visualizes the mean scores per trait and ethnic group, excluding ingroup scores. It shows that, in line with common stereotypes, the Kikuyu were perceived to be the least trustworthy; the Luo were rated the most intelligent, as well as violent; and the Maasai were perceived to be the least intelligent. Further analyses showed that teachers' stereotypic attitudes showed no significant variation among schools, despite notable differences in school organization, and were not influenced by teachers' age, education level, teaching experience, or gender (see Kuppens et al., 2018). The interviews demonstrated that these stereotypes were not unknown to teachers:

> Whenever it comes to matters of doing business, they [i.e., the Kikuyu] want to make profit. So whenever it comes to that side, they look at them as untrustworthy, not as hardworking. (Biology teacher, Embakasi, 2016)

> When you look at the performance per term you find Luo students dominate in the top. You can actually see but we do not really like to tell them that. (Mathematics teacher, Dagoretti, 2016)

> In our country, mostly, the ones who will go to the streets are the Luo. They want to fight and they want to throw stones. I think it is their nature. (Mathematics teacher, Lang'ata, 2016)

> When you are known to be a Maasai, they consider them to be illiterate. So when they come with those attires, they won't [hesitates] … Ok, most people won't look beyond their attires. They just look at what they have in their mind. They just treat them generally as, they consider them as illiterate and more concerned with pastoralism. Learning, there is little learning with them. (English teacher, Kasarani, 2016)

What is more, teachers acknowledged that they too were raised with negative images of the 'other': "When I was growing up, I was told my tribe does not like this tribe and this information I received from my parents" (History & government teacher, Njiru, 2016). Still, teachers were usually very quick to refute these stereotypes. After confiding that she perceived Luo to be violent, the mathematics teacher above continued, "when we come to school, I don't really have cases of the Luo being more violent. It is probably based on the political view, but in school, they don't fight" (2016). Interestingly, another teacher tried to mitigate the stereotype after conforming to it: "Indiscipline issues come more from the Luo tribe. Personally, I attribute it to the state of life. Most students from that community here they are poor. They are poor and I think background translates into indiscipline" (Mathematics teacher, Westlands, 2016). Furthermore, while many teachers admitted that they held some stereotypes, they also expressed their motivation to renounce them:

> As teachers, we are not immune from that. When I hear you come from this community you know back in my mind I have those stereotypes, so sometimes you, I identify them. Sometimes you have to totally ignore them you know. (Arts teacher, Kamukunji, 2016)

Teachers were also prone to ingroup bias. Figures 3.2. to 3.4. show that ingroup ratings were consistently more positive than outgroup ratings. Still, these biases were also affected by societal stereotypes: even though the Kikuyu, for example, rated their own group more trustworthy than other groups did, it was still lower than the ratings the Luo and the Kalenjin attributed to their own groups. All in all, the presence of stereotypes and biases raise some questions regarding the ability of teachers to foster social cohesion through (in)direct peace education.

98 EMPIRICAL EVIDENCE

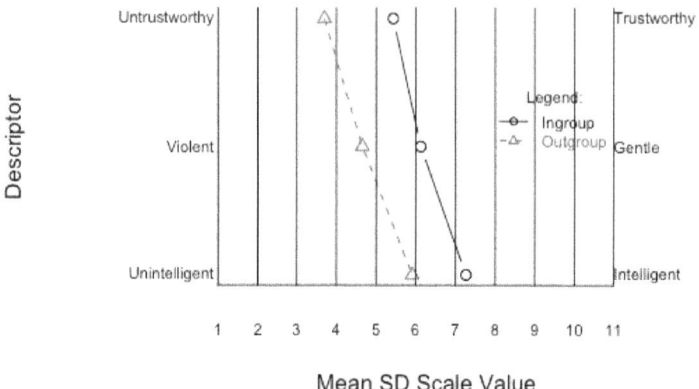

Figure 3.2. Kenyan teachers' attitudes towards ethnic Kikuyu differentiated by in- and outgroup belonging (from Kuppens et al., 2018)

Mean SD Scale Values: Luo

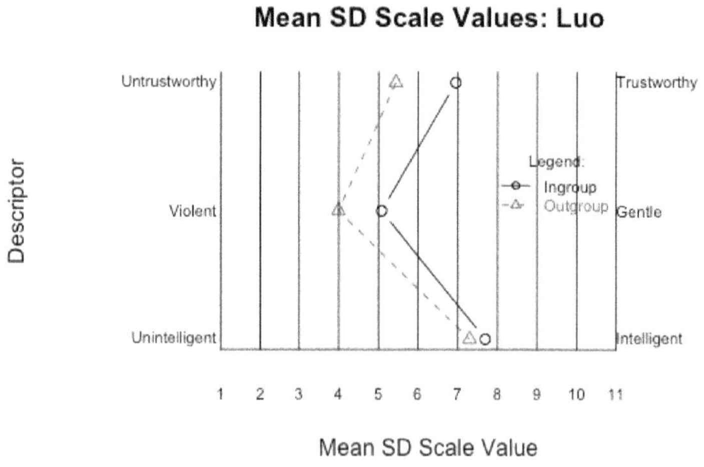

Figure 3.3. Kenyan teachers' attitudes towards ethnic Luo differentiated by in- and outgroup belonging (from Kuppens et al., 2018)

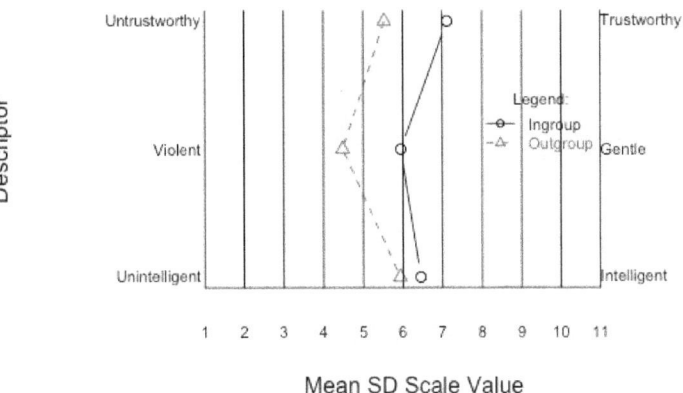

Figure 3.4. Kenyan teachers' attitudes towards ethnic Kalenjin differentiated by in- and outgroup belonging (from Kuppens et al., 2018)

3.6.2. Ethnic favouritism in the classroom

To gain insight into the incidence of ethnic favouritism in the classroom, we included a list experiment in our survey by which we hoped to establish the prevalence of attitudes or behaviour that are subject to a social desirability bias, and are therefore commonly underreported when asked about directly (these results were first published in Kuppens & Langer, 2022). Teachers were presented with a list of more and less common teaching situations and had to indicate the number of situations that applied to them. For all teachers, this list included the following situations:

- I have skipped a small part of the curriculum due to time concerns;
- I have used video material in class;
- I have made a spelling error on the blackboard;
- I have invited an external speaker to my classroom;

For half of the teachers, a fifth situation was added: "I have favoured a student from my own ethnic group". Since teachers were asked to indicate how many rather than which statements applied to them, they had no incentive not to be truthful about the fifth, sensitive situation about favouring certain students. By subtracting the mean sum of applicable situations in the first group (control group) from the mean sum of applicable situations in the second group (experimental group) – a difference-in-means test – we could extrapolate the percentage of teachers in Kenya who would already have favoured a student from their own ethnic group, which was 26% (see Table 3.5.; for more information on the method, see Holbrook & Krosnick, 2010; for a detailed description of the analysis, see Kuppens & Langer, 2022).

Table 3.5. Observed data from list experiment

Number of statements that apply to teacher	Control group (4 situations; N = 431)		Experimental group (5 situations; N = 463)	
	Frequency	%	Frequency	%
1	128	29.7	142	30.7
2	115	26.7	92	19.9
3	113	26.2	99	21.4
4	75	17.4	83	17.9
5			47	10.2
Mean (SD)	2.31 (1.077)		2.57 (1.353)	

Note: an adapted version of this table was first published in Kuppens & Langer (2022).

During the interviews, teachers confided that ethnic favours do occur, but that such favours were generally well-intended. Examples included showing more supportive behaviour, and providing more tangible support; as if they constituted acts of 'loyal subversion' (Levinson, 2015) exclusively towards students from their ingroup:

> You find that he (cf. a Luo teacher) has a lot of patience with the students from the Luo community, but no patience with the ones from the Kikuyu community or from other communities. (English, Life skills education and Christian religious education teacher, Dagoretti, 2016)

> I'm a Kikuyu, you find that all the Kikuyu students will come to me whenever they have a problem. Or…the students from the Luhya community will be

going to that person, and whenever they are together, they talk in their native language. (Mathematics and Biology teacher, Embakasi, 2016)

The Luhya, Kisii and Luo are here [in school], but the Kikuyus are dominant because the owner is a Kikuyu. So, she is trying to help the needy students from her region. (KiSwahili teacher, Lang'ata, 2016)

These favours can also be understood as expressions of solidarity with one's kin – respecting tradition. Still, even well-intentioned favours can be detrimental in the classroom, which teachers seemed aware of: "If a teacher does that (cf. giving ethnic favours), most of the students will not perform well, the students of the other communities" (Mathematics and Biology teacher, 2016). Most teachers, moreover, dismissed ethnic favouritism, stressing instead that teachers "should be able to bring equality, equity between students so that you can eradicate the issue of tribalism" (KiSwahili teacher, 2016).

Whereas teachers generally felt that ethnic favouritism was a marginal phenomenon in the classroom, most were not convinced that the school environment was immune to ethnic favouritism. Yet in their view, it largely occurred at management level and higher. For instance, teachers complained about ethnic discrimination in teacher appointments at privately-funded schools (generally, teachers at privately-funded schools are appointed by the management board, unlike teachers at government-funded schools who are appointed by the TSC): "I was discriminated just because I did not belong to that community. I was not given a job and I qualified, I knew I qualified" (KiSwahili teacher, Starehe, 2016). A further example related to the politics of resource distribution at the constituency level. As one teacher explained:

The area MP [Member of Parliament] and MCE [Metropolitan Chief Executive] happened not to be of the same ethnic group of our former principal. So, the principal would ask for assistance but they could say they would not help him because he is not from their ethnic background. (Science teacher, Makadara, 2016)

Another teacher gave an example of regional differences caused by policies favouring some groups at the expense of others: "if you go to central Kenya you find teachers with master's degrees are so many. But if you go to Turkana with a bachelor's degree you are far much ahead" (KiSwahili teacher, Dagoretti, 2016). Notably, these forms of ethnic favouritism can significantly increase grievances and cause a breakdown in social cohesion.

3.7. Situating Kenyan teachers within the framework of conflict-history education

Our findings suggest that eight years after the 2007-2008 post-election violence, the majority of Kenyan secondary school teachers was convinced of the social utility of integrating direct peace education. Whereas some preferred integrating it at the level of primary education, others had a preference for the secondary school level. Yet despite this support, two issues emerged that could affect the effective implementation of teaching about the causes and consequences of the post-election violence. First, a number of teachers felt very uncomfortable about this. They either feared that conflict-history education would increase instead of decrease the politicization of ethnicity; or dreaded making students relive the trauma they suffered. Second, stereotyping and ethnic favouritism remained prevalent among a substantial number of teachers. Although many teachers were aware of their stereotypes and consciously decided not to act on them – key preconditions to effectively eliminate prejudiced behaviour – we found that about one quarter of the teachers extended largely well-intended favours to students of the same ethnicity, which we deem harmful in the broader context of the politicization of ethnicity in Kenya. This suggests that our sample included both 'containers' and 'risk-takers' (and all positions in between). We therefore place the Kenyan teachers we interviewed partly in the upper right and partly in the lower right quadrants of our framework. The lack of electoral violence during the 2017 and 2022 presidential elections, along with the reduced emphasis on ethnicity in recent campaigns, may meanwhile have helped more teachers overcome their discomfort.

Even though some teachers felt sufficiently prepared (see box 3.1.), our results suggest that more teacher training is required to transform Kenyan teachers into 'critical design experts'. Tellingly, one teacher attested: "we never even considered that tribalism can be practiced in schools. I think it was assumed that it does not exist. So they do not prepare the teachers for that" (Mathematics teacher, Lang'ata, 2016). Another teacher suggested that training in multicultural education, and culturally sensitive teaching practices in particular, could help overcome ethnic favouritism in school:

> We have not been trained to handling people with regards to where they come from. Maybe if that could be put in as part of the curriculum, then change may start from schools with everyone being able to look at the other as the same; not as you come from this community or that. (Economics teacher, Stahere, 2016)

CHAPTER 4

Teaching about the violent past in Côte d'Ivoire

> During the crisis (...) we were at each other's throats. At each other's throats, I am not telling you, because at once the clans, the two clans were visible. In the same way that things were going in the city, it was like that at school. In fact, engaging in the debate on the causes of the Ivorian crisis (...), everyone already has his point of view. The debate would already be biased at the base. The teachers supporting Ouattara say that Ouattara's right. Those of Gbagbo say that Gbagbo is right. They will give causes in favour of the Gbagbo camp. (French teacher, Yopougon, 2015)

In April 2011, the post-electoral violence in Côte d'Ivoire ended when the then President Laurent Gbagbo was removed from power with the help of French and UN forces, and his opponent Alassane Ouattara assumed office. While both leaders claimed to have won the preceding December 2010 presidential elections, the international community recognized Ouattara as the legitimate president. The post-electoral violence was the most recent episode in a longer history of conflict that had its roots in the xenophobic politics of the 1990s and, from a longue durée perspective, in the ethnic patronage of the country's first post-independence president, Félix Houphouët-Boigny. In the first section of this chapter, we trace back this history of conflict and discuss the diverse interpretations of this history by various groups within Ivorian society. As the above quote shows, these competing narratives have survived the conflict. In spite of a range of peacebuilding initiatives, including a Truth and Dialogue Commission, Ivorians loyal to Gbagbo still claim that "their" candidate won, which leaves one to conclude that reconciliation remains an ongoing process.

Against this background, we examine teachers' support for conflict-history education and focus on their own interpretations of the past to explain their position on the integration of the violent past in the classroom. However, to provide context, we will first outline the structure of the education system in Côte d'Ivoire and describe the profile of the teachers who participated in our research. We will conclude the chapter by interpreting our findings through the lens of our theoretical framework.

4.1. Conflict dynamics

From independence in 1960 up until his death in 1993, Côte d'Ivoire was led by Félix Houphouët-Boigny. His presidency was characterized by economic growth and relative political stability through promoting ethnic patronage networks (Langer, 2010). However the so-called Houphouët compromise also set the stage for future conflicts, among other things by promoting uneven economic and social development across different regions and ethnic groups. This disparity meant that some areas and communities benefited more from state resources and infrastructure, while others were marginalized (Akindès, 2011). Whereas ethno-regional tensions had already surfaced against the background of the economic recession of the late 1970s, nativist struggles only came to the fore once the power vacuum left by Houphouët's death created a bitter contest between Henri Konan Bédié, the leader of Houphouët's *'Parti démocratique de Côte d'Ivoire'* (PDCI; Democratic party of Côte d'Ivoire), and the then prime minister, Alassane Ouattara. As the PDCI primarily drew its support from the south, Bédié, also a southerner, feared the electoral threat of his former party member's newly established *'Rassemblement des républicains'* (RDR; Rally of the republicans), which had a strong following among northerners, Muslims and migrant workers from neighbouring states who had come in large numbers to work in Côte d'Ivoire's predominantly southern based plantation economy (Arnaut, 2012). To defeat Ouattara, who, like many of his followers came from the north, he employed the ethno-nationalist ideology of *'Ivoirité'* to prevent him from standing. A group of academics and intellectuals close to President Henri Konan Bédié had framed *Ivoirité* as a cultural concept meant to distinguish the Ivorian "us" from the non-Ivorian "them" in response to concerns about authenticity following decades of mass migration. However, its controversial use led to the idea of citizenship becoming overly simplified and associated with a particular group of people, which created division (Babo, 2017; Cutolo, 2010). Consequently, the new 1994 electoral code imposed strict nationality requirements for presidential candidates and voters. The law effectively disenfranchised many northerners and prevented Ouattara from standing for president amid rumours about his alleged Burkinabé origins (Akindès, 2011; Langer, 2010). More broadly, northern Ivorians became increasingly marginalized due to their cultural ties with immigrant communities in Côte d'Ivoire and the misleading stereotype that all northerners are Muslim. As a result, they were often considered second-class citizens or *'Ivoiriens de circonstance'* ('Ivorians of circumstance') rather than *'Ivoiriens de souche'* ('native Ivorians'), shorthand for Ivorians of southern, Christian descent (Banégas, 2006; Bassett, 2003; Marshall-Fratani, 2006; see also Kuppens & Langer, 2023). Guillaume Soro, one of the leaders of the 2002 rebellion (see below), summarized the politics of *Ivoirité* as follows: "a word that in its true sense means nothing more than 'Côte d'Ivoire to Ivorians', that is to those who originate from the South, northerners were foreigners in their own country (...) what was called *Ivoirité* was merely invented to prevent that disturbing man [i.e., Ouattara] from running" (Soro, 2005, pp. 20-21; own translation). Once elected, Bédié further fuelled resentment by invoking *Ivoirité* to amend laws on land ownership that advantaged *'Ivoiriens de souche'* at the expense of northerners and immigrants. So ordinary citizens were forced to deal with laws that were designed by certain political elites to target specific political rivals (Babo, 2017).

In 1999, an army general called Robert Guéï ousted Bédié, but his rule was short-lived. In the subsequent elections that were organized one year later, he lost to Laurent Gbagbo, leader of the socialist *'Front populaire ivoirien'* (FPI; Ivorian popular front) – Ouattara was still disqualified. Although Gbagbo could count on support outside of his core ethnic base (which included the Bété, Gouro, and Guéré), largely because of the appeal of his anti-colonial discourse (Arnaut, 2012), ethnonationalism continued under his presidency (Babo, 2017; Bassett, 2011; Cutolo, 2010). By 2002, mounting frustrations resulted in disadvantaged sections of society, mainly northerners, joining forces and attempting to overthrow Gbagbo's administration in September of that year. While they failed to oust him, the rebels did seize control of about 60% of the territory in the north of the country (Akindès et al., 2010; McGovern, 2011; Popineau, 2017). In the subsequent five years, the country remained divided. Importantly, the anti-colonial Gbagbo denounced the rebels' grievances, and depicted the rebellion as a foreign intervention instead. He claimed that the rebellion was set up by the government of neighbouring Burkina Faso, which would have acted on behalf of France, the former colonizer. Victory over the rebels was therefore presented as a "true" or "second" independence from neo-colonial France (Förster, 2013).

While fighting only continued sporadically between 2002 and 2007, the signing of the Ouagadougou Peace Agreement in 2007 ushered in a new time of *"ni guerre, ni paix"* ('neither war nor peace'; see McGovern, 2011; Piccolino, 2017). The opposing parties agreed that sustainable peace would require new presidential elections and for the first time would include Ouattara. As such, the elections would be a landmark in the struggle for equality by the north (Akindès et al., 2010, p. 94). They did eventually take place in 2010, but they reignited conflict instead of bring peace. Violence erupted after incumbent president Gbagbo contested the electoral victory of Ouattara, claiming that the results had been rigged (Bouquet, 2011). He argued that the international community, and France in particular, preferred "a president from the IMF that understands their interests [...] to a Laurent Koudou Gbagbo" (Gbagbo & Mattei, 2014, p. 65; see also McGovern, 2011, p. 88). The crisis lasted until pro-Ouattara forces captured Gbagbo on 11 April 2011. An estimated 3,000 Ivorians lost their lives during the fighting (Amnesty International, 2013, p. 8).

Since Ouattara assumed the presidency in 2011, the country has been experiencing economic growth, at least at macro level, and relative political stability. Yet, so far, Ouattara's policies have failed to address the legacies of the conflict successfully, particularly the issue of land rights, the restructuring of the army, and the advancement of reconciliation and social cohesion (Piccolino, 2017). In spite of setting up the Dialogue, Truth and Reconciliation Commission (*Commission de Dialogue, Vérité et Reconciliation*, CDVR) and granting amnesty, Côte d'Ivoire seems tainted by a sense of 'victor's justice' that continues to threaten its fragile peace (e.g. Akindès, 2017; Amnesty International, 2013, p. 56; Bovcon, 2014, p. 71). Notably, the CDVR's report, when published two years after its conclusion, did no longer contain testimonies concerning the electoral support for Gbagbo, or concerning Ouattara's role in the post-electoral crisis (Piccolino, 2017, p. 54), and, apart from a few exceptions, only perpetrators associated with Gbagbo have been indicted and prosecuted. Furthermore, many former rebels were given important positions in government and state institutions, thereby enjoying de facto impunity for their suspected abuses committed during the Ivorian conflict (Akindès, 2017, p. 12; Tiemessen, 2014, p. 453). At the time of writing, Ouattara is completing his third term in office, which was vehemently contested by opposing parties many of whom boycotted the 2020 elections. While his candidacy followed the unexpected death of presidential candidate and former prime minister

Amadou Gon Coulibaly, his third term is evidence, Richard Banégas and Camille Popineau argue (2022), of the frailty of the peacebuilding process in the country, and revealing of an intensifying authoritarian turn of the post-conflict regime.

4.2. Education, conflict & peace

4.2.1. *Côte d'Ivoire's educational system*

Côte d'Ivoire's educational system is modelled after the old French system, which consists of six years of primary education and seven years of secondary education. The primary level is divided into three: two preparatory years, two years of elementary school and two years of middle school. At the end of middle school, pupils take national examinations to obtain the *Certificat d'Etudes Primaires et Elémentaires* (Certificate of Primary and Elementary Studies). Secondary education starts with the *'premier cycle'*, or lower secondary education, that runs from sixth year (expected school age of 12-13) to third year (expected school age of 15-16). It is followed by the *'second cycle'* (16 to 19 years old), or higher secondary education, which runs from second year (expected school age of 16-17) to *'la terminale'* or senior year (expected school age of 18-19). As they transition from lower to higher secondary education, students opt for general or technical education. To complete secondary education, students must pass their *'baccalaureate'* (Sany 2010, p. 2).

    Primary school teachers are trained by the *Centres d'Animation et de Formation Pédagogique* (Centres for Pedagogical Support and Training). Across the country, there are 14 such centres (amounting to 7,000 places in 2016). Notably, nearly 100% of primary school teachers in Côte d'Ivoire are trained (GEM, 2017). To become a secondary school teacher, aspiring teachers interested in working in the public sector attend the renowned *'Ecole Normale Supérieure'*. For aspiring teachers specializing in technical and physical education or the arts, there are dedicated institutes (the National Pedagogic Institute for Technical and Professional Education, the National Institute for Youth and Sports, and the National Higher Institute for the Arts and Cultural Action, respectively). Secondary school teacher training takes four (*'professeur de collège'*, lower secondary education) to six years (*'professeur de lycée'*, higher secondary education), apart from technical education teacher training which takes two years. Prospective teachers in the private sector typically complement their university degree in a relevant field of study with a two-week pedagogical training and internship organized by the Autonomous Service for the Supervision of Private Institutes. Teaching in a privately-funded school is generally less attractive than teaching in a public school, however: instead of the permanent contract offered public school teachers, most teachers at privately-funded schools are employed on a temporary basis and are merely remunerated for the number of hours they teach (*'les vacataires'*).

4.2.2. Education & conflict

The 2002-2007 civil war significantly disrupted the Ivorian education system. As a result of the country falling apart, 80% of the teachers left their post, and an estimated 50% of all pupils was deprived of education (Sany, 2010, p. 7; Popineau, 2017; government estimates). In areas occupied by the rebels, all educational investments and personnel allocations were frozen as part of the Gbagbo administration's strategy to discredit the rebels (Chelpi-den Hamer, 2014, p. 188). To ensure the continuity of education in spite of all this, the rebels set up an alternative system of education with the help of NGOs and donors (Lanoue, 2003, p. 130). Notably, high-school and university students who volunteered to teach were later officially accredited to teach in public schools (Popineau, 2017).

The flux of refugees from north to south also put pressure on the education system in the south of the country. To accommodate as many pupils as possible, a double-shift system was introduced (*'écoles de relai'*): a first group attended school in the morning and a second group in the afternoon. In addition, emergency schools (*'écoles de sauvetage'*) were set up (Chelpi-den Hamer & ROCARE, 2013, pp. 7-11). Also in the southern region, French schools and institutes were looted and burned down by young supporters of Gbagbo, allegedly to express their hatred towards neo-colonial France (Lanoue, 2007, p. 99). All in all, the disruptions caused by Côte d'Ivoire's civil war (2002-2007) resulted in an overall decline of 0.94 years of schooling among children and adolescents in areas affected by violence compared to those living in other areas (Dabalen & Paul, 2014, p. 1644).

Although more confined, the 2010-2011 post-electoral crisis had a heavy toll on the education system too, particularly in and around Abidjan. Throughout the country, 180 schools were looted and 173 (partially) destroyed, of which, respectively, 72 and 92 in Abidjan. Another 23 schools, of which 13 in Abidjan, were occupied by armed forces (Education Cluster, 2011, pp. 4-6). Although school was briefly interrupted, the Ministry of Education reorganized the year in semesters instead of trimesters and delayed the summer holidays to allow students to complete the year. Despite these efforts, many students dropped out of school as they fled the violence.

Besides suffering from the violence, the education system also contributed to escalating conflict dynamics. Although research did not identify any inappropriate content in the Ivorian curricula that could have fuelled the conflict (Chelpi-den Hamer & ROCARE, 2013, p. 26), the country has a history of unequal access to the education system and uneven allocation of educational funds, in particular disadvantaging the northern region. For example, by 2001, the net enrolment rate for primary education was only 50% in the north compared to 80% in the southwest (Sany, 2010, p. 3). Langer (2005) also highlighted a similar north-south divide in terms of primary school enrolment, primary school completion and literacy levels. Additionally, during the conflict, the educational sector became highly politicized. The 'Fédération Estudiantine et Scolaire de Côte d'Ivoire' (FESCI) – i.e. the country's then largest student organization – became actively involved in the Ivorian conflict (Sany, 2010, p. 8). Since its inception in 1990, the FESCI has been highly politicized, initially aligning with the then opposition parties (FPI and RDR) and serving as a platform for political dissent (see e.g. Popineau, 2017). Notably, both Guillaume Soro, a former rebel leader and later President of the National Assembly, and Charles Blé Goudé, Gbagbo's so-called 'youth general', served as the Secretary-General of the FESCI. After the former had rallied behind Gbagbo, their rivalry culminated in the infamous machete war in 2003 (see Popineau, 2017).

4.2.3. *Education & peace*

While the country's educational structures and curricula have largely remained the same throughout the political turmoil, a new decree saw the introduction of human rights and citizenship education to the curriculum following the end of hostilities in 2011, called *'Education aux Droits de l'Homme et à la Citoyenneté'* (EDHC) (Decree No. 2012-884, Presidency of the Republic of Côte d'Ivoire, 2012). The government described the subject as "a real opportunity" to bring about "a transition to a culture of peace and achieve together the ultimate objective of national reconciliation" after the country was "destabilized by the war that has been raging since September 2002, and culminating in the serious post-election crisis of November 2010" (Sacanoud et al., 2012, p. 6; own translation).[9] Notwithstanding this rationale, the subject had been in the pipeline for about a decade – also note that civic and moral education had already been part of the curriculum since 1983, but did not discuss human rights, peace or reconciliation. In 2002, notions of peace were first introduced into the Ivorian school curriculum through the primary school subject 'Issues of Daily Life' (Kanon, 2012, pp. 184-185). A year later, the UNICEF-supported 'Education for Peace and Tolerance' (PEPT) programme was implemented at the primary level, covering topics like tolerance, non-violence, conflict resolution, national integration, children's rights, and international humanitarian law (Ivorian National Commission for UNESCO, 2005, p. 4). Human rights were added in 2004, after Côte d'Ivoire signed up to the World Programme for Human Rights Education (United Nations resolution 59/113). At that point in time, discussions to develop and integrate EDHC were also initiated, but it was only in 2009 that the Ministry of National Education decided to integrate EDHC as a discipline alongside mathematics and French (OHCHR, 2010, p. 2). Developed in collaboration with the International Red Cross, UNICEF, and various NGOs, the subject has been part of the curriculum since 2012 (for a discussion, also see Kuppens & Langer, 2018).

EDHC is taught one hour per week from primary school up until the end of junior secondary school (expected age 15-16). The junior secondary school curriculum of EDHC is built around five core competencies: (C1) Children's rights, human rights and international humanitarian law, (C2) Citizenship and democratic principles, (C3) Road safety education, entrepreneurship and community life, (C4) Health preservation and sex education, and (C5) Environmental sanitation and environmental protection (MEN, 2012a; 2012b; see also Kuppens & Langer, 2018). These competences are taught based on age-specific themes. During the last year of lower secondary school, for example, students (expected age 15-16) study, among other things, the instruments and legal mechanisms that exist to protect vulnerable people from violence (C1), what constitutes responsible behaviour towards political parties and the institutions of the Republic (C2), which ethnic alliances exist and why (C3), what are the benefits of HIV testing (C4), and how to protect national parks and forest reserves (C5) (MEN, 2012b, p. 6). At no point, however, does the curriculum focus on the history of Côte d'Ivoire's violent disintegration. The subject is best described – as its name suggests – as an example of human rights and citizenship education, and thus as a type of indirect, rather than direct, peace education. Still, the subject does offer some opportunities to discuss the country's violent past. Pupils learn, for example, about the reintegration of child soldiers into society and the preservation of social peace (Grade 4; expected age 14-15), and about the rules to protect victims of armed conflict (Grade 5; expected age 13-14).

Note that other subjects also address the peace and conflict-related competencies of EDHC. In history-geography, grade 5 students (expected age 13-14), for instance, study the codes of conflict regulation, and grade 4 (expected age 14-15) students discuss traditional mechanisms to prevent and resolve conflict. The curriculum for Spanish even includes a hypothetical scenario that involves the arrival of a Spanish Red Cross team that comes to help war victims and instructs students to assist this team as interpreters (Grade 3; expected age 15-16). In French, students are likely to read the book '*On se chamaille pour une chaise*' ('Fighting over a seat') (Grade 4; expected age 14-15), a story about electoral tensions between a father and his daughter who are both running for local office. The arts curriculum also addresses conflict-related topics. In third grade, for example, students draw a pamphlet promoting humanitarian law, and in music class, pupils sing songs about anti-personnel mines (Grade 3; expected age 15-16) and child soldiers (Grade 5; expected age 13-14). And finally, in addition to both world wars, the curriculum of history-geography includes the Rwandan genocide (Grade 3; expected age 15-16) – in the past, the Rwandan genocide was alternated with the Biafra conflict. Still though, the curriculum materials do not make any relevant comparisons to Côte d'Ivoire's own conflict dynamics (see Kuppens & Langer, 2018).

4.3. Survey data

In 2015, which is to say four years after the end of the post-electoral crisis, we visited 77 schools in the de facto capital of Abidjan to survey teachers' support for (in)direct peace education, covering the neighbourhoods of Abobo, Adjamé, Attécoubé, Cocody, Koumassi, Marcory, Plateau, Treichville and Yopougon. A total of 984 secondary school teachers took part, ranging in age from 22 to 71. The majority of teachers were male

(84.3%), consistent with the national proportion of male secondary school teachers at that time (85.4%, see DPES-MENET, 2014, p. 22). The ethnic distribution of the teachers somewhat reflected the national distribution of the five largest and politically most relevant ethnic groups in the country (see Langer, 2005), although there was a notable bias towards southern ethnic groups. Abidjan being located in the south of the country, this is representative of the local context. Most teachers identified with one of the two largest southern ethnicities: 50.4% were Akan (compared to 42% nationally), and 18.7% Krou (compared to 13% nationally). Eight percent indicated belonging to the Mandé Sud (compared to 10% nationally). Among the northern groups, 10% were Gur or Voltaïc (compared to 18% nationally), followed by 8.6% Mandé Nord (compared to 17% nationally). Teachers from other ethnic groups primarily identified with those that had migrated from neighbouring states to Côte d'Ivoire over the last decades. In terms of religion, the majority of teachers (75.9%) were Christian. This confirms the southern bias in the data, since Muslims constitute the majority nationally (Bassett, 2003).

Sixteen percent attended the prestigious teacher training institutes for public schooling, although only 11.1% were teaching in a government-funded school. The large majority, however, attended university and obtained a complementary teaching certificate. Forty-one point nine percent of teachers taught one of the national subjects as their primary field of study, which includes French, history-geography and EDHC. Mathematics or one of the natural sciences constituted the main subject of the second largest group (29.8%), followed by teachers of other social sciences (22.6%). Many teachers taught multiple subjects, however. Notably, nearly one fifth (17.1%) taught EDHC, often as a secondary subject. This included teachers who specialized in French, history-geography, but also in mathematics. On average, teachers had been teaching for about 9.5 years. An overview of teachers' background characteristics can be found in Table 4.1.

Table 4.1. Teacher Characteristics of the Ivorian sample (N=984)

Variable (Response rate)	%	Mean (SD)	Min.	Max.
Age (95.12%)		38.2 (8.16)	22	71
Teaching experience (in years) (98.27)		9.46 (7.74)	0	40
Sex (99.7%)				
Male	84.3%			
Female	15.7%			
Ethnicity (99.5%)				
Akan	50.4%			
Krou	18.7%			
Mandé Nord	8.6%			
Mandé Sud	8.0%			
Gur	10.0%			
Other	4.4%			
Religion (99.19%)				
Christianity	75.9%			
Islam	15.5%			
Other[a]	8.6%			
Education level (99.60%)				
MA degree	74.2%			
BA degree	7.1%			
Secondary level teacher college	16.0%			
Other	2.7%			
Primary subject taught (96.54%)				
National subjects[b]	41.9%			
Other social sciences[c]	22.6%			
Math & natural sciences[d]	29.8%			
Other[e]	5.7%			

Notes: [a]includes Buddhism, animism, no religion; [b]includes French, history-geography, EDHC; [c]includes the foreign languages German, English and Spanish, as well as philosophy; [d]includes mathematics, physics, and life & earth sciences; [d]includes physical education, technical education, arts.

4.4. Support for (in)direct peace education

The omission of the violent past from Côte d'Ivoire's official secondary school curriculum suggests that, at the time of our data collection, there was no political appetite for, or consensus on, openly dealing with the country's violent collapse into ethnic strife and conflict. The current authoritarian turn of the post-conflict regime (Banégas & Popineau, 2022) also suggests that this is unlikely to occur soon. This does not, however, foreclose society's, and in particular teachers', readiness to support direct peace education. Which is why, in this section, we aim to explore support for direct peace education among secondary school teachers in Côte d'Ivoire. We do so by establishing the position of teachers along the horizontal continuum of our new conflict-history education framework. First, we will take a brief look at teachers' views on the purpose of indirect peace education. We combine survey data with insights from teacher interviews and FGDs.

4.4.1. Support for indirect peace education

To measure support for indirect peace education, we included a set of items on the peacebuilding potential of education in general, and on the EDHC course in particular (for an analysis of results, see also Kuppens & Langer, 2018). Teachers responded on a five-point Likert-scale ranging from 1 = 'Strongly disagree' to 5 = 'Strongly agree'. Nearly 95% of secondary school teachers in Côte d'Ivoire who participated in our 2015 survey (strongly) agreed that school is the ideal place to learn about peace and tolerance, and 92.5% of the teachers believed that schools can have a positive influence on student behaviour (see Table 4.2.). Still, a majority (60.7%) considered the impact of schools on student behaviour second to that of family and friends. Ethnically diverse schools, moreover, can help refute prejudice according to the large majority (81.6%), and would not lead to more tensions (79%). Finally, 88.9% of the teachers (strongly) agreed that schools can play an important role in the process of national reconciliation. We thus conclude that there was rather strong consensus among teachers concerning the peacebuilding potential of education in a society in transition such as theirs (meaning that teachers acknowledged the social utility of education), which puts them on the right end of the horizontal axis of our framework.

Table 4.2. Percentage of teachers by extent of agreement with the survey statements on the peacebuilding potential of education in Côte d'Ivoire (N=984)

Item (response rate)	Strongly disagree	Disagree	Neither disagree nor agree	Agree	Strongly agree
School is the ideal place to learn about peace and tolerance. (98.37%)	2.1%	0.2%	3.0%	24.2%	70.6%
School plays an important role in national reconciliation. (97.66%)	2.2%	1.6%	7.4%	33.7%	55.2%
School can change student behavior positively. (96.65%)	1.5%	1.1%	5.0%	25.9%	66.6%
Friends and parents influence a student's behaviour more than school. (95.83%)	4.6%	7.7%	26.9%	35.9%	24.8%
Diversity at school helps to refute prejudice. (95.33%)	3.5%	3.1%	11.8%	36.7%	44.9%
Contact between different ethnic and religious groups at school leads to tensions. (96.96%)	49.6%	29.4%	12.4%	4.2%	4.5%

When considering EDHC specifically (see Table 4.3.), similar patterns emerged. Before presenting the results, it is important to note that teachers could indicate not to have an opinion on the matter. After all, not all teachers had experience with the subject and could therefore abstain from answering. 86.7% and 76.6% of the teachers were of the opinion that the subject contributed to students' knowledge of civic and moral values, and to peaceful and tolerant attitudes, respectively. The content was deemed appropriate and meaningful (72.3%) to the extent that 58.8% of the teachers supported including it in other subjects. The large support (77.4%) for extending the subject until the final year of secondary education was also indicative of their appreciation of it. Similarly, during FGDs, teachers suggested to "introduce the EDHC subject in the second cycle" because "we can discuss more with students in the second cycle" (FGD, Bouaké, 2015). Besides integrating it in higher secondary education (expected age 16 to 19), many teachers seemed to support increasing the number of hours the subject is taught. After all, a main criticism was that "it's only one hour, one hour per week. If it is through this subject that we can talk about peace to children, what will the child learn in only one hour?" (FGD, Abobo, 2015). Another teacher confirmed and added that in consequence: "we skim over it [i.e., the course content]" (Music & EDHC teacher, Yopougon 1, 2015). We thus conclude that support for indirect peace education was high among Ivorian secondary school teachers.

Notwithstanding high overall support levels, we examined whether there were any systematic differences between teachers in terms of support for indirect peace education, looking only at those teachers who expressed their views on EDHC. As in the case of Kenya, we analysed the correlations between the statements and teachers' gender, age and teaching experience using Kendall's τ-b, as well as primary subject taught using Cramer's V (see Table A.2 in appendix) – we did not look at differences between teachers from different ethnic groups. The results showed that older and more experienced teachers were somewhat less convinced of the content of EDHC, and of extending the course until the end of higher secondary education. Across subjects, further, there were no notable differences between teachers when it came to their views on the potential of EDHC. There was significantly less support among mathematics and natural science teachers however for integrating the content of the course across the curriculum – about half of them still supported doing so. Similarly, these teachers were more opposed to extending the course until the end of secondary education.

Table 4.3. Percentage of teachers by extent of agreement with the survey statements on the peacebuilding potential of EDHC in Côte d'Ivoire (N=984)

Item (response rate)	Strongly disagree	Disagree	Neither disagree nor agree	Agree	Strongly agree	No opinion
EDHC contributes to students' knowledge of civic and moral values. (97.05%)	1.6%	1.2%	4.8%	40.6%	46.1%	5.8%
EDHC contributes to peaceful and tolerant student behavior. (97.05%)	1.5%	2.8%	13.0%	40.5%	36.1%	6.1%
The content of the EDHC is appropriate and meaningful. (95.53%)	1.3%	2.8%	15.4%	42.8%	29.5%	8.3%
The content, including civic and moral values, should be incorporated into all other courses. (96.54%)	7.4%	10.8%	16.3%	28.5%	30.3%	6.6%
EDHC should be extended to the final year of secondary schooling. (97.76%)	4.4%	4.8%	7.9%	26.2%	51.2%	5.5%

4.4.2. Support for direct peace education

However, direct peace education would be much more effective in promoting reconciliation than indirect peace education. To gain greater understanding of teachers' support for engaging with it the questionnaire included questions about whether teachers thought it would be desirable to teach about the Ivorian crisis, and, if so, at what levels of education. The results showed that 22.9% of teachers felt it would be appropriate to introduce the topic at the primary level, while 52.7% supported its inclusion at the lower secondary level, and 78.4% at the higher secondary level (see bar chart 4.1.). One teacher provided the following explanation:

> We need to talk about it so that we never experience the same symptoms again [...] The conflict started when we began insulting each other, and saying "such and such an ethnic group is not good", "such and such an ethnic group does not like another ethnic group". If we hide these causes, we will fall into the same trap again tomorrow [...] We must not necessarily judge, but in fact, we must forgive and not forget. If I forget, tomorrow the same thing will happen. (History-geography teacher, Yopougon 3, 2015)

His peer concurred and added that there are already openings to integrate teaching about the country's violent past when teaching about other conflicts:

> Take the example of the Rwandan crisis, and the example of the Biafra crisis. When we do these lessons, the children are not blind. Maybe they have not experienced exactly the same thing, but they recognize many the elements. There are some who say "well during the crisis, this, that". Knowing the causes can be helpful, so that we do not do them again. (History-geography teacher, Yopougon 1, 2015)

Importantly, many teachers seemed to consider students' maturity an important precondition for direct peace education – even if support at one level was significantly correlated with support for direct peace education at another level.[10] Neither sex, age, nor teaching experience could explain differences between teachers in terms of their support for direct peace education by level of education. Support appeared slightly higher however among teachers of the national subjects.[11]

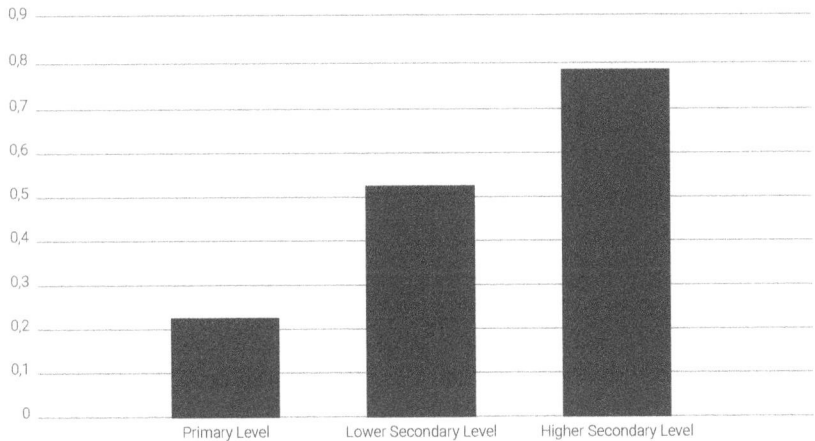

Bar chart 4.1. Support for direct peace education by level of education among Ivorian teachers (N=984)

Still, not all teachers supported conflict-history education. Even at higher secondary level, around one-fifth of teachers opposed its integration. These teachers did not want to "open a wound that was already healed" (French teacher, Yopougon 2, 2015) or they just wanted to "forget and move on" (Music and EDHC teacher, Yopougon 1, 2015). Others specified that it needs to be "contained", not to deviate too much from the course objectives of the official curriculum (History-geography teacher, Bouaké, 2015; emphasis added).

To further unravel teachers' support for direct peace education, but also teachers' past experiences with curricular-instructional gatekeeping when it comes to dealing with the violent past, the Ivorian survey included another set of relevant questions. More particularly, teachers could indicate whether they had undertaken one of the following actions:

- Taught, on their own initiative, the causes and consequences of the country's conflicts.
- Facilitated a class discussion on the topic, encouraging every pupil to express themselves freely and openly.
- Used pedagogical tools, such as documents, texts, articles, or pictures related to the crises.
- Instructed students to read a book that directly or indirectly dealt with the conflicts.

Teachers could respond with one of the following options: (1) No, I did not, and I do not think it is necessary; (2) No, I did not, but I would like to; (3) Yes, I did, and it went badly; or (4) Yes, I did, and it went well. Teachers who had not taken a particular action were also asked whether they thought it would be desirable to do so in the future (these results were previously published in Kuppens & Langer, 2016a). Notably, almost one in five teachers had already used their curricular-instructional gatekeeping powers to either teach their students about the causes and consequences of the Ivorian crises or to organize a class discussion on the topic (see Table 4.4.). A French teacher, for instance, assigned conflict-related essay topics: "What are the causes of the crisis? Then the child has to argue these are the causes, here you go. And what are the consequences in society? And how do we avoid it? Similar strategy" (French teacher, Adjamé, 2015). A substantial group (45.9% and 41.6% for teaching a lesson and organizing a discussion, respectively), had not yet endeavoured to do so, but was willing to. The share of teachers who had used educational materials or asked their students to read a conflict-related book was considerably lower, just like fewer teachers thought it was desirable to do so in the future. Still, some teachers of "the languages, philosophy, human sciences, history-geography" had already made "an opening to study a text that talks about the war, for example, to pass on a message", as one Spanish teacher shared (Abobo, 2015). Indeed, using such materials is not as straightforward in other subjects.

More generally, there were rather weak, but highly significant differences between teachers depending on the subject taught (see Table A3 in appendix).[12] Cross-tabulation of subject taught and the various activities shows that the group of teachers who already taught in some way about the violent past is consistently greatest among teachers who teach one of the national subjects (French, history-geography, or EDHC) as their primary subject and lowest among teachers whose main field of study is mathematics and natural sciences. Illustratively, 28.6% of teachers of the national subjects had already taught a lesson about the causes and consequences of the crises back in 2015 (amongst whom only 17 out of 109 thought it did not go well), compared to 9.9% of mathematics and natural sciences teachers (among whom 3 in 27 said it did not go well). Similarly, 31.6% of national subject teachers had already organized a classroom discussion related to the crisis (amongst whom 27 out of 118 thought it did not go well), compared to 9.2% of mathematics and natural

Table 4.4. Percentage of Ivorian teachers that has implemented/supported activities implementing direct peace education (N=984)

Item (response rate)	No, I did not & not necessary	No, I did not, but desirable	Yes, I did & it went badly	Yes, I did & it went well
I taught my students about the causes and consequences of the Ivorian crises. (94.5%)	33.5%	45.9%	3.2%	17.3%
I organized a class discussion on the crises which allowed students to express themselves freely. (94%)	35.5%	41.6%	5.5%	17.4%
I have already used documents, texts, articles, or photos related to the crisis in the classroom. (92.58%)	57.3%	34.0%	1.4%	7.2%
I asked my students to read a book that speaks (in)directly about the crisis. (93.39%)	51.1%	36.9%	2.7%	9.2%

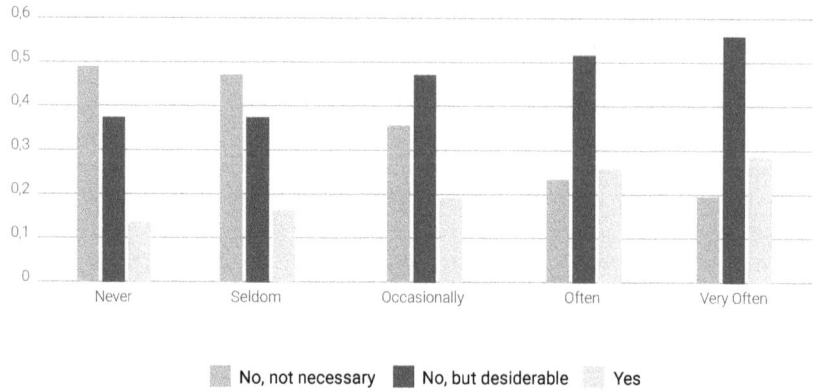

Bar chart 4.2. Share of Ivorian teachers who had already taught a lesson on the Ivorian crises by frequency of engaging in political discussions at home (N=984)

sciences teachers (amongst whom 7 out of 25 thought it did not go well). Finally, 13.7% and 19.7% of those who taught one of the national subjects had already used pedagogical materials or asked their students to read a conflict-related book (mostly teachers of French), compared to 2.2% and 4.4% of the mathematics and natural science teachers – who may also have done so in a secondary subject they were teaching at the time (it will be recalled that there was a significant group of mathematics teachers teaching EDHC as a secondary subject). Still, even among mathematics and natural science teachers there was substantial support for the activities. Among those who had not yet taught a lesson or organized a classroom discussion, 55.51% (136 out of 245) of the first group and 52.42% (130 out of 248) of the second thought it would be desirable to do so.

We also examined how gender, age, and teaching experience could explain differences in teachers' attitudes towards conflict-history education. This didn't expose any significant correlations, except for a very small one between gender and the question of reading a conflict-related book. Cross-tabulation of the results showed that more women (17.1%) than men (11%) had asked this of their students (with most female and male teachers considering it a good experience). Finally, we also looked at any significant differences in attitudes based on political interest, assessed based on the frequency of engaging in discussions about politics at home. We had expected that teachers who are more interested in politics, would be more likely to have taught about the Ivorian crises in some

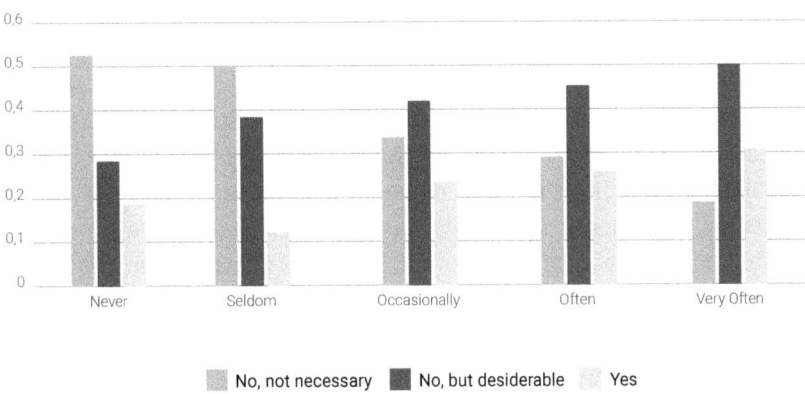

Bar chart 4.3. Share of Ivorian teachers who had already organized a discussion on the Ivorian crises by frequency of engaging in political discussions at home (N=984)

way. In effect, there was a significant correlation for all items, except for the question that students read a book that speaks of the crisis (see Table A3 in appendix).[13] In short, teachers who discussed sociopolitical issues at home on a (very) regular basis, were significantly more likely to have taught or have supported teaching their students about the causes and consequences of the Ivorian crises (see bar chart 4.2.); to have organized or to have supported organizing a class discussion on the theme (see bar chart 4.3.); and to have used or to have supported using documents, texts, articles, or photos related to the crisis in the classroom. Teachers who said they discuss politics at home occasionally, which were the majority, also tended to be more favourable towards direct peace education.

4.5. (Dis)comfort

So far, our results suggest that the sociological time was 'ripe' for direct peace education in Côte d'Ivoire in 2015. In this section, we will examine whether this premise holds when looking at the comfort level of teachers with regard to direct peace education. We do this by combining quantitative and qualitative evidence and focus on two main concerns: retriggering trauma and political polarization within the classroom and beyond.

We will first examine to what extent teachers' own traumatic experiences affected their view on conflict-history education. With Abidjan, the location of our research, being the hotbed of the post-electoral crisis, we asked teachers about the impact the crisis had had on their lives. To this end, the survey included a general, subjective assessment of its impact using a five-point Likert scale (1= 'Not affected at all' to 5= 'Strongly affected'), as well as a set of questions about specific consequences. These items ranged from the loss of a direct family member and/or friends, to financial issues caused by the violence. Generally, more than half of the teachers (60.5%) considered the impact of the crisis had (strongly) affected them, compared to a mere 10.9% who said it did not affect them at all (response rate of 96.6%; 15.8% and 12.8% indicated that the impact was small and neither small, nor large, respectively). That the impact was substantial for a great many, clearly showed in the rest of the data. First, no less than 72.6% of the teachers had to flee their house at the time of the violence (response rate of 93%). Further, whereas the loss of a direct family member was less common (13.6%, response rate of 83%), 60.9% of the teachers (response rate of 88.6%) had lost a close friend. While few had experienced physical and sexual violence (12.9% and 1.7%, respectively; response rates of 84.9% and 82.7%, respectively), many reported psychological injuries (64.8%, response rate of 89.3%), including intimidation and threats. Materially, teachers suffered substantially as well. 44.5% (response rate of 87.0%) indicated they had their property damaged, while a staggering 76.4% reported financial problems (response rate of 91.8%). Hence, the participating teachers clearly suffered at the time of the conflict. Notably, two thirds (66.5%) said they were still sufferering from the psychological consequences of the crisis at the time of the survey (response rate of 90.8%). For instance, one teacher even shared: "I hold a grudge against those who brought war to this country, sincerely. It hurts me. Because we lived in a very peaceful way. It's true that we had some small problems, but it wasn't like that" (History-geography teacher, Yopougon 3, 2015). Against this background, the risk of retraumatizing teachers needs to be taken seriously. Still, there was no significant correlation between the subjective impact of the crisis (general assessment) and support for direct peace education whether at the lower or higher level of secondary education[14], nor between the subjective impact of the crisis on the one hand and (support for) teaching a lesson about the past conflict; organizing a class discussion; using pedagogical materials; and reading a book that refers to the conflict on the other (see Table A.3. in appendix). Beyond being victims, some teachers participated in the violence themselves, making conflict-history education even more challenging: "There are plenty [of teachers] who were militiamen, by will, by force, or by their will to defend a political opinion. They found themselves in the midst of war. So, addressing the causes, it will create a bomb" (French teacher, Yopougon 2, 2015). While seven teachers in our sample admitted to having personally taken part in the violence, this could be an underestimation of the real share of teachers who took part.

Students too were affected by the violence, and are therefore at risk of retraumatization as well. A French teacher who assigned students to debate about peace, for instance, had to navigate the trauma of a girl who said she could never forgive because her brother was killed. Whereas dealing with traumatized students is challenging, most interviewed teachers were of the opinion that they knew how to go about it. One teacher explained: "We ask them a little: 'when were you displaced, how did you live there?' He [a student] replies, 'when we went to the village, there were mosquitoes everywhere'. Oftentimes, students feel relieved [after sharing]" (EDHC teacher, Adjamé, 2015). Other teachers argued to leave the past in the past instead. One teacher shared the following message with her students: "It's over, forget it, it's only the past. There are no Bétés here, there are no Dioulas. We are all the same" (EDHC teacher, Abobo, 2015).

More than fear of retriggering trauma, interviews and FGDs with teachers showed that they feared negative reactions both within and outside of the classroom. Although teachers generally did not think that tensions between students from different ethnic or religious groups had increased since the post-electoral violence (see Table 4.5), there had nonetheless been more or less heated debates within the classroom: "Well, there was someone talking about the 'The Hague Prisoner' [i.e., Gbagbo] and then his neighbour said that he is not a prisoner. Now, another one talked of him as 'the president', another reacted: 'no, not president, ex-president'" (History-geography teacher, Bouaké, 2015). Which is why many interviewed teachers preferred to restrict topics that could be considered sensitive, even when included in the official curriculum:

> Even when you talk about the UN, the children interpret what their parents tell them at home: "The UN, they're the ones who attacked Gbagbo". When you teach, the child tells you that. If you say the Security Council, they say "Yes, that's right, France and the United States, they're the ones behind it!" As teachers, we thus have to channel it so as not to let it overflow. (History-geography teacher, Cocody, 2015)

> Teaching the history-geography lesson on the establishment of the peoples of Côte d'Ivoire can be delicate because some communities think that they have a certain primacy over others because not all the peoples of Côte d'Ivoire arrived at the same time. Are the first to arrive more Ivorian than those who arrived later? It is a question and it is delicate. (FGD, Bouaké, 2015)

More than fearing tensions within the classroom, teachers feared direct peace education could sour relations with colleagues outside the classroom. Notably, distrust between teachers was considered more of an issue than distrust among students: 36% of teachers (strongly) agreed that there was a sort of distrust between teachers from different groups since the post-electoral crisis (see Table 4.5.). Finally, teachers also feared negative reactions beyond the school walls, such as from parents:

> Even if you want to do good when speaking of politics, you could not get by because they themselves [cf. pupils] will tell their parents that mister [cf. the teacher] did politics in class. Since the father has it already fixed in his head that he [cf. the teacher] is FPI, RDR, or PDCI, he thinks directly that they are going to pull his child towards their political party. (English teacher, Cocody, 2015)

> At home, each has its own political preferences. There's dad who even turns off the TV when he sees someone he doesn't like, "Ah this guy, he's getting on my nerves". The child who observes him, he's formatted. Children copy their parents, that's it. Coming back to school to reopen [past wounds], it's a risk. (French teacher, Yopougon 2, 2015)

Table 4.5. Percentage of teachers by extent of agreement with the survey statements on changed relations within schools since the post-electoral crisis in Côte d'Ivoire (N=984)

Item (response rate)*	Strongly disagree	Disagree	Neither disagree nor agree	Agree	Strongly agree
Since the post-election crisis there has been some sort of distrust between students from different groups. (76.9%)	32.5%	22.2%	21.4%	15.1%	8.9%
Since the post-election crisis, students no longer talk about political issues among themselves. (76.2%)	16.7%	21.3%	33.5%	15.6%	12.9%
Since the post-election crisis there has been some distrust between teachers from different groups. (77.6%)	32.3%	13.1%	18.6%	18.7%	17.3%
Since the post-election crisis, teachers no longer talk about political issues in the teachers' room. (77.5%)	23.2%	20.8%	23.2%	14.8%	18.0%

Note: * response rates are much lower since teachers who were not yet teaching prior to the post-electoral crisis, could indicate 'not applicable' (respectively 18.3%, 19.8%, 17.5% and 18.9% of the total samples indicated this response option).

> **Box 4.1. About containers and risk-takers: Focus on François (pseudonym), history-geography teacher in Bouaké (2015)**
>
> *Researcher:* Do you think that it would be a good thing to study the causes and the consequences of the Ivoirian crises in the 2nd cycle?
>
> *Teacher:* During the course, talk about politics? Generally, children are very interested in that. For example, earlier *[cf. the teacher was analysing the book 'how I became a rebel' of Guillaume Soro in class; he later explained also using a book by Gbagbo, yet one that does not address his motivations to engage in conflict]*, if I wasn't careful, they were going to drag me into it. So I know that they really want to bring it out, to talk about that. But, well, we have to *contain* them [emphasis added]. For example, there was a student, who generally doesn't talk much. But the day I gave that text, I felt in him that he wanted to get a lot of things out. I knew that, in fact, he had suffered things during the crisis that were really not at all pretty to see. So, he really wanted to free himself. But I had to channel it since that is not our objective, *it is not in the curriculum* [emphasis added]. That is to say that if there is a possibility for students to talk about it in class, they will do it. Now it is up to the teachers to be able to channel these things.
>
> *Researcher:* Would it be interesting to let students express themselves on the crisis?
>
> *Teacher:* On the one hand, I would like that, let the children express themselves. But what we have to fear in this is the teacher's opinion. Because, when you're in a room, well, there are two sides, right?! There are people who are for and there are people who are against. Now if the teacher tries to take one side, it forces the debate. Yet, as the educator, he should always remain in the middle. But if the teacher now wants to impose his way of seeing or his political way, no, then I think that it's not worth it. […] Thus, it will depend on us. If we are given the opportunity, what are we going to do? That's it, and everyone has their own opinion, and everyone has their own nature, so. The teacher has to be neutral to discuss these things so that these kinds of things do not repeat themselves. I think that will be welcome. It will be very important even.
>
> *Researcher:* Are there any initiatives to raise awareness among teachers, especially in history-geography classes, on teachers' neutrality?
>
> *Teacher:* No, there aren't any. But when we do seminars, we are told to be neutral. That's all. But it's a debate at the same time. Last week for

> example, as I am the head teacher of history-geography, the students came to see me to tell me that there are colleagues who take political sides too much. So I had to organize a meeting to try to ensure that students don't feel that teachers take this side or that side. Now, we discussed it, but will they apply it? I don't know. I know that it's also the difficulty of our subject. As little as you say, you already end up in politics, especially in the final year.
> *Researcher:* What was the reaction of the other teachers during this meeting?
> *Teacher:* They asked me, what proves that they had a political bias? I explained that students in their final year of high school are no longer children. They learn certain things. (...) So, I told them that they must arrange to be neutral when they give their lessons. Because you never know where information can go. Well, they understood, they said they were going to make an effort. Well, I hope so.

4.6. (In)competence

Because of the risk of retriggering trauma and causing polarization, teachers require a set of pedagogical skills to deal with the trauma students experienced and de-escalate heated classroom situations. Although challenging, dealing with these negative emotions constructively is necessary. It is also important that they develop the skills to engage with multiple perspectives on their country's history of conflict. Teachers, however, may have very biased interpretations of what happened in the past. In the context of Côte d'Ivoire, we plotted teachers' narratives of conflict to reflect on teachers' position along the vertical axis of (in)competence to teach about the violent past. We complement this enquiry with a discussion of their support for relevant professional development for teachers.

4.6.1. *Focus on competing narratives of conflict*

Engaging with multiple perspectives is central to direct peace education. However, teaching about the opposing narrative can create dissonance, such that teachers may struggle to constructively analyse the past through the lens of the 'other', as case studies have shown. Anecdotally, Ivorian teachers in our study have themselves indicated fear that their colleagues would not have the competence to overcome partiality and engage with multiple perspectives: "The teachers of Ouattara will say that Ouattara is right. Those of Gbagbo will say that Gbagbo is right. They will give causes in support of the camp of Gbagbo" (French teacher, Yopougon 2, 2015). In this section, we want to examine systematically how prevalent conflict narratives remained in the post-conflict environment of Côte d'Ivoire in 2015, and whether their presence affected teachers' stances towards direct peace education. To that end, we will first analyse how teachers interpreted the causes of conflict in Côte d'Ivoire. Second, we will assess how teachers' openness to teaching direct peace education varies by their views on the past. It should be noted that the level of analytical complexity is kept to a minimum. For a more in-depth analysis of teachers' conflict narratives and their relationship with direct peace education, the reader is invited to refer to an earlier publication (Kuppens & Langer, 2020).

To expose different conflict narratives, teachers were asked to indicate on a scale from 1= 'Not at all' to 5= 'A great deal' to what extent they agreed that a set of "real" or "invented" causes drawn from different political discourses on the conflict had contributed to causing conflict in their country (e.g. Akindès, 2011; Bouquet, 2011; McGovern, 2011; note that the results were first published in Kuppens & Langer, 2016b). Two main narratives underpinned the list. We expected supporters of Ouattara, who are mainly northerners, to trace the roots of the crises back to a struggle for equality between the north and the south after years of discrimination against northerners. Meanwhile supporters of Gbagbo would emphasize foreign interests, particularly French ones (Akindès et al., 2010, p. 94; McGovern, 2011, p. 91). We also included the main actors to assess whom teachers primarily blamed for the violence. In addition, a set of less controversial causes of conflict that are typically cited in the scholarly literature, like the economic hardship of the 1980s and the political transition following the death of the first president, Félix Houphouët-Boigny (FHB). Figure 4.1. illustrates the various causes and conflict actors by narrative.

Among our sample of teachers, the most agreed-upon causes of conflict were French interests (M=4.07, SD=1.26), the cornerstone of the discourse of Laurent Gbagbo (see Table 4.6.). A significant majority (73.6%) believed that French interests were a major cause of the outbreak of violent conflict in Côte d'Ivoire. Other high-scoring elements included the transition upon the death of FHB (M=3.68, SD=1.36), and other foreign

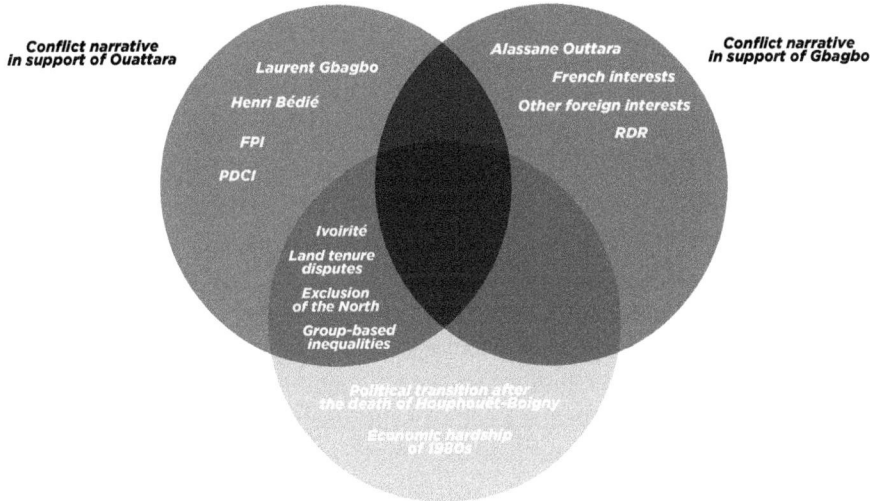

4.1. Venn diagram of Ivorian conflict narratives (by authors)

interests (M=3.55, SD=1.37). When asked who should be held responsible, 64.9% of teachers indicated that the current president, Alassane Ouattara (M=3.71, SD=1.43), played an important role, while only 43% attributed significant blame on his opponent, Laurent Gbagbo. Many teachers believed Gbagbo only played a minor role (16.5%) or no role at all (30%). Similar sentiments were expressed about Henri Konan Bédié. The same is true for their political parties: more teachers blamed Ouattara's RDR, than Gbagbo's FPI. Furthermore, a significant number of teachers indicated the importance of Bédié's PDCI, which formed a coalition with the RDR in 2010. Finally, problems with land ownership and the economic decline in the late 1980s divided teachers, just like inequalities based on group membership, the exclusion of the north, and *Ivoirité*. About half of the teachers attributed a (major) role to these factors, while the other half believed they played only a minor role, if any. One teacher argued, whose words are representative of the latter group:

> They claim the south is more developed than the north, but in reality who developed the south? [...] They say, look there has not been a minister from the north. But, they must not abuse and say, "We are minimized" – it's nonsense. The real truth about the crisis in Côte d'Ivoire is that at one point they wanted

this gentleman to be at the head of the country. Mr. Alassane Dramane Ouattara was thirsty for power. (History-geography teacher, Yopougon 3, 2015)

Similarly, he argued that "people turned it [i.e. *Ivoirité*] pejorative. Otherwise, it was a very good concept." These admissions suggest that Gbagbo's conflict narrative was prevalent among the teachers surveyed. This could be due to the overrepresentation (compared to national statistics) in our sample of teachers of southern origin. Notably, significant differences emerged when taking the ethnic and religious backgrounds of teachers into account (see Table 4.6.). Teachers who identified as belonging to northern ethnic groups had higher mean scores on elements reflecting discrimination in the country, such as group-based inequalities, exclusion of the north, and *Ivoirité*, compared to teachers from southern ethnic groups. Conversely, teachers from southern ethnic groups scored much higher on French and foreign interests. Regarding leaders, teachers belonging to northern ethnic groups predominantly blamed Gbagbo, while teachers from southern ethnic groups primarily pointed at Ouattara. These differences are statistically significant.[15] Further, the perceptions of Muslim teachers aligned with the views of teachers from northern ethnic groups, whereas the views of Christian teachers aligned with those of southern groups. These differences were also significant.[16] Note that the northern ethnic groups are predominantly Muslim, while the southern groups are mainly Christian.[17] There were no significant differences between teachers in terms of their acknowledgement of the structural causes of conflict, including the economic hardship of the 1980s, and the political transition after the death of FHB, but also land ownership problems. As regards actors, there were no significant differences between teachers as concerned blaming the political elite in general, or Henri Konan Bédié and his PDCI in particular.

Teachers who interpret the past conflict through an ethno-religious lens are more likely to experience dissonance when having to address the other perspective in the classroom and may therefore reject doing so. To further test the prevalence of two opposing conflict narratives among teachers and examine their impact on their support for direct peace education, we ran a Structural Equation Model (SEM) in a different publication (Kuppens & Langer, 2020). Apart from conducting a confirmatory factor analysis to measure how the different causes and/or actors correlated with either the Gbagbo or Ouattara narrative, this

Table 4.6. Teacher attributions as to the causes of the conflict in Côte d'Ivoire by ethnic and religious group (N=984)

Items representing perceptions on conflict	Mean (SD)	Mean (SD) by ethnicity		Mean (SD) by religion	
		South	North	Christian	Muslim
Inequalities between population groups	3.06 (1.52)	2.79 (1.48)	3.92 (1.30)	2.84 (1.48)	4.08 (1.18)
Failure of justice system	3.34 (1.39)	3.20 (1.41)	3.85 (1.17)	3.26 (1.40)	3.95 (1.12)
Exclusion of the north	2.46 (1.59)	1.99 (1.54)	3.94 (1.35)	2.10 (1.42)	4.17 (1.20)
Concept of *Ivoirité*	3.19 (1.54)	2.84 (1.50)	4.30 (1.06)	2.94 (1.49)	4.50 (0.85)
Land tenure problems	3.23 (1.44)	3.18 (1.47)	3.43 (1.30)	3.19 (1.45)	3.39 (1.35)
Economic hardship since 1980s	2.82 (1.45)	2.81 (1.47)	2.86 (1.40)	2.85 (1.46)	2.73 (1.35)
Political elite	3.90 (1.24)	3.84 (1.27)	4.06 (1.12)	3.87 (1.26)	4.07 (1.12)
Political transition upon death of FHB	3.68 (1.36)	3.64 (1.41)	3.83 (1.20)	3.7 (1.36)	3.68 (1.29)
FPI and its ideology	2.94 (1.51)	2.64 (1.45)	3.94 (1.25)	2.7 (1.45)	4.16 (1.15)
RDR and its ideology	3.53 (1.38)	3.67 (1.36)	3.04 (1.36)	3.65 (1.34)	3.03 (1.41)
PDCI and its ideology	2.87 (1.35)	2.8 (1.37)	3.14 (1.27)	2.86 (1.34)	3.13 (1.35)
French interests	4.07 (1.26)	4.32 (1.11)	3.21 (1.37)	4.3 (1.11)	2.99 (1.39)
Foreign interests	3.55 (1.37)	3.76 (1.31)	2.84 (1.36)	3.75 (1.27)	2.6 (1.34)
Culture of violence propagated by FESCI	3.11 (1.48)	2.85 (1.45)	4.01 (1.23)	2.89 (1.44)	4.24 (1.08)
Laurent Gbagbo	2.88 (1.56)	2.58 (1.51)	3.87 (1.29)	2.64 (1.52)	4.06 (1.20)
Henri Konan Bédié	2.82 (1.39)	2.79 (1.41)	2.93 (1.34)	2.83 (1.39)	2.90 (1.43)
Alassane Ouattara	3.71 (1.43)	3.93 (1.36)	2.99 (1.42)	3.9 (1.35)	2.92 (1.47)

Note: Results by ethnicity and religious group first published in Kuppens & Langer (2016b).

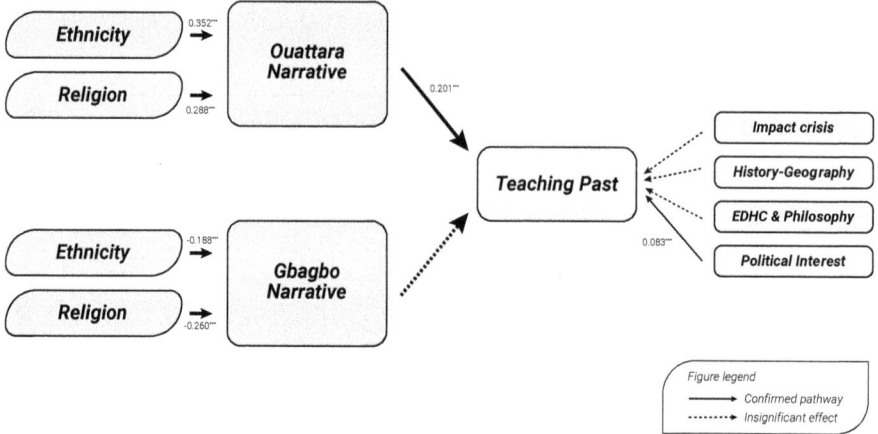

Figure 4.2. Structural path model including standardized coefficients measuring the effect of Ivorian teachers' conflict narratives on their willingness and past practices of discussing the country's violent past in the classroom, by religious and ethnic group belonging (adaptation of Kuppens & Langer, 2020, p. 45)

model tested the effect of teachers' social identity (ethnicity and religion) on their support for either narrative. It also examined how the two narratives affected teachers' attitudes towards teaching about the violent past (structural paths), as measured by a binary variable where '0' equalled 'I have never discussed the causes and consequences of the conflict in the classroom and I do not want to'; and '1' equalled 'I would like to discuss the causes and consequences of the conflict in class, or I have already done so'. The model also controlled for the subjective impact of the crisis, the subject taught and teachers' political interest (again measured against the frequency of political discussions at home).

Figure 4.2. visualizes the model.[18] It confirms that two underlying conflict narratives existed at the time. The items that allowed the narrative in support of Ouattara to take hold (so items with factor scores of >0.40) included inequalities between different groups in the population, the exclusion of the north, inequitable justice, the concept of *Ivoirité*, the FPI and its ideology, Laurent Gbagbo, and the culture of violence propagated by the student organization FESCI; note that the student movement is popularly perceived to be connected to the FPI (McGovern, 2011, p. 18). The interests of France, other foreign interests, the RDR and its ideology, and Alassane Ouattara had high factor scores for the narrative in support of Gbagbo. As expected, there was a negative correlation between the two conflict narratives, which means that an increase in support for the one means a decrease in support for the other. However, the correlation was not so strong as to be mutually exclusive either.[19] The model confirmed that teachers belonging to an ethnic group from the north and Muslim teachers were more likely to adhere to the conflict narrative of Ouattara, and less likely to that of Gbagbo. It further showed that teachers who interpreted the past along the lines of the discourse of Ouattara, were more likely to support direct peace education. Arguably, this shows the importance of the sociopolitical context: teachers in support of Ouattara may have been more confident to discuss the past since they supported the narrative of the ruling president. This research also confirmed there is a positive correlation between political interest and the general readiness to discuss the history of conflict. Whether teachers felt that the crisis had substantially impacted their lives or not, or the subject they taught, did not affect their support for conflict-history education (see Kuppens & Langer, 2020).

Teachers' biased interpretations of the past raise questions regarding their ability to engage constructively with multiple perspectives in the classroom. According to the survey results, 75.4% of the teachers nonetheless (strongly) agreed with the statement that they always try to present all the different points of view on an event they are explaining in class [response rate of 95.5%; 13.2% (strongly) disagreed]. This question was not specific to the history of conflict, however. Classroom observations and interview data further suggested that these results should be taken with a grain of salt: notably, a history-geography teacher from Bouaké whose class we were sitting in on while discussing the book 'Why I became a rebel' by former rebel leader Guillaume Soro (see also box 4.1.), responded as follows when we enquired about the use of other resources in class which provide different perspectives:

> Another text I used was a text by Laurent Gbagbo. But the difference is that it only speaks about history. But [...] I have explained a little bit about him, as a political character, a little. This morning I thought it would be interesting to take the opposite of Laurent Gbagbo.

The book he referred to is not about the Ivorian conflict. So no comparisons were made between the motives of Soro and the motives of Gbagbo.

Table 4.7. Percentage of Ivorian teachers that had participated in/supported teacher professional development (TPD) in the field of direct peace education (N=984)

Item (response rate)	No, I did not participate yet & not necessary	No, I did not participate yet, but desirable	Yes, I did participate & it went badly	Yes, I did participate & it went well
TPD on dealing with the Ivorian crises in the classroom. (91.8%)	19.3%	66.0%	6.5%	8.2%
TPD on dealing with traumatized children. (92.8%)	12.5%	72.1%	6.7%	8.8%

His students may have interpreted this as silent support for the narrative of Soro. Still, the teacher himself was convinced that "the teacher should be in the middle. (…) Now, if the teacher wants to impose his views or political opinion, then, no, no, that is not good."

4.6.2. Support for teacher training

Direct peace education requires that teachers have certain skills. Therefore, we asked them if they would support professional development training (Teacher Professional Development or TPD) focused on teaching their country's conflict history and managing traumatized children in the classroom. If relevant, teachers were also able to indicate whether they had already participated in such training, and how they had experienced it. Notably, a large majority of teachers thought that TPD aimed at preparing teachers to teach about their country's conflict history in class (66.0%) and to deal with traumatized children (72.1%) was desirable (see Table 4.7.). Some teachers indicated that they had already followed a teacher-training course on addressing the violent past in class (14.9%), or on dealing with traumatized children in class (15.5%). Given that the Ivorian Ministry of Education had not yet organized such courses at the time, it is likely that these teachers had participated in trainings by NGOs, such as Amnesty International or SOS Exclusion, or religious organizations.

4.7. Situating Ivorian teachers within the framework of conflict-history education

As of 2015, most secondary school teachers in Côte d'Ivoire believed that their country's history of conflict should be included in the official school curriculum. In practice, however, the large majority avoided this sensitive topic. These teachers shared their experiences of discomfort engaging in direct peace education, fearing negative reactions within and outside the classroom. We therefore situate Ivorian teachers in the lower part of our framework towards the right quadrant. Besides the hesitant containers, there were nonetheless some teachers who had already experimented with direct peace education activities. Since our analysis exposed some risks when it came to constructively presenting multiple perspectives in the classroom, these teachers have been positioned as risk-takers. All in all, this suggests that 'support from below' was present among secondary school teachers as of 2015, but that efforts to implement direct peace education require teacher training provided 'from above' (or 'from outside') to strengthen the necessary competences – measures that the teachers themselves supported.

CHAPTER 5

Teaching about ongoing violence in the eastern Democratic Republic of Congo

> If our youth today are not well educated, we are preparing a time bomb. We currently see how young people behave; even children when they play they use things like weapons. However, through the training that children receive at school they will know how to behave in the future, so it is a means of prevention. Here at school with the course they receive in civic and moral education, we are already preparing our children to behave like good citizens, which will have a positive impact on security itself. (FGD with secondary school teachers, Goma, 2016)

Violence remains widespread and enduring in the Democratic Republic of Congo (DR Congo), and its eastern provinces of North and South Kivu more specifically. Among the causes of conflict that have plunged the country into ongoing conflict, scholars have identified the bankruptcy of the state following a long period of dictatorship (Titeca & De Herdt, 2011; Trefon, 2013) and the competition over natural resources (Autesserre, 2012; Ntanyoma & Hintjes, 2022). Also political and identity-related tensions have increased in the Kivus since the influx of Rwandan Hutu refugees after the 1994 genocide and the change of political regime in Rwanda (Verweijen & Vlassenroot, 2015; Autesserre, 2006; Kaganda, 2013; Trefon, 2013). The persistent climate of insecurity and tensions raises important questions regarding the sociopolitical conditions leading teachers to (partially) support or reject peace education. In particular, research by Paluck (2010) demonstrated that media outreach programmes that aim at promoting intergroup reconciliation in eastern DR Congo backfired because of the inhospitable environment. Extending our research to a society in conflict, like eastern DR Congo, will therefore be revealing in terms of the challenges teachers face when engaging in direct peace education.

This chapter will begin with an outline of the conflict dynamics in the Kivu provinces and will provide some background on the Congolese education system. This will be followed by an examination of the support offered by secondary school teachers' for indirect peace education and conflict-history education. After discussing the areas of discomfort teachers experience and their attitudes towards participatory pedagogies and corporal punishment, we will consider their competences in implementing 'Uprooted', an educational tool that was designed to support Congolese teachers in teaching about pervasive and chronic violence in Congo.

5.1. Conflict dynamics

After 75 years of brutal colonization and exploitation, the DR Congo gained independence in 1960. The First Republic was short-lived, lasting only five years before Colonel Mobutu seized power. As president, Mobutu ruled as a dictator, consolidating his authority through force and exacerbating social, political, and economic inequalities. When large numbers of Rwandan Hutus fled their country in 1994, they settled in eastern DR Congo. In an attempt to stop the fleeing *'génocidaires'*, Rwanda supported the *Alliance des Forces Démocratiques pour la Libération du Congo-Zaïre* (Alliance of Democratic Forces for the Liberation of Congo-Zaire; AFDL) of future President Laurent-Désiré Kabila to dismantle Hutu refugee camps. The AFDL had been created around that same period to contest the marginalization of the Banyarwanda – Congolese Tutsi, Hutu, and Twa who live predominantly in the province of North Kivu (Masisi and Rutshuru territories) and speak Kinyarwanda, the official language of Rwanda. The ensuing 'liberation war' (1996-1998) led by Kabila resulted in President Mobutu being removed from power (Verweijen & Vlassenroot, 2015). Once in power, Kabila broke with his allies in Rwanda and Uganda, who were then forced to withdraw from Congolese territory. These armies subsequently turned against him, creating another major armed conflict which was at least partially economically motivated. After all, the competition for access to natural resources intensified when Kabila adopted a nationalist stance (Kennes, 2000). In addition to Rwanda and Uganda, Burundi's army was involved, supporting new rebel movements in eastern DR Congo, including the *Rassemblement Congolais pour la Démocratie*. For his part, Kabila was being supported by Angola, Zimbabwe, Chad and Namibia (Autesserre, 2006; Verweijen, 2015). Because of the involvement of seven foreign armies and the large number of casualties, this war is sometimes dubbed Africa's World War.

The signing of the Sun City Peace Agreements in South Africa in 2003 marked the formal end of the war. However, even though large-scale fighting did not resume, insecurity and violence have remained rife in eastern DR Congo with the proliferation of armed groups such as the *Forces Nationales de Libération* (National Forces of Liberation), the *Forces pour la Défense et la Démocratie* (Forces for Defence and Democracy), the Allied Democratic Forces – National Army of Liberation of Uganda (ADF-Nalu; see, e.g., Bucyalimwe, 2006; Stearns & Botiveau, 2013), the 'March 23rd Movement' (M23), and Mai-Mai armed groups (Kaganda, 2013b). In North Kivu, for example, the town of Beni has seen a series of massacres committed by Ugandan ADF-NALU rebels since 2014, with an average of two people killed every day (Berghezan, 2018). In South Kivu, violent clashes recur between Mai-Mai groups and the regular army in the territories of Fizi, Shabunda, Mwenga and Kalehe (Kaganda, 2013; Verweijen, 2013; 2015). Most recently, the M23 movement reemerged in both Kivu provinces with the alleged support of Rwanda after having been militarily defeated in 2013 (IPIS, 2024; Mukwemulere, 2024).[20] Officially, these armed groups were formed to defend their communities (Verweijen, 2015; see also Brandt, 2021). The Mai-Mai militias, for instance, aim to "cleanse" the region of the ethnic Banyamulenge to defend the autochthonous Babembe, Bafuliiru, and Banyindu ethnic groups. Although the Banyamulenge have been living in eastern DR Congo for centuries, like the Banyarwanda, they are typically depicted as Rwandan refugees who fraudulently obtained Congolese citizenship and profit from Congolese resources to the detriment of the Bantu "natives" (Ndahinda & Mugabe, 2022).[21] Notably, while some claim that Mai-Mai is a shorthand for *Mayi Mayi* ('Water Water' in KiSwahili) thereby referring to a ritual of pouring magic water over someone to protect him or her from bullets (Brandt, 2021), others have suggested that it is an acronym for *"Mututsi Aende Inje– Mkongomani Aongoze Inchi"* which is KiSwahili for "Tutsi Get Out – Congolese Guard Your Country!" (Jackson, 2006). In turn, the M23 movement (formerly known as the *Congrès National pour la Défense du Peuple*, CNDP; National Congress for the Defence of the People), fights for the protection of the Tutsi, which include the Banyamulenge living in South Kivu, Tutsi in Nord Kivu and Hema in Ituri Province. Yet notwithstanding alleged identity-related motivations, in practice these groups are deeply implicated in the control and plundering of natural resources and have become self-sustaining (Stearns, 2022).

Significant political progress has nonetheless been made in the past two decades, with the organization of four electoral ballots. The first two rounds of elections (in 2006 and 2011, respectively) were won by Joseph Kabila, son of Laurent-Désiré Kabila who was murdered in 2001. Even though a change in leadership was highly anticipated in 2016 – Kabila could no longer run because of presidential term limits – the new presidential elections were postponed until 2018, causing major unrest across the country resulting in arrests and convictions of political opponents and members of citizen movements like Lucha, Filimbi, and *Réveil des Indignés* (Awakening of the Indignant). The 2018 elections, just like the subsequent 2024 elections, were won by the son of a former key opposition figure, Felix Antoine Tshisekedi Tshilombo, although his victory was disputed.[22] To ensure a peaceful transition, Tshisekedi made a deal with former president Kabila, thereby enabling the latter to retain significant power in parliament and beyond.

5.2. Education, conflict & peace

5.2.1. The Congolese education system

A colonial legacy of the Belgian education system (André & Poncelet, 2013; Poncelet et al., 2010), the Congolese education system comprises three cycles: three years of preschool, six years of primary education, and six years of secondary education (with the exception of vocational secondary education, which takes only five years). Secondary education is divided into two cycles. After two years of general secondary education, students opt for general, technical or vocational education. Upon completing secondary education, students take part in national examinations to obtain their state diploma. Whereas four national languages (KiSwahili, Kikongo, Tshiluba and Lingala) are taught in elementary school, the official language of instruction is French (Ndugumbo, 2014). Since 2014, education is compulsory and free for the first 8 years of basic education – before 2014, household financial contributions to the running of schools was estimated at 77% (MINEPSP, 2013; see also De Herdt, Marivoet & Muhigirwa, 2015). Yet in practice, parents continue to pay tuition fees. Originally entirely Catholic, the education system now includes government-funded schools, privately-funded schools, and schools run by Protestant (34.7%), Catholic (17.9%), Kimbanguist, Islamic and other religious communities. Schools have been coordinated at the provincial level since the system was decentralized in 2006. Like elsewhere on the continent, there is a ban on all types of corporal punishment (see Kalolo & Kapinga, 2023 for a review on relevant legislation across Africa).

Primary school teachers require a state diploma (D6) or a four-year post-primary diploma (D4) from the former secondary education system in DR Congo. Secondary school teachers require either a diploma from a Higher Pedagogical Institute or Higher Technical Institution (3 years post-secondary), or a bachelor's degree in a pedagogical discipline (5 years post-secondary). Whereas teachers specialize in a particular subject, all teachers are trained in citizenship education, logic and philosophy, English and oral and written expression techniques. In addition to training secondary school teachers, Higher Pedagogical Institutes also conduct research into applied pedagogy to improve the quality of teaching in primary and secondary schools, and contribute to developing textbooks (DRC, 2014; Ntoto 2013). In total, there are 151 institutions of higher education in North Kivu and 69 in the neighbouring province of South Kivu, including the renowned Higher Pedagogical Institute of Bukavu (*Institut Supérieur Pédagogique*, ISP/Bukavu) which was established in 1961. Still, many secondary school teachers are not qualified: out of 253,929 registered secondary school teachers in the 2010/2011 academic year, 168,728 (66.6%) only had a secondary school diploma (UNESCO, 2014).

5.2.2. Education & conflict

Decades of armed conflict have significantly impacted schooling in the eastern DR Congo. At the height of conflict, schools were used by the military and armed groups to house and train soldiers, as well as to collect communal taxes (HRW, 2015). Especially schools in rural areas were affected, but the displacement of large groups of the population also put pressure on the education system in urban areas such as Goma. To accommodate all students, many refugee-receiving schools were forced to operate in shifts. Schools were also set up in camps for internally displaced persons, often under precarious learning conditions. Other students dropped out of school completely and were recruited by armed groups (Nfundiko, 2013; 2015; see also Kaganda 2013, Odden & Tonheim 2013). Between 2009 and 2012, 2,145 children, predominantly from North Kivu and including 142 girls, were recruited by force. Another 7,069 joined armed groups voluntarily seeking refuge (Nfundiko, 2013). Other students, particularly girls, dropped out fearing rape and/or abduction on their way to school (Rudahindwa, 2020). In 2010, 16.3% of girls and 13.1% of boys still felt unsafe in school, while a combined 35% felt unsafe on their way to or from school (Search for Common Ground, 2012). Finally, dropout rates were also high among children whose families had difficulties paying school fees (MINEPSP, 2013; UNESCO, 2015). Thus, unsurprisingly, the highest rates of Congolese children and adolescents not in school were living in provinces affected by conflict, and in the provinces of North and South Kivu in particular (MINEPSP, 2013). Teachers were affected, too. As perceived representatives of political and administrative authorities, they were (and continue to be) regularly targeted by armed groups (Marchais et al., 2023).

5.2.3. Education & peace

Concomitant to the political transition following the signature of various peace agreements, a series of educational reforms were carried out. In 2007, notably, a course on 'Civic and Moral education' (ECM; *Education Civique et Morale*) was developed with the support of UNESCO and the United Nations Office for Human Rights. It replaced an older course on civic education (successively called 'Civic and Moral Education' and 'Civic and Political Education') that propagated the one-party-state ideology of "Mobutism" during the period of authoritarianism (1970-1997) (Musuasua, 2006). Although it includes notions of peace and non-violence, the 2007 course remains predominantly civic-oriented, as its foreword illustrates:

> This course introduces learners to practicing the good habits recommended by civics, patriotism, and nationalism. In short, Civic and Moral Education develops learners' knowledge and behaviour for good social conduct, through respect for the laws and the implementation of social values and principles. (MINEPSP, 2007, p. 5)[23]

Previously (in 2005), there had been a revision of the history-teaching curricula, also with a view to including notions of democratization. More recently, a new framework law was adopted (Education Framework Law No. 14/004 of February 11, 2014) which furthermore acknowledges human rights and the fight against discrimination in education as cornerstones of the curriculum.

ECM is taught one hour per week (which works out to 37 hours per year, and 10 points per semester) from the first year of primary school up until the end of secondary school (expected age of 18). Rather than a course-specific training, all trained teachers have studied ECM as part of the general component of their training. They use 'My Fatherland' as a textbook, which was developed by secondary school inspectors in collaboration with members of *'Groupe Jérémie'*, a non-governmental human rights organization based in eastern DR Congo. The textbook is written around seven themes: (i) knowledge of oneself, others and one's environment; (ii) morality and social peace; (iii) the culture of peace; (iv) the rights and duties of citizens and respect for human rights; (v) civic education, patriotism and nationalism; (vi) the highway code; and (vii) good examples and models to follow in a changing society (MINEPESP, 2007). Every year, students study these various themes. For instance, students in their first year of secondary education (expected age of 12-13) study the culture of peace and the factors that promote or hinder it, as well as the associated notions of tolerance, mutual understanding, assistance and generosity. In their second year, this is followed, among others, by the study of UN resolutions and the UNESCO declaration on the culture of peace (expected age of 13-14), an analysis of the distinction between positive and negative peace in their fourth year (expected age of 15-16), and by an exploration of all forms of discrimination and of the national and international legal provisions prohibiting discrimination in the final year of secondary education (expected age of 17-18; see also Nfundiko, 2020). Themes related to civic education include learning about the principles and pillars of democracy (years 3, 4 and 5; expected age of 14 to 17), national unity (years 3,4 and 5; expected age of 14 to 17), civic rights and duties (year 5; expected age of 16-17), and the constitution (years 2, 5 and 6; expected age of 13 to 18). In their final year, students examine the roles, functions and modus operandi of political parties, and the organization of democratic, free and transparent elections. Although the course is rich in conceptual definitions, it has only few concrete examples from the Congolese context that would help learners to connect theoretical concepts with their own lived experiences (Nfundiko, 2020).

Notably, and in contrast to the EDHC curriculum in Côte d'Ivoire, the Congolese ECM curriculum does focus on the history of DR Congo's violent disintegration. In the fifth year of secondary education (expected age of 16-17), it includes a chapter that focuses on the political history of the

DR Congo and the institutional destabilization that followed its independence. This chapter does not only list the various crises, mutinies and wars that broke out after Lumumba's death, but also comprises more recent conflicts between 1990 and 2000. With respect to the war of liberation, the textbook notes for instance that: "These four men [i.e., Laurent Désiré Kabila, Anselme Masasu Nindaga, André Kisasu Ngandu and Déogratias Bugera] were in the service of the Americans and their main mission was to lead the war from eastern Congo to Kinshasa and thus overthrow the regime of Marshal Mobutu, who was suffering from prostate cancer (...)" (Teacher textbook, My Fatherland 5, 2012c; p. 64). In total, the textbook mentions 25 key dates, including days on which important cities were seized and important figures such as the Archbishop of the Catholic Church of Bukavu, *Monseigneur* Christophe Munzihirwa, were murdered. In other words, the curriculum does include some limited and episodic content of past conflicts.

Note that other subjects, such as history, languages, geography, and African sociology, also include notions of peace, non-violence and democracy. The French curriculum, for instance, includes mandatory readings on democracy, war and friendship (MINEPESP, 2002). The study of migration, further, which is part of the history curriculum instructs teachers to "explain that there is no such thing as a pure race, whatever the linguistic or morphological differences... Today's peoples are the products of the mixing of populations" (National history programme, 2005). The subject also addresses conflict-related topics more explicitly. Notably, apart from studying (pre)colonial conflicts and tensions in the early days of independence, the history curriculum in the final year (expected age of 17-18) traces the main historical events, dates and figures involved in conflicts in Congo up to 2006. However, for fear of tensions, the teacher training programme for aspiring history teachers does suggest caution on this subject. The geography curriculum, too, touches upon conflict dynamics. In the second year (expected age of 13-14), for instance, students look at ethnic conflicts in North Kivu between Hutu or Tutsi populations, who speak Kinyarwanda, and indigenous populations like the Bahavu, Batembo, Bavira, Bafuliiru, and Babembe. The chapter also focuses on border disputes. In North Kivu, students look at the borders between the city of Goma and Rwanda, and between the territory of Rutshuru and Uganda. In South Kivu, students examine the Gatumba border between DR Congo and Burundi. However, students do not engage in-depth with these dynamics. It is striking, for instance, that the study of migratory movements to and within DR Congo and of the formation of Congo's major ethnic groups in the first year of secondary school (expected age of 12-13) does not include the arrival and settlement of waves of Rwandophone ethnic groups. In view of the vicious autochtony/allochtony discourse (involving the Hutu, Tutsi and Banyamulenge ethnic groups) that is rife in Bukavu and Goma (Jackson, 2006; Büscher & Vlassenroot, 2010; Solhjell, 2015), it is clear that the absence of these ethnic groups in the curriculum and in school textbooks presents teachers with significant challenges in their classrooms. It also helps explain why young people in Kivu were found not to distinguish between Rwandan and Congolese Tutsis, or contest the so-called "Congolese" identity of these "Tutsis from Rwanda" (Bentrovato, 2014).

Aside from government sanctioned peace education, it is interesting to note that many schools in the conflict-affected provinces are involved in peace education initiatives led by NGOs and civil society organizations. These organizations typically support extracurricular activities aimed at creating spaces for dialogue and learning about the culture of peace and peace values (Ciribuka, 2022). Because of a lack of coordination, these activities are often concentrated in urban schools, despite having been less affected by conflict than their rural counterparts.

5.3. Survey data

To measure secondary school teachers' support for direct peace education in contexts of ongoing tensions and widespread and enduring violence, we visited 114 secondary schools out of the 565 registered schools in the cities of Bukavu and Goma in the spring of 2018, only a few months before the much anticipated general elections that should already have taken place in 2016. Bukavu is the capital city of the province of South Kivu. It is primarily inhabited by members of the Bashi, Balega, Babembe, Bavira, and Bafuliiru ethnic groups, but also houses a significant Banyamulenge community. It was the first major city in eastern DR Congo to come under the control of the Kabila-led AFDL rebels in 1996. Between 1998 and 2004, another rebel group – the Congolese Rally for Democracy – took control of the city. It was subsequently attacked by the mutinous troops of Laurent Nkunda and Jules Mutebutsi in an alleged attempt to stop the "massacre" of members of the Banyamulenge community in the city (Solhjell, 2015).

After about two decades of relative calm, the city was recently taken by M23 rebels. Goma is the capital of North Kivu province and is predominantly inhabited by ethnic Hutus, Banande, Bahunde, and Nyanga. Between 1998 and 2004, it housed the headquarters of the political and administrative institutions of the rebellion. Compared to Bukavu, the city and its surroundings always remained more volatile after open fighting ended. Most recently, Goma was also the first of the two cities to fall under the control of the M23 movement.

In total, 1,642 secondary school teachers took part, of whom 792 (48.2%) and 850 (51.8%) were working in Goma and Bukavu, respectively. Notably, the large majority of teachers was male (91.1%), which is representative of the overall gender distribution in the education sector in the provinces: women only represent 8.9% of the teaching force in North and South Kivu (RDC, 2014b; CTSE, 2015). The youngest teacher was 19 years old and the oldest was 72 years old at the time of data collection. In terms of ethnicity, most teachers identified with one of the groups indigenous to Bukavu and Goma: Bashi (37.9%), Balega (13.0%), Hutu (11.6%), Banande (10.3%), Bahavu (10%) and Bahunde (4.9%). All other groups accounted for less than 3% of the sample. Notably, there were only four teachers who identified as Tutsi, and none that identified as Banyamulenge. Nearly all teachers were Christian (97.8%). An overview of teachers' background characteristics can be found in Table 5.1.

The teachers in our sample were more qualified than the average teacher in North and South Kivu, which is probably due to the urban bias. Almost half (48.4%) of the participating teachers obtained a university degree. A slightly smaller, but still significant group (44.0%) obtained a graduate degree. 7.7% of teachers only had a secondary school degree. On average, teachers had been teaching for about 10 years. The most experienced teacher had been doing the job for 50 years. In terms of the subjects taught, there was a bias towards the national subjects (44.5%) and other social sciences (30.6%). Only a quarter (25.5%) of the teachers taught mathematics, physics, chemistry, biology or another subject in the natural sciences. Note that many teachers taught multiple subjects.

Table 5.1. Teacher characteristics of the eastern Congolese sample (N=1642)

Variable	%	Mean (SD)	Min.	Max.
Age		36.2 (10.26)	19	72
Teaching experience (in years)		10.2 (8.54)	0	50
Sex				
Male	91.1%			
Female	8.9%			
City of residence				
Bukavu	51.8%			
Goma	48.2%			
Ethnicity				
Bashi	37.9%			
Balega	13.0%			
Bahavu	10.0%			
Banande	10.3%			
Bahunde	4.9%			
Hutu	11.6%			
Other	12.4%			
Religion				
Christianity: Catholic	50.5 %			
Christianity: Other	47.3%			
Islam	0.8%			
Other	1.4%			
Education level				
MA degree	48.4%			
BA degree	44.0%			
Secondary school	7.7%			
Subject taught (combinations possible)				
National subjects[a]	44.5%			
Other social sciences[b]	30.6%			
Math & natural sciences[c]	25.5%			
Other[d]	46%			

Notes: [a]includes French, history, religion, ECM, geography and life skills; [b]includes English, philosophy, sociology, psychology; [c]includes mathematics, physics, biology and chemistry; [d]includes physical education, technical education, arts, accounting, etc.

5.4. Support for (in)direct peace education

Notwithstanding the enduring climate of insecurity, the inclusion of some elements regarding the history of recent conflict suggests that there was at least some political support for dealing openly with the country's history of violence. Yet to what extent do Congolese teachers at the frontline of violence share this openness? In this section, we will explore the support for direct peace education among secondary school teachers in Bukavu and Goma back in 2018. Again, we will do so by assessing the position of teachers along the horizontal continuum of our framework. We will first have a brief look at the views of the participating teachers on the purpose of indirect peace education, before turning to direct peace education. We will combine survey data with insights from teacher interviews and FGDs.

5.4.1. Support for indirect peace education

Like in Côte d'Ivoire, we included three items on the peacebuilding potential of education in general, and three items on the ECM course specifically, to measure support for indirect peace education, using five-point Likert scales ranging from 1 = 'Strongly disagree' to 5 = 'Strongly agree'. Nearly all teachers (strongly) agreed that school is the ideal place to learn about peace and tolerance (93.7%), but also that school can improve students' behaviour (94.7%; see Table 5.2). Similarly, 87.1% of teachers (strongly) agreed that schools can advance reconciliation. Notwithstanding the socializing role of schools, 71.8% of the teachers thought that friends and parents influence students' behaviour more (note that these results were published previously in Nfundiko et al., 2025). Still, these results provide compelling evidence that back in 2018, teachers in eastern DR Congo were convinced that schools can contribute significantly to the reconciliation effort. So far, this puts them on the right end of the horizontal axis of our framework.

When asked about ECM specifically, nearly all of the questioned teachers (97.8%) believed it contributes to students' knowledge of civic and moral values. Besides knowledge, the large majority (84.4%) also believed it could promote peaceful and tolerant attitudes. The content was furthermore deemed appropriate and relevant, so that 82.1% of the teachers supported including it in other subjects (see Table 5.3.). This outlook contrasts with results from a previous study, according to which

Table 5.2. Percentage of teachers by extent of agreement with the survey statements on the peacebuilding potential of education in Eastern DRC (N=1642)

Item	Strongly disagree	Disagree	Neither disagree, nor agree	Agree	Strongly agree
School is the ideal place to learn about peace and tolerance.	0.5%	2%	3.7%	32.6%	61.1%
School is the ideal place to foster national reconciliation.	1.4%	4.3%	7.2%	42.1%	45%
School can change student behaviour positively.	0.7%	0.7%	3.8%	31.1%	63.6%
Friends and parents influence a student's behaviour more than school.	3.2%	9.1%	16.0%	33.9%	37.9%

teachers considered the course as a "stopgap" *(bouche trou)* or "filler of the schedule" (Kihangi, 2013) because of the low number of hours allocated to the course. In our interviews, too, teachers expressed some reservations, though largely of a different nature: some teachers feared that the notions of peace included in ECM would ring hollow to students who were confronted with a different reality on a daily basis; much like Davies (2016) observed in other conflict-affected societies:

> "What does it mean for us?" That is mainly the reaction of the students. "Here at home where we live in rather troubled environments", they now ask, "what must be done here at home, so that these elements are put to practice?" We can clearly see that they are surprised by the fact that there are tensions all the time, all the time, that there are endless wars; so often when we approach the notions [of peace], they seem not to be very convinced. [They think] that it is not effective because we do not experience that in our environment […] Yes, there is this feeling of despair, very sceptical, even when you talk about very positive things, they say "not here, not in the Congo". (Geography and ECM teacher, Goma, 2016)

> Students themselves tell you, "sir we have learned this, we have learned that, we have learned for example that there is freedom of expression, but there are people who have been put in prison for that. But you, you tell us this" [i.e., that students have the right to express themselves freely]. So they know what is happening around them. (ECM and Arts teacher, Goma, 2016)

When checking for systematic differences between teachers in terms of support for indirect peace education (see Table A.4 in appendix), it appears that teachers who taught at least one of the national subjects were generally more positively inclined towards ECM than other teachers, although the differences were very small (most teachers were overwhelmingly in support). Also, experienced teachers in particular felt that ECM contributes to developing peaceful and tolerant attitudes amongst students. This group was also slightly more supportive of incorporating some of its content in all other subjects.

Table 5.3. Percentage of teachers by extent of agreement with the survey statements on the peacebuilding potential of ECM in Eastern DR Congo (N=1642)

Item	Strongly disagree	Disagree	Neither disagree, nor agree	Agree	Strongly agree
ECM contributes to students' knowledge of civic and moral values.	0.6%	0.2%	1.5%	18.4%	79.4%
ECM contributes to peaceful and tolerant student behavior.	1.8%	3.8%	9.9%	44.9%	39.5%
The content of the ECM is appropriate and meaningful.	2.7%	7.5%	11.7%	42.9%	35.2%
The civic and moral values included in ECM should be incorporated into all other courses.	3.4%	7.1%	7.4%	27%	55.1%

5.4.2. Support for direct peace education

To measure teachers' support for direct peace education, the survey included two sets of questions. First, there was a general question that enquired about teachers' support, irrespective of the students' level of education. On a scale of 1= 'Strongly disagree' to 5= 'Strongly agree', a large majority (86.7%) (strongly) agreed that the causes of conflict in eastern DR Congo should be taught at school (2.7% strongly disagreed, 4.8% disagreed, 5.7% neither agreed, nor disagreed). One teacher explained the need for direct peace education in relation to students' lived experiences:

> If we talk to the students about it, it can go down very well because these are things that happened when they were already conscious [of what was going on around them – Ed.]. They heard the explosions here, they experienced that. When we talk to them about things like Laurent Désiré Kabila, the escape from the AFDL and all that, well, they understand, but they can understand even better. (ECM and Arts teacher, Goma, 2016)

Even more recurrent was the idea of 'never again': "Such education is necessary because it can help us avoid future conflicts in our societies. By learning from the past, understanding what caused these conflicts, we can prevent conflicts in society" (Teacher trainer, Bukavu, 2016). Many teachers were glad that the curriculum included at least some references to the country's violent past, and implemented them without hesitation:

> I only teach in 6th grade and there we talk about the different wars: the liberation war of 1996, the AFDL war of 1998, the M23 war. We explain students that an agreement was concluded on March 23, but that some say that this agreement was not respected, which caused the war. We try because they must know about our country. (History and ECM teacher, Sake, 2016).

Still, recent conflicts are largely glossed over in the current curriculum: "They [i.e., the Ministry of Education] only give themes, themes to develop but often without sufficiently detailed works, which are needed to help the teacher and help the students too" (subject unknown, Bukavu, 2016). The curriculum was furthermore considered too packed, making it difficult to cover direct peace education materials in sufficient depth: 74.7% of teachers (strongly) agreed that because the curriculum is too packed, they didn't have sufficient time to address these issues (14.1% disagreed, 11.3% neither agreed nor disagreed). Some teachers nonetheless tried to integrate it to some extent by actively linking past and present (what also prompted the development of the risk-taking continuum by Kitson and McCully, 2005 in Northern Ireland) when teaching about more distant conflicts:

> After having given the material which concerns for example the course and consequences of the First World War, the Second World War, we combine it with what happened in Kaniola. There are some students who lived through it, there are others who were still too young, but when you do that, they easily understand what happened in Kaniola. (History teacher, Kaniola, 2016)

> The first republic in our country was characterized by mutinies, rebellions, secession of Katanga, Kasai, the political division of September 5, 1960. When we talk about these rebellions, that is where we are also referring to the M23 rebellion […] When we teach about the Berlin conference, we talk about the Goma conference of 2008 with agreements made between the government and the Rwandans, of which the M23 say that we did not respect. (Geography, History and ECM teacher, Goma, 2016)

This approach did not suffice for all however:

> You will hear people say that there are some Banyamulenge here who are Rwandans, but these people have been here for many, many years. Clearly, people don't understand well their history. Yet, instead of including that [history] in the national curriculum, what do we put? Always the French Revolution. (History teacher, Goma, 2016)

We also asked teachers at what level of education they thought it was appropriate to incorporate direct peace education. Generally, support was high for all levels. At the primary, lower secondary and higher secondary level, 60.5%, 58.2% and 73.1% of the teachers were in support of incorporating direct peace education, respectively (see bar chart 5.1.), with a significant incidence of teachers who support direct peace education at one level also supporting it at at least one other level.[24] This does not mean that teachers felt direct peace education was void of age considerations though:

> If we talk about it in the first grades, we can say something, but we are not going to go into details or give examples that we could give to students in 5th or 6th grade. For instance, the photos there that were taken when people were

massacred here in Kaniola – these photos are often shown when there is for example a conference at the parish, so we can show that – we cannot fail to show them, but we must see at what age we must show these photos. That's it. (History teacher, Kaniola, 2016)

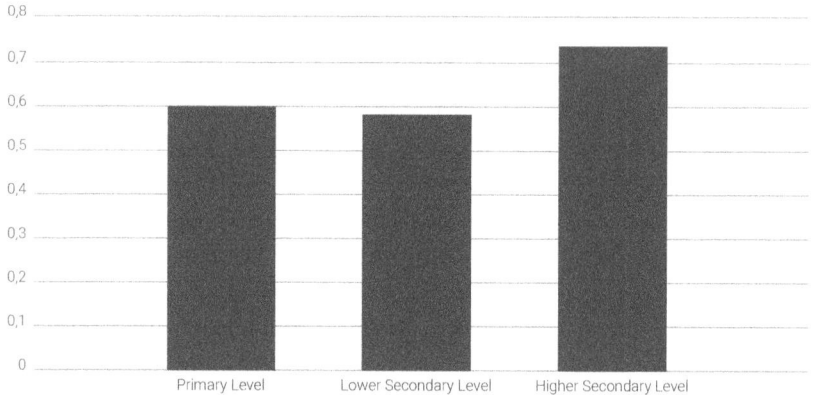

Bar chart 5.1. Support for direct peace education by level of education among Congolese teachers in Bukavu and Goma (N=1,642)

Although there were no significant differences between male and female teachers or according to subject taught, more experienced teachers showed somewhat stronger support for direct peace education, particularly at the lower secondary level of education.[25] Teachers in Bukavu were also somewhat more supportive of starting to teach about the past from an early age onwards[26], just like teachers who regularly engaged in political discussions at home. The latter were also more supportive than other teachers of direct peace education in higher secondary education.[27]

Interestingly, there was opposition from teacher trainers. Two teacher trainers of the ISP of Bukavu explained their position as follows:

We do not agree with [the teaching of] recent history! That's our stance... you will see that, even in Belgium, opening archives on a subject such as the murder of Lumumba took up to 50 years, and in France, 30 years. There are good reasons for taking such measures. (Teacher trainer in history, Bukavu, 2016)

Personally, since I have been teaching this course [ECM], I have never included a chapter dedicated to controversial issues such as massacres in a region or the war we experienced. We can give examples, but not focus on something that happened in the country. The school environment is primarily apolitical. When you address topics related to massacres and wars in a particular region, you cannot avoid leading to political discussions, which is strictly prohibited. (Teacher trainer in ECM, Bukavu, 2016)

5.5. (Dis)comfort

Against the background of enduring tensions, the sociological time in eastern DR Congo could be considered less 'ripe' for direct peace education. Still, the teacher data indicates high levels of support. In this section, we will examine how comfortable teachers felt offering direct peace education by combining quantitative and qualitative data. Again, we will look at concerns of retraumatization and of the politicization of the school environment.

To assess the traumas teachers experienced, the survey, like in Côte d'Ivoire, included both a general, subjective means of impact assessment of the past conflict (ranging from 1= 'Not affected at all' to 5= 'Very much affected'), as well as a set of questions enquiring about the specific consequences they experienced. Generally, slightly over half of all teachers interviewed (54.1%) shared that the past conflicts in eastern DR Congo had (very) much affected them, whereas 39.9% indicated that it had not (16.6%) affected them at all or only little (23.3%) – 6% indicated that the impact was small or neither small, nor large. Notwithstanding the different contexts of Goma and Bukavu, there were no significant differences between teachers from both cities. Clearly, the impact of the conflict was substantial: notably, 42.1% of the teachers lost a direct family member and 53.8% lost a close friend. Of the teachers themselves, 25.6% were physically harmed by the conflict, while 57.1% suffered from intimidation and threats. 41.2% continued to suffer from the psychological consequences of their lived experiences at the time of data collection. At 20.8%, there was even a rather high incidence rate of sexual violence (including male teachers whose wife or children had been victims). On a material level, 44.9% had had their property damaged and 61.3% struggled with financial problems. 42.5% at at least one point in time fled their house. One teacher explained how many people were affected in multiple ways: "the AFDL war found me at the ISP, they took everything I had and our house was systematically looted, there are also uncles who died during this war: uncle Ndongozi, uncle Chaburwa and uncle Magabe" (Geography and ECM teacher, Goma, 2016). While we expected that traumatized teachers would be more reluctant to engage with direct peace education, it appeared that those who were affected more – with higher scores on the subjective impact assessment – were actually more likely to agree that the causes of conflict in eastern DR Congo should be taught at school, and to start already at the primary level.[28] This could indicate that teachers who are heavily affected by conflict are more likely to consider discussing the past and seeking reconciliation even more deeply than less affected peers.

Also, most of the teachers we interviewed seemed keenly aware of the extent of trauma experienced and the negative impact thereof on students' schooling. Some even had participated in training offered by NGOs on how to deal with such trauma. As a result, these teachers were not afraid to address the trauma:

> Well, you know, sometimes we say *"Dawa ya moto ni moto"* ("the medicine for fire is fire; fighting fire with fire"). So if a child has suffered trauma because he himself was raped for example or because one of his parents or relatives was raped, it is not by hiding, by hiding it, by not talking about it that we help this child, we must rather talk about it and get this child to open up, to talk about his wounds, to talk about what bothers him, I believe that that is the solution. (ECM and Arts teacher, Goma, 2016)

A director of studies added that only

> when parents hide information about their child's past from us, we have problems managing them because maybe instead of talking to him slowly, I will raise my voice and he remembers a lot of stories, so instead of solving his problem we only make the situation worse. (Study director, Goma, 2016)

In terms of sociopolitical tensions in and beyond the classroom, the Congolese survey included questions gauging the extent to which teachers agreed that tensions in the classroom and the school in general, would stand in the way of direct peace education. Importantly, 55.2% of teachers agreed that fears to incite tensions among students made teaching about the past conflicts difficult (31% disagreed, 13.8% neither agreed nor disagreed). Classroom situations could turn particularly tense for Banyamulenge students, interviews showed:

> When I asked "what is the motto of our army [the national army of Congo]?", my students did not know, except for a munyamulenge. [...] He knew the motto *"makila na biso pona Congo"* [Our blood will be shed for Congo]. I wanted to show that you have to be a nationalist to die for the country. The other students said "teacher, do you accept that? It is not for them". (History and ECM teacher, Bukavu, 2016)

> I remember, we had two Banyamulenge students. When you mention the name of these students when there was a conflict, the others started to say M23... (Physics teacher, Goma, 2016)

> There are things that you can introduce in your class and you feel the children get tense. For example, when discussing the role that the military must play, we teach that they must protect the national borders, they must protect the national integrity, but we also show that a citizen can protect his country and how he can protect it. Then, students give examples to protect from "infiltrators who come from Rwanda". At that moment, you feel that all those who have to do with Rwandans are getting tense. (Geography and ECM teacher, Goma, 2016)

However, ethnic tensions were not limited to classrooms with Banyamulenge students. A history and ECM teacher from the closeby village of Sake (2016), where "Hunde and the Hutu still live at daggers drawn", explained:

> When the villages were burned here up in the hills... teachers and students kept talking about it. I overheard how some Hunde students told their Hutu colleagues: "you have just burned our houses; do you think we are happy, are we going to kill each other here???" I tried to calm them down: "you are children, you must not fight for what happened." Yet, the other child [Hutu] said: "be careful, there are a lot of us, don't dare because we are going to massacre you." Children cannot develop such a language of hatred. (History and ECM teacher, Sake, 2016)

In addition to causing tensions among students, 51.3% thought that teaching conflict history could cause problems with other colleagues (34.8%

disagreed, 13.9% neither agreed nor disagreed). Others still deemed the staff room a safe space, especially in comparison to the broader neighbourhood: "(…) we can talk among ourselves here, among teachers, but in the neighborhood we keep to ourselves, yes" (Physics teacher, Goma, 2016). Indeed, more than fearing negative reactions within the school environment, most teachers in eastern DR Congo were concerned about their security outside of the classroom. This is not surprising in a context where former warlords occupy important political and administrative positions. Notably, previous research shows that teachers are commonly perceived as representatives of the state and thus suspected by local militias of being informants for the state (Brandt, 2021).

> We are in a danger zone when we teach history (…) There are parts that can lead to certain criticisms. When there are criticisms, agents from the National Intelligence Agency can come after us. (Geography, History and ECM teacher, Goma, 2016)

> We are especially fearful when engaging in a historical biography of someone who is still alive. For example, when you denounce their abuse, what they have done to consolidate their power, this can lead to the person feeling exposed and wanting to protect themselves by creating other catastrophic situations. That's why we historians prefer to stay away from immediate history. (Teacher trainer in history, Bukavu, 2016)

One inspector of history education therefore recommended caution when addressing the violent past – though not avoidance:

> We ask teachers not to refrain from dealing with recent wars, even if it can create conflicts. However, we cannot state who armed whom, or who was recruited by whom… It is at this level that we reserve ourselves, we wait for the actors to disappear to talk about it…What is also sensitive, is insisting on tribe. We must not say Bisimwa or Runiga from South Kivu are bad … that will create conflicts between those peoples and the Bashi … (Inspector history education and ECM, Goma, 2016)

Yet, some teachers commented in this respect that "children spontaneously speak of names that are common here" (ECM and Geography teacher, Goma, 2016).

Box 5.1. Between just 'doing the job' and containing: Focus on Philemon Mapendo (pseudonym), Geography and ECM teacher in Goma since 2001 (2016)

Researcher: Have you ever tried addressing any of the recent conflicts that have affected the region, such as the M23 rebellion?

Teacher: No, I did not address it in a class lesson because I withhold myself from all political commentary. Where did the M23 come from? Who are the sponsors of the M23? Children cannot understand that. Still, they know that all wars come from the Rwandans.

Researcher: Where do they learn that from then?

Teacher: This is often information that circulates in the city and there are certain families which talk about politics because you get questions, such as "sorry sir, where have Laurent Nkunda and the others gone?" I answer them that *"petit* [little one], that's a question for outside the classroom".

Researcher: It seems that the educational system hides a lot of things from children, can this solve the problem?

Teacher: No, in principle we must be aware of everything that happens in our environment. If there was a war, children should know that there was a war, so that these children do not make the same mistakes that our elders and we ourselves made. If there are armed groups, then these children should be informed about why these armed groups exist, and who pushes them to make war, so that one day they do not become part.

Researcher: Where should we talk about this then?

Teacher: We really need to organize conferences where we can raise awareness and inform the grassroots about everything we have experienced and are experiencing, and that is the very role of civil society. As educators we can also look for opportunities to train and inform, but the school authorities must organize this as it is not a subject that is included in the official curriculum [...]

Researcher: Would we not risk poking wounds, throwing oil on the fire?

Teacher: We must avoid naming people. Take the war of M23, CNDP, we know its origins but we must not tell children the actors were such and such. Instead, we show the consequences of this war and tell them that war never has advantages for the population. We can ask students the question, should we encourage others to join armed

> groups? In the end we could discourage children from joining these movements.
>
> *Researcher:* Imagine you are appointed to the Ministry of Education in charge of peacebuilding through schools. Based on your experience as a geography teacher and having lived in the sub-region, what is your priority?
>
> *Teacher:* It is to create a mechanism that can bring together teachers because it would be necessary for teachers to be more aware and informed. Yet, we must develop the materials to give to teachers. So, we must set up a project based on what we have just covered on wars and conflicts at the Ministry and try to insert some basic concepts into the civic and moral education course.

5.6. (In)competence

Our survey results indicate that 9% of teachers in Bukavu and Goma have taken part in the violence in eastern DR Congo. Bearing in mind the results of the previous chapter, important questions arise regarding the ability of these teachers to teach about the past from multiple perspectives. However, rather than examine teachers' biases, this section focuses on teachers' pedagogical skills. Beyond being familiar with and open to discussing divergent perspectives on the past, teaching about past conflicts from multiple perspectives requires pedagogical skills that emphasize participation and interaction. There is also a need to reject corporal punishment, since it not only violates children's fundamental rights but also contradicts the message of non-violence promoted by both direct and indirect peace education. Notably, besides detrimental effects on students' self-esteem, academic motivation, and their relations with teachers, it normalizes violence as a method of conflict resolution (Kalolo & Kapinga, 2023; Oben & Hui, 2025).

While Congolese teachers almost unanimously agreed (98.6%) that participation is crucial to promoting mutual understanding (see Table 5.4.), about half (51.2%) considered overcrowded classrooms an issue in this respect. Admittedly, participatory pedagogies are difficult to implement in such settings. Clearly, teachers require tailored strategies that enable participation with large groups. While their support for participatory pedagogies was nonetheless promising, there were also some indications that some teachers failed to fully understand participatory pedagogies: nearly one third (29.2%) of teachers still believed that allowing students to express their views undermined their authority as teachers.

Although corporal punishment has been banned in the DR Congo, it is worrying that a substantial percentage of teachers (31.9%) still agreed that the practice is necessary to ensure good conduct. Interestingly, one teacher we interviewed expressed regret at no longer being able to use corporal punishment:

> So here, sometimes children were whipped, those who misbehaved were whipped, but since 2013, we followed training in PAP (*Pédagogie Appliquée et Participative*; [Applied and Participative Pedagogy]), we were forbidden to insult, punish and do anything to the child. Now we see that discipline is really slipping away from us, school discipline. (French teacher, Goma, 2016)

Perhaps unsurprisingly then, roughly the same proportion of teachers (36.6%) admitted to still applying it every now and then: "I know it's forbidden but from time to time I do it when I find it's getting a bit out of hand" (School principal & teacher of Social, educational and commercial sciences, Goma, 2016). Accordingly, 18.5% of teachers believed that it still occurred regularly at their school. Taking social desirability effects into account, these proportions could even underestimate the real share of teachers that still reverted to corporal punishment. In many parts of sub-Saharan Africa, studies have similarly exposed the persistent use of corporal punishment (Lanoue, 2007; Sayed et al., 2018), which some have attributed to the colonial roots of educational systems (Kalolo & Kapinga, 2023; Oben & Hui, 2025). After all, colonial forces used schooling as a disciplinary method to maintain discipline and provide itself with soldiers, artisans, and so on (André & Poncelet, 2013; Ocobock, 2012). Nevertheless, more recent investments in teacher training programmes on positive disciplining seem to have paid off:

> A disruptive student for example, or a student who does not participate in class, I often give them work. I give them novels to go and read, and within a week they have to write a summary. That is their punishment, because today's students do not like to read. So for them, it becomes a big job that you give them, but it is a punishment that is constructive. (French teacher, Goma, 2016)

Table 5.4. Percentage of teachers by extent of agreement with the survey statements on peace pedagogy in Eastern DR Congo (N=1642)

Item	Strongly disagree	Disagree	Neither disagree, nor agree	Agree	Strongly agree
Participatory pedagogies are important for promoting mutual understanding.	0.4%	0.2%	0.9%	23.0%	75.6%
Providing space for students to express their views diminishes the power of the teacher (-).	24.9%	36.5%	9.4%	13.2%	16.0%
Participatory pedagogies are difficult to implement because of overcrowded classes.	10.3%	24.7%	13.9%	25.3%	25.9%
Corporal punishment is necessary to ensure good conduct at school (-).	21.4%	32.2%	14.6%	18.1%	13.8%
Sometimes I use corporal punishment to reprimand students (-).	21.3%	31.5%	10.5%	26.1%	10.5%
Corporal punishment is regularly used in this school to correct students (-).	30.1%	39.5%	11.9%	12.4%	6.1%

Our results therefore suggest that many teachers still lacked the necessary skills to teach conflict-history education. Even though civic education is covered in national teacher training programmes, and despite the participation of a great many teachers in one or more training programmes organized by the many NGOs that are active in the region, 77.4% of teachers were themselves also of the opinion that they did not have the required training to provide direct peace education (14.1% disagreed, 8.5% neither agreed nor disagreed).[29]

5.7. Uprooted

Although there have been some opportunities to address the violent past, teaching materials are scarce and superficial – a view that teachers expressed (see section 5.5.). Against this backdrop, we developed and piloted educational resources over the course of 2023-2024 to help teachers implement conflict-history education as part of the 'Uprooted' project. In this section, we present the growth trajectories of teachers who have used these materials. First, however, we provide some brief background information.

5.7.1. Background on 'Uprooted'

With the support of the Provincial Ministry of Education and the Education Justice and Memory Network (EdJAM), the 'Uprooted' project literally aimed to 'uproot' conflict dynamics in the region by raising awareness of the complexity of the situation and encouraging students to understand the perspectives of other ethnic groups by adopting multiple viewpoints. To this end, the research team co-created a set of educational tools to teach students about the violent past of eastern DR Congo. To ensure the initiative was implemented effectively, we also provided training for 20 history and civic education teachers from ten secondary schools in and around Bukavu. The selection of schools considered the diversity of the Congolese educational system, including government-funded, faith-based and privately-funded schools. While the ultimate objective was to assess changes in students' attitudes towards peace, their knowledge about the past, and their critical thinking skills after being exposed to the materials, this section looks exclusively at the outcomes of the teacher training and experiences of teachers with the newly developed materials.

We first developed the materials in close collaboration with the participating teachers, selected students from the schools involved, and local experts and practitioners in the field of reconciliation. Each group of stakeholders participated in a micro '*arbre à palabres*' (palaver tree), a practice of communal dialogue and conflict resolution which in the past brought together community elders and other members under large, often ancient, trees. During these sessions, the stakeholders identified key conflict events, which included elite assassinations (of traditional authorities, religious leaders, politicians, and members of civil society organizations), conflicts over land and between ethnic groups, but also the consequences of conflict (such as forced displacement and migration, mass killings and conflict-related sexual violence). Compiling each group's timeline of events, this resulted in an online[30] and paper-based timeline of the history of conflicts, which can largely be sub-divided into five sections:

1. Violence under Congo's independent state: This includes chapters on the collection of "red" rubber and people forced into labour by agents of Leopold;
2. Conflict and violence during the Belgian colonization of Congo: These events retrace forced labour, as well as the struggle for independence with a particular focus on the martyrs of independence;
3. Conflict and violence in the post-independence period: This section covers events such as the Katangese secession, Pierre Mulele's rebellion, the revolt led by Jean Schramme and the two Shaba wars;
4. The 1996 war: This section covers the massacres of the Kiliba population, the rebellion of the AFDL, the assassination of *Monseigneur* Christophe Munzihirwa, and the Kaniola-Nindja massacres;
5. From 1998 to present: The final section focuses on the emergence of the different rebel movements that continue to affect eastern DR Congo up until this day.

For each selected conflict event, the materials bring together a selection of relevant historical documents, photographs, and testimonies from those involved in, or affected by, the occurrence. Teachers can use these materials to facilitate discussion, and they are accompanied by an educational note on how to use them. The research team collected many of these materials during visits to sites where atrocities occurred. These included Fizi, Uvira, Walungu, Kabare, Mwenga, Bukavu, and Goma and its surrounding villages.

In a second step, teachers spent two months experimenting with the materials as part of their history and/or ECM courses in 5th and 6th grade (expected age of 16 to 18). Throughout the implementation period, the teachers participated in a Community of Practice (CoP). Teachers met regularly to reflect on and share their experiences and emotions when using the 'Uprooted' tool. Apart from physical meetings, the CoP was facilitated by a WhatsApp group. From the CoPs, it emerged that teachers mainly discussed the events that occurred after 1996, and the Kiliba, Kasika, Mutarule, and Kishishe massacres, primarily using the collected photos (i.e., of memorial sites of massacres, or historical pictures of the victims themselves). Teachers only used the documentation (i.e., reports, peace agreements) to prepare. Due to time constraints, most teachers only inserted the materials occasionally, while others consistently integrated the material in each lesson, however short. As regards student responses, teachers generally noted two types of reaction. On the one hand, discussing the materials resulted in students expressing remorse and empathy, and focussing on forgiveness and justice as pathways forwards. On the other hand, there were students who expressed resentment and spoke of revenge.

5.7.2. Fostering critical design experts through 'Uprooted'

To reflect on their professional development while implementing 'Uprooted', 15 out of 20 participating teachers positioned themselves on the conflict-history education framework prior to and after having experimented with the materials. Table 5.5. presents their various trajectories, as experienced by the teachers themselves. We discuss three emerging insights.

First, prior to using the 'Uprooted' materials, a minority did not consider the potential of education for reconciliation as revealed by the number of avoiders and teachers just 'doing the job'. This corresponds with our broader survey findings. One avoiding teacher explained that

> because of my religious belief, I thought that returning each time to past conflicts would overheat the minds of certain people who had already forgotten the atrocities of which they were victims and this would always lead to tearing society apart and depriving it of the peace it always needs, all the more since I did not have all the necessary knowledge. (teacher 9)

Table 5.5. Congolese teachers' position on the conflict-history education framework (n=15)

	Prior to Uprooted				Post Uprooted			
	Avoiding	Doing the job	Containing	Critical expert	Avoiding	Doing the job	Containing	Critical expert
1			X					X
2		X						X
3		X						X
4			X					X
5			X					X
6				X				X
7				X				X
8			X					X
9	X							X
10			X					X
11				X				X
12	X							X
13		X	X			X		
14		X						X
15				X				X

The teachers just 'doing the job' simply "didn't think we would find solutions to peace even if we taught history in schools" (teacher 2); "sincerely thought that just reminding students of the past conflicts was enough to make peace" (teacher 3); or merely "implemented what was in the programme" (teacher 14) – just like teacher 13, who nonetheless appreciated drawing lessons from the past for the future (hence his double position in the table). In contrast, while most teachers acknowledged the peacebuilding potential of conflict-history education, they were reluctant to implement it (six containers compared to four critical design experts): "Before using 'Uprooted' I wanted to contribute to telling the truth to the students, but the fear of doing, to avoid any revolution among the students prevented me from doing that" (teacher 8). Containing teachers also mentioned, as a hindrance to implementing direct peace education, the lack of documentation to support them in their endeavours.

Second, four teachers regarded themselves as critical design experts even before the project had been implemented. Among these teachers, one was involved in his school's peace club and had a long history of working with, and following training programmes of, NGOs and human rights organizations. Thanks to this experience, he was able to "defy fears" (teacher 11). Prior to implementing 'Uprooted', he taught about the atrocities that had shaken the country in his ECM classes "because ECM is a current affairs course. So every time they talk about massacres that are happening here on the radio, we talk about it with students and sometimes even discuss up to an hour." Another teacher (15), who perceived himself as a critical design expert from the outset, was simply so convinced of the need that he could not be stopped:

> The wine produced should only be drunk. I have no fear of approaching its history. To better treat an illness, one must know its origin and cause. There is nothing wrong with learning about one's past. Teaching people to live in peace also requires discussing war and conflict.

Third, and most notably, all teachers except for one considered themselves critical design experts after having used the materials. Promisingly, seeing that his "students were interested and gave constructive ideas" convinced a teacher just 'doing the job' that "this [i.e. conflict-history education] could in the long run provide solutions" (teacher 2). More generally, teachers noted a great deal of interest among students. For instance, on returning from a short break after having introduced a lesson about the war between Germany and France, another teacher noticed how students had changed the subject on the board to "the war between Rwanda and the DR Congo". For the second teacher previously just 'doing the job', the materials themselves "encouraged me to consider the history of conflicts as a means of imposing peace and changing the behaviour of learners" (teacher 1). Former containers largely explained that learning about the conflicts and having the necessary materials available helped them to no longer be "afraid of teaching what we do not master" (teacher 8). Similarly, teachers who already considered themselves critical design experts did still believe to have "even more necessary knowledge and skills to teach how to avoid conflicts" upon concluding the pilot project (teacher 7). Only one teacher did not identify as a critical design expert afterwards. Oscillating between a teacher just 'doing the job' and a container at the start, he did become more convinced of teaching the history of conflict "for the cause of educating society in the context of resolving social conflicts", but "caution" was still warranted.

While these results suggest that such programmes as 'Uprooted' can foster critical design experts, the key question is whether observers would also position all teachers (except one) as critical design experts after participation in 'Uprooted'. Classroom observations, but also student interviews could shed more light on the actual trajectories of the teachers. Nonetheless, it is fair to assume that not all teachers have fully come to terms with the inherent challenges. Earlier discussions during the CoPs revealed that at least some teachers continued to fear reprisals from perpetrators. As such, one teacher mentioned a former rebel governor who became a leading partner of the ruling regime. Other teachers also shared not knowing how to react to students' expressions of vengeance after learning more about the past – clearly, they did not want to further 'root' instead of 'uproot' conflict dynamics. Finally, there was the issue of institutional support that came up at least once during each CoP. Undoubtedly, the participating teachers would feel more comfortable if the programme was accepted and authorized by the Ministry of Education. However, as Pingel (2008) noted, official reform projects typically adhere to a strict hierarchy from curriculum revision to textbook development to teacher training. Such a long process can result in the reform effectively being shelved and prevent conflict-history teaching within such a project as 'Uprooted' from ever being added to the curriculum. This is even more likely now the conflict has flared up again.

5.8. Situating Congolese teachers within the framework of conflict-history education

Notwithstanding, or perhaps because of, the violence that is rife in eastern DR Congo, our research demonstrated that, in 2018, most teachers in Bukavu and Goma supported conflict-history education, often starting as early as primary school. Accordingly, we situate eastern Congolese teachers predominantly on the right side of our framework. This 'ripening' of the sociological time may have been prompted by political time. Although it was a rare occurrence, the Ministry of Education agreed to include in the official curriculum recent conflicts that had taken place in the region. Teachers even went beyond the formal curriculum, however, using other conflict-related themes to draw parallels with their own context of conflict. Still, significant hurdles remained. Ethnic tensions were at times palpable in the classroom, particularly affecting Rwandophone students. Importantly, the physical integrity of teachers was at risk, given that many of those involved in the conflict are still alive and sometimes occupy influential positions. Moreover, our results revealed that a substantial number of teachers still supported corporal punishment and that many struggled to implement participatory pedagogies, which are crucial to direct peace education. This suggests that most teachers involved in direct peace education may not only place themselves at physical risk but also risk modelling behaviours that undermine the principles of non-violence and participation. However, on a more positive note, the discussion of the 'Uprooted' teacher training demonstrated that these positions can change with the right support, with teachers moving towards becoming critical design experts.

PART 3
Conclusions & Policy recommendations

CHAPTER 6

Main findings and conclusions

> Education is, quite simply, peacebuilding by another name. It is the most effective form of defense spending there is. Efforts must be made to save posterity from the adverse effects of war and conflict. (Kofi Annan, 1999)

Conflict-related curricular reforms seldom involve teachers within war-torn, war-born or war-threatened societies. Nevertheless, research shows that teachers can still refuse, subvert, adapt or defy policies and reforms that they consider unjust or with which they are uncomfortable. This is particularly true of sensitive policies like the integration of conflict-history education, or direct peace education, in societies affected by armed conflict. Direct peace education involves learning about the causes, course, consequences and costs of conflict from multiple perspectives, with the aim of increasing understanding of the grievances and motivations of the former opponents, and reducing mistrust and hatred towards the 'other'. At the very least, it was argued, it should contribute to 'political generosity', as defined by Emerson (2012) as the ability to recognize the cultural and political identities of those with opposing views. Alternatively, it could contribute to 'historical perspective-taking', which is the willingness to consider how other groups view the violent past (Bilali & Vollhardt, 2013). Furthermore, we posited that effective implementation of such education requires 'support from below', namely, from teachers. This book's main objective was therefore to systematically and rigorously evaluate teachers' support for direct peace education in African countries transitioning from conflict to peace.

Although previous research has already focused on identifying the challenges and opportunities encountered and perceived by teachers in conflict-affected societies, the data we presented in this book is unique in combining qualitative insights with large-scale, systematic, empirical research in three under-examined case study contexts in sub-Saharan Africa: Kenya, Côte d'Ivoire and the eastern Democratic Republic of Congo (DR Congo). These case studies are also enlightening when viewed in a comparative context. Although all three countries were affected by identity-based conflict, the degree and duration of the conflict varied significantly, with violence being more or less temporally removed from the present. Moreover, to systematically interpret the data, we employed an original analytical heuristic: the conflict-history education framework, that was inspired by Kitson and McCully's (2005) risk-taking continuum. Our framework positions teachers on two axes, showing how their attitude towards the peacebuilding role of conflict-history education intersects with their perceived level of (dis)comfort and competence to engage critically and constructively with multiple perspectives on the history of conflict in their own country, alongside their students.

In this chapter, we summarize the positions of secondary school teachers in Kenya, Côte d'Ivoire and the DR Congo using this framework, and examine which individual traits and experiences explain differences in teachers' stances regarding conflict-history education, or direct peace education, within and across the three country contexts. We also reflect on the role of temporal distance and type of violence. Finally, we synthesize the support that teachers thought they needed to gain the confidence and skills to promote reconciliation in their own classrooms. We will also evaluate the analytical value of our theoretical framework in measuring the readiness of groups that have previously been in conflict to address the past. Finally, we will discuss the limitations and outline recommendations for future research.

6.1. Situating teachers in terms of their support for direct peace education

To systematically examine support for direct peace education and make comparisons across countries, we carefully searched the existing body of research prior to writing this book to identify an appropriate analytical lens. However, it soon became apparent that most relevant studies did not make use of a well-delineated theoretical framework, despite researchers' efforts to devise categorizations that could be applied across contexts. In this respect, the work of Kitson and McCully (2005) stood out. Based on teacher observations in Northern Ireland, the risk-taking continuum was developed to distinguish between three types of teachers: those who avoid conflict-history education (avoiders), those who take the sting out of conflict-history education (containers) and those who actively encourage students to explore multiple perspectives on the violent past (risk-takers). Fundamentally, they assumed that teachers' practices differed because of their views on the societal role of education. In contrast to risk-takers and containers, avoiders consider peacebuilding to be outside the remit of teaching. Furthermore, what sets containers apart from risk-takers is the discomfort faced by the former. Out of fear of retriggering trauma or polarising views, they prefer to study emotionally distant conflicts rather than their own context. Alternatively, they prefer to apply teacher-led methods to maintain control. However, their continuum failed to convey clearly this essential difference in motivations between teachers who (partially) support direct peace education and those who do not. Moreover, it presupposed that risk-taking was an inherently positive endeavour, despite the importance of having the necessary skills to do so without causing harm.

To address these shortcomings, we have developed a new framework which illustrates how support for, and engagement with, direct peace education depends on three key factors: (1) teachers' beliefs regarding the purpose of education as a tool for reconciliation, (2) their (dis)comfort in addressing sensitive societal topics, and (3) their ability to engage critically and constructively with multiple perspectives on the history of conflict in their own country, alongside their students without (re)traumatizing the latter. We subsequently proposed mapping teachers' positions with respect to these elements on two intersecting continua. This resulted in the identification of four ideal-type positions: (1) 'avoiders', who do not consider peacebuilding to be part of their duty as teachers and who would be uncomfortable taking on this responsibility if asked to do so; (2) teachers just 'doing the job', who in principle do not consider it their responsibility either, yet who would feel confident and be competent if asked to do so; (3) 'containers', who acknowledge the reconciliatory potential of education, but are reluctant to put it into practice for fear of (re)traumatization and/or polarization, and (4) 'critical design experts', who also acknowledge the peacebuilding potential and feel confident and competent in taking on this responsibility. We distinguished critical design experts from risk-takers. The latter were confident but not necessarily competent, in teaching about the violent past constructively. We used this framework to examine support for direct peace education in each of the three case study contexts.

With respect to teachers' beliefs about the role of education, it emerged that, regardless of context, teachers generally recognized the potential of education to contribute to reconciliation and sustainable peace. In Kenya, where ethnicity has been heavily politicized since (and prior to) independence, teachers largely agreed that schools are the ideal place for pupils to learn how to respect other ethnic groups, and that diversity at school contributes to the debunking of stereotypes. Similarly, in Côte d'Ivoire, where identity-based grievances led to a civil war and post-electoral crisis, nearly all teachers believed that schools are the ideal place to learn about peace and tolerance, and that they play an important role in national reconciliation. This was also the case in the eastern DR Congo, where violence remains rife to this day. Such acknowledgement, however, does not necessarily translate into support for direct peace education even though our data showed that support was substantial: in all three case studies, a majority of teachers supported direct peace education. When asked whether their country's history of conflict should be taught at primary, lower and/or higher secondary school, there were differences of opinion. Whereas in Kenya and eastern DR Congo, the share of teachers in support of teaching about the violent past was high across all education levels – notwithstanding slightly higher levels of support at (higher) secondary level – in Côte d'Ivoire support steadily increased with the level of education, and thus student maturity: whereas "only" 22.9% of teachers considered it appropriate to include the history of the violent disintegration of their country at the primary level, 78.4% was in favour of including it at the higher secondary level. The differences between the three case studies regarding the appropriate level of inclusion could suggest that, when plotted against the degree of violence a society has experienced, the perceived appropriate level of education could follow an inverted U-shape, but for different reasons: in societies with low-intensity violence (like in Kenya), direct peace education can be integrated from a younger age because it is deemed less controversial than in societies with higher intensity violence (like in Côte d'Ivoire). However, in contexts where violence has become so rife (like in eastern DR Congo), the perceived urgency to address it and its daily impact on students' lives may lower the age bar again. It is interesting to note in this respect that the topic of genocide is introduced at primary school level in Rwanda (although only in the final year; Russell, 2019). Although it did not specifically pertain to conflict-history education, but to teaching about ethnic diversity more generally, a Kenyan teacher made another compelling argument to start at the primary level, one that we would like to share to encourage further reflection:

> At primary level, I think it will go a long way to discourage or mitigate some of these problems. Because most of the population does not even go to the higher level. We have some wastage at the secondary level. So by the time people exit Form IV [i.e., final year of secondary education, expected age 18] we only have a small fraction. So dealing with that at the secondary level alone you might not do much. The bigger population is down at primary level. (Chemistry and Mathematics teacher, Kasarani, 2016)

Uniquely, the Ivorian data also showed that about one fifth of secondary school teachers had already experimented with direct peace education or had organized a class discussion on the crisis and most of these teachers thought back to it as a positive experience. In eastern DR Congo too, teachers had already discussed recent conflicts in the classroom. The main difference, however, is that the history of conflict is not integrated in the official Ivorian curriculum, while it is in the Congolese curriculum, although in a very limited and fragmentary way. So while the Ivorian teachers of our research took the initiative and showed themselves exemplary at curricular-instructional gatekeeping (see section 2.1.), Congolese history and ECM teachers are just 'doing their job' when teaching about the violent past. Some Congolese teachers nonetheless tried to go beyond the formal curriculum as well – which they considered too superficial – by making the link between other conflict-related themes in their textbooks and the conflicts in eastern DR Congo. This strategy was also applied by some Kenyan teachers, who used curricular themes such as the political history of Kenya and land management to make the link with their country's post-election violence.

Others refrained from doing so because they weren't comfortable with it. While relevant survey data was not available for Kenya, interview data showed that Kenyan teachers feared retriggering the trauma students suffered (even though the risk of that increasingly abated as time went by) and politicizing ethnicity (which they perceived to occur more and more). Teachers in Côte d'Ivoire shared these concerns. More than fearing tensions between students, however, the Ivorian data showed that teachers were wary of tensions between teachers from different groups. Concerns were most substantial in Bukavu and Goma. Notably, slightly more than half of teachers appeared to fear inciting tensions among students and among teachers if they were to teach about the history of conflicts. Yet what Congolese teachers feared most, were reprisals from outside of school if they mentioned the name of conflict actors who are still alive and still involved in the country's dealings. Finally, any decision to integrate direct peace education should also take stock of the traumatic experiences of teachers – like students, they are also at risk of retraumatization. Notably, survey data showed that 60.5% and 54.1% of Ivorian and Congolese teachers, respectively, felt that the impact of (the) past conflict(s) had (very) much affected them. Note that experiencing widespread and enduring violence seems to move the yardsticks of what is considered a heavy toll: the share of teachers who had been physically harmed by the violence or who had lost a direct family member was substantially higher in eastern DR Congo than in Côte d'Ivoire, in spite of the fact that the teachers from DR Congo felt less affected generally. In Kenya too, teachers had been affected by the violence.

In terms of teacher competences, third, each case study highlighted other aspects. In Kenya, we demonstrated how teachers, who themselves grew up in a heavily ethnicized environment, are not immune to ethnic stereotyping and ingroup favouritism, although it was not blatant. Teachers said, for instance, only to give into favouritism in solidarity with their ethnic group. Yet even well-intentioned benefits risk conveying the message that ethnic favouritism is normal and socially acceptable. In Côte d'Ivoire, we focused on the teachers' interpretations of the violent past, or their narratives of the conflict. After all, it is debatable whether very biased teachers can constructively and critically engage with other perspectives on their country's violent past. The data showed that teachers attributed the past conflict to different causes and blamed different actors in the conflict to different extents. Notably, teachers' conflict narratives depended on whether their ethno-religious group leaned to southern, Christian teachers adhering closer to the conflict narrative of former president Gbagbo, or to northern, Muslim teachers adhering closer to the conflict narrative of president Ouattara. In Kenya, too, teachers expressed concerns that such partiality could stand in the way of direct peace education:

> It will be very tricky for the teacher to involve in this directly because from the homes our parents have failed to give us neutral grounds about the governance of Kenya. I will not be taken seriously by the younger generation. I will be taken as if I am talking in favour of who I support politically. (History & government teacher, Njiru, 2016)

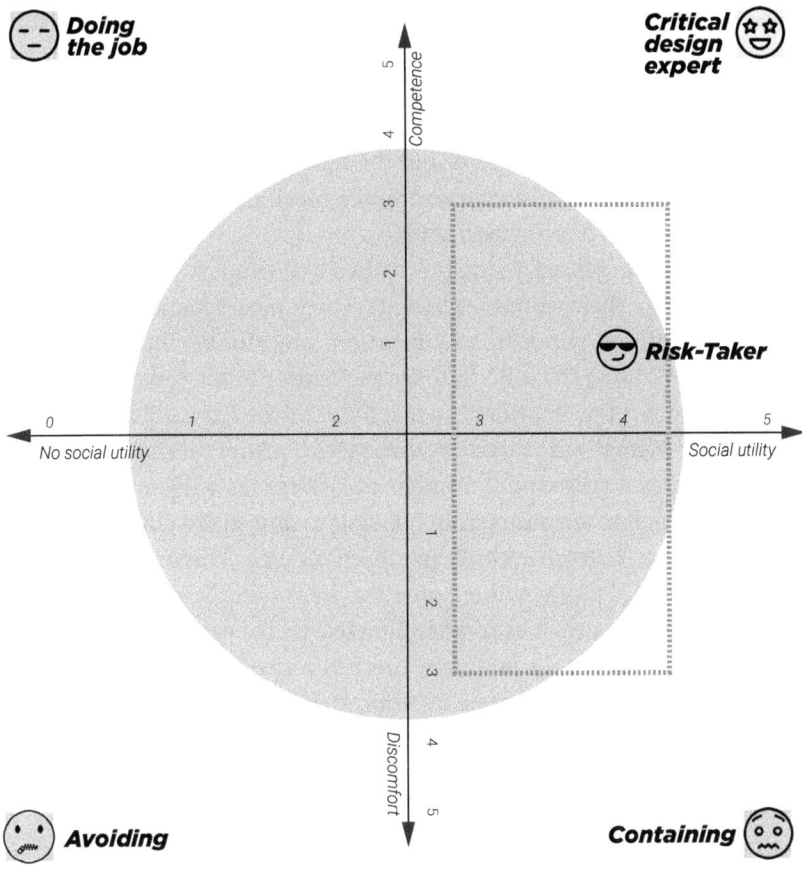

Figure 6.1. Situating Kenyan, Ivorian & Congolese secondary school teachers on the conflict-history education framework

In eastern DR Congo, finally, we enquired about teachers' pedagogical competences. While the results showed that nearly all teachers recognized the importance of participatory pedagogies to establish mutual understanding, notwithstanding the difficulties of implementation in overcrowded classrooms, close to one third of teachers still believed such approaches to undermine their authority. More worrying is that an equal share of teachers was also of the opinion that corporal punishment remains necessary to ensure good conduct at school, thus contributing to a normalization of violence as a method of conflict resolution rather than contributing to a normalization of non-violence (Oben & Hui, 2025).

Interviews with Kenyan and Ivorian teachers suggested that, in these countries too, a significant number of teachers continued to support corporal punishment. This suggests that the fundamentally authoritarian values, structures and processes of conventional schooling remain deeply embedded in the consciousness and the basic assumptions of teachers – which could represent a major stumbling block for education achieving its peace potential (see Harber, 2019).

All things considered, we demonstrated that support 'from below' was high across the three country contexts. Since most teachers considered the peacebuilding potential of education, the number of avoiders (or teachers just 'doing the job') thus seemed closer to the lower end. Many teachers did not feel confident to teach the history of conflict, however, positioning themselves closest to containers. Further, our study suggests that there was a substantial number of risk-takers who could do more harm than good when addressing the violent past in the classroom if not supported to do so from multiple perspectives using student-led activities (see figure 6.1.). Finally, while some teachers identified themselves as critical design experts, observational research is needed to corroborate their self-assessment. In addition, there is a need to assess the ethical dilemmas involved in direct peace education (see section 2.3.), including a risk assessment regarding teachers' physical and professional security.

6.2. Explaining differences

To explain differences in teachers' stances regarding conflict-history education, we assessed the correlations between support for direct peace education and a set of teachers' individual traits. In all three case studies, we examined whether there were any systematic differences in terms of gender, age, teaching experience and subject taught. Remarkably, these characteristics could hardly explain variation. In Kenya and eastern DR Congo, more experienced teachers nonetheless appeared to favour direct peace education slightly more, which was also the case for teachers of the national subjects in Côte d'Ivoire. In Côte d'Ivoire and eastern DR Congo, we also looked at the effects of subjective impact of conflict on teachers' lives, as well as teachers' political interest. While we expected that teachers who were affected more strongly by the past conflict(s) would be more reluctant to support direct peace education, we did not find any significant correlation between subjective impact and support for conflict-history education in Côte d'Ivoire. In eastern DR Congo, there was a small correlation, but in the other direction: teachers who experienced higher levels of victimization were more in favour of direct peace education. This suggests that, at least in the Congolese context, the more a teacher was affected, the more (s)he considered it fundamental to foster reconciliation through the education system. In terms of political interest, the data showed a small, but significant effect on teachers' support for direct peace education in both countries. Notably, Congolese teachers who engage more often in discussions about politics at home were more supportive of integrating conflict-history education both at primary and secondary level, whereas politically interested teachers in Côte d'Ivoire were more likely to have already implemented some form of direct peace education. In a related manner, Ivorian teachers who interpreted the past through the prism of the president in power, Ouattara, were also more confident in implementing direct peace education. This suggests that the socio-political context plays an important role for teachers in assessing their curricular-instructional gatekeeping. Beyond our case studies, Russell (2019) observed a similar trend that especially Hutu teachers in Rwanda were careful to adhere to the official curriculum and textbooks, in contrast to Tutsi teachers who were less concerned about being accused of divisionism or genocide ideology.

Finally, our analysis showed scarcely any variation at the school level. This is somewhat surprising, especially in Kenya, where schools vary considerably in terms of student population and educational resources. However, convergences were to be expected, particularly as regards student diversity: notwithstanding the regional quota for schools, Nairobi is very diverse in itself (see above), as are Abidjan, Goma and Bukavu.

6.3. Teachers' professional development needs

Although some teachers felt confident and skilled enough to take on the responsibility of promoting reconciliation in their own classrooms, many teachers in each country context felt that they were not sufficiently prepared and skilled to teach peace in general, or to address their country's history of conflict in particular. One Kenyan teacher, reflecting on the teaching of Kenya's divisive ethnic politics, meaningfully explained:

"Many people don't want to talk about [it] because they don't even know how to handle it" (Music and Economics teacher, Kenya, 2016). Accordingly, there seemed to be rather widespread support for organizing teacher professional development (TPD). Although teacher training did not figure prominently in the Kenyan survey, 66% and 72.1% of the Ivorian teachers thought that it was desirable for TPD to include training on conflict-history education and dealing with traumatized students, respectively. In eastern DR Congo, the workshops to help prepare teachers for implementing the 'Uprooted' materials, and the community of practice that was organised at the same time were greatly appreciated. Teachers enthusiastically shared how this training helped them change their attitude from avoiders, teachers just 'doing their job' or containers to critical-design experts.

Questions remain, however, about the ability of teachers to assess their own skill level. Teachers in Kenya rejected ethnic stereotyping and ingroup favouritism, while a list experiment showed that a quarter of the teachers had already shown favouritism to a student of the same ethnicity. Teachers in Côte d'Ivoire still held diametrically opposed views on the past, including on who was the main culprit for the recent violent conflict. When expressed one-sidedly, these views may shape pupils' interpretations of the violent past or cause frictions between teachers and pupils with contrasting views. Notably, we observed a teacher who claimed to teach even-handedly about the violent past, discussing two books of a very different nature with his students: whereas the book written by former rebel leader Guillaume Soro was explicitly political, the book authored by former president Laurent Gbagbo was not. It is important to note in this regard that teachers are no tabula rasa. Many teachers in Côte d'Ivoire, Eastern DR Congo and Kenya have experienced conflict first-hand and have been raised according to divided worldviews. Some teachers even actively participated in the conflict – in eastern DR Congo even up to 9%, not accounting for social desirability bias! While teachers may be careful not to let their biased views and attitudes inform their classroom behaviour, teachers are not necessarily aware of their biases. Finally, in eastern DR Congo, about a third of Congolese teachers still believed that corporal punishment was necessary to address misconduct, and that providing space to students to express their views diminished their classroom authority. These results clearly call for more and/or better TPD.

6.4. Limitations & future research directions

In the introduction to this book, we identified three main shortcomings in the literature on 'education, peace and conflict' that we sought to address: a limited geographical focus on a few "typical" cases; a dearth of systematic, large-scale research; and the lack of an analytical lens. With this book, we are taking the first steps towards addressing these gaps without fully closing them. In this section, we will discuss the limitations of our approach and propose next steps along these three avenues of research.

First, the book sheds light on three underexamined cases in the field of 'education, conflict and reconciliation': Côte d'Ivoire, eastern DR Congo and Kenya. While we outlined the similarities in the introductory chapter (i.e., the experience of identity-based conflict), we also emphasized the differences, most notably with respect to the intensity of fighting, its duration and scope, and the temporal distance of conflict to the present. It is telling that, notwithstanding these differences, we generally found high levels of support for conflict-history education, and that, across contexts, we could scarcely expose any background characteristics that could explain differences between teachers. Still, important differences were revealed, not the least regarding the appropriate level to address the violent past. This demonstrates that every violent context is unique, and it raises questions regarding the representativeness of our case studies for other conflict-affected countries across the continent. We therefore recommend replicating this research on a country-by-country basis. Importantly, researching an ever-expanding set of case studies will provide us with more insight into the relationships between conflict dynamics and support for direct peace education, but also into the sociological time of coming to terms with the past in conflict-affected settings on the continent. With the latter in mind, we would also recommend replicating this research over time. It would be insightful to understand how support for direct peace education increases – or decreases – as conflict becomes increasingly distant (or resurfaces), or as important political events unfold.

Second, and related, while the insights presented in this book draw on the attitudes, practices and experiences of over 3,000 secondary school teachers in Nairobi, Abidjan, Bukavu, and Goma, our findings remain first and foremost descriptive of the major urban contexts of Kenya, Côte d'Ivoire and eastern DR Congo. In each of these contexts, fighting was heavily concentrated in the urban areas, at least at specific times. The data are therefore representative of teachers who have been affected by conflict dynamics. Still, violence was not limited to these localities. In Kenya, the Rift Valley was the scene of some of the most horrific atrocities during the post-election violence; in Côte d'Ivoire, experiences during the country's civil war diverged substantially between the government-controlled south and the rebel-controlled north; and while violence eased in Bukavu and to a lesser extent Goma until recently, it continued unabated in the rural areas. Conflict dynamics are expected to influence teachers' attitudes towards conflict-history education significantly, and may therefore differ in rural, but also semi-urban areas compared to major cities. Other characteristics may also account for differences in attitudes, practices and experiences. Because of the smaller size and perhaps more entangled social networks in rural areas, discomfort experienced when addressing the history of conflict could be higher, for instance. Further, teachers (and students) in the city have had much more intergroup contact than their peers in rural areas. Indeed, more than once, teachers explained how much more diverse their city was than the rest of the country. Pointedly, a Kenyan history and government teacher stated: "Being in an urban set up has actually brought us national unity as compared with the rural areas" (2016). Similarly, a Congolese teacher said:

> In the city, children have friends who are not necessarily of their cultures, who are not of their ethnic group, of their village; it helps putting things into perspective a little, they actually have more chances than the children who are in remote areas [to understand that conflict is not merely about ethnicity]. (ECM and Arts teacher, Goma, 2016)

It follows that future research could expand the scope of the study to nationally representative samples, including teachers from urban, semi-urban and rural areas.

Third, we recommend that future studies in the selected case studies or other conflict-affected settings in sub-Saharan Africa and beyond use our framework. Previous research lacked a common theoretical framework, which limited the ability to draw conclusions across socio-political settings. We believe that our framework builds on the valuable insights provided by this literature, while providing a platform for a more systematic examination of how social, political, temporal, geographical, and cultural characteristics affect the opportunities available to teachers to promote reconciliation. However, our framework was developed a posteriori. In other words, we collected our data based on measures formulated before the new conflict-history education framework was developed. Furthermore, the measures we used varied across context. While our data has provided interesting results, which we interpreted through the prism of our framework, a systematic comparison of the results requires the use of a set of standardized measures that fully capture all dimensions of the framework. To conclude this chapter, we have therefore developed a set of items to accompany research based on our new conflict-history education framework (see Table 6.1.). Prior to conducting research aimed at examining teachers' positions on the framework in a country of interest, we recommend testing the scale in a variety of contexts with a view to validating it.

Table 6.1. Scale to measure teachers' stances on the conflict-history education framework

On a scale of 1 = 'Strongly disagree' to 5= 'Strongly agree', to what extent do you agree with the following statements:

Support for direct peace education:

1. The school is an ideal place to improve relations between [group 1 previously in conflict] and [group 2 previously in conflict] in [name of country/region].

2. At school, students must be taught about the causes and consequences of conflict in [specify name of country/region].

3. When teaching about the history of conflict, it is important to discuss <u>critically</u> and <u>constructively</u> the perspectives of all sides involved on why conflict occurred and who is to blame.

4. In addition to achieving the course objectives as outlined in the curriculum, it is my responsibility as a teacher in [specify name of country/region] to contribute to promoting peace and reconciliation among my students through teaching about the causes and consequences of [past conflicts/the past conflict].

5. It causes too much confusion to allow expressions of different perspectives on the history of conflict in [specify name of country/region]. *(Item from historical perspective-taking scale; Bilali & Vollhardt, 2013)*

6. As a teacher, my <u>only</u> responsibility is to improve students' knowledge and skills in the subject(s) I teach.

7. It is more constructive to teach about conflicts that took place in other countries, than to teach about the causes and consequences of conflict in [name of country/region].
8. It is more constructive to teach about conflicts that took place in the distant past, than to teach about the causes and consequences of conflict(s) that occurred in recent years.

Experienced (dis)comfort:

1. I fear that teaching about the history and legacy of my country's conflict will cause tensions <u>between students</u> from different groups.
2. I fear that teaching about the history and legacy of my country's conflict will cause tensions <u>between teachers</u> from different groups.
3. I fear negative reactions or reprisals <u>from the school administration</u> when teaching about the history and legacy of my country's conflict.
4. I fear negative reactions or reprisals <u>from parents or other caretakers</u> when teaching about the history and legacy of my country's conflict.
5. I fear negative reactions or reprisals <u>from actors (previously) involved in conflict</u> when teaching about the history and legacy of my country's conflict.
6. I fear that teaching about the history and legacy of my country's conflict will retrigger trauma among students.
7. I fear that teaching about the history and legacy of my country's conflict will reawaken the trauma I experienced myself during conflict.
8. I am uncomfortable teaching about the causes, consequences and actors of the conflict in [specify name of country/region] <u>with students from other groups</u>.

Perceived competences to engage critically and constructively with the violent past in the classroom:

1. I have tried to learn about the history of conflict(s) in [specify name of country/region] from the other groups' perspectives. *(Item from historical perspective-taking scale; Bilali & Vollhardt, 2013)*
2. I am sure that the history of conflict(s) in [specify name of country/region] that I have learned from my family and peers is the only true history. *(Item from historical perspective-taking scale; Bilali & Vollhardt, 2013)*
3. My [specify salient identity] group is better than other groups. *(Item from Vollhardt & Bilali, 2015)*

4. Participatory pedagogies are important for promoting mutual understanding between students from different groups.
5. When teaching about the history of conflict, it is important to encourage students to disclose their position on the conflict or share their lived experiences during conflict.
6. I have the necessary pedagogical skills to manage a classroom discussion that is becoming very heated.
7. I have the necessary pedagogical skills to support students when they become overwhelmed by emotions in the classroom.
8. Sometimes, I use corporal punishment to ensure good conduct in the classroom.

CHAPTER 7

Promoting critical design experts?
Policy recommendations

> Who they engage most with is the headteachers, but you find that headteachers are not much loved by the teachers (...) So the headteacher, the majority of them, they don't get the information directly from the teacher and then take it to their meetings, but they plan in advance their own agenda. There is no transparent information. Then whatever happens, the teachers down here are left to their own advises (...) So they [i.e., the Ministry of Education] need to include the stakeholders (...) You have the parents on the one hand, the peers on the other hand, and the teachers yet on the other hand. So the three have to be involved so that the system works. Because if any one of the three thinks he is disadvantaged, then we will not achieve whatever we want. (Geography and Mathematics teacher, Kenya, Dagoretti, 2016)

> You see, the government doesn't involve teachers in the development of the curriculum, and everything to do with education. They just decide. I don't know which groups organize these things, because they don't involve teachers. Even if they did, I think they see it at the highest level, not the lowest teachers who are the real implementers of the curriculum. (English teacher, Kenya, Kasarani, 2016)

While we exposed examples of continuing negative aspects of teaching, many teachers still envisioned schools as the ideal setting for promoting reconciliation. In this final chapter, we want to open discussions on innovative and prospective educational policies which can promote the peacebuilding potential of education through critically and constructively engaging with multiple perspectives on the violent past in the classroom. To this end, we have set some first steps by inviting two policymakers from Kenya and Côte d'Ivoire to reflect on the main lessons learned from this book, its relevance to policymaking and its feasibility. We also formulated a range of actionable policy recommendations that we believe could help to fulfil the potential of education in this respect. However, it is teachers, rather than policymakers, who remain at the heart of this work. We therefore conclude by proposing teaching strategies to support teachers in conflict-affected countries in dealing with the legacies of violence in the classroom. It is our hope that these strategies will inspire teachers to embrace their role as peacebuilders while safeguarding their own well-being.

7.1. Reflections from the field

We invited (former) policymakers to engage with this book and reflect on its policy implications, drawing on two case study contexts. As first readers, they were asked to summarize the book's main takeaways, and share which insights puzzled them and which were to be expected. They were also asked to formulate policy recommendations that they believed were feasible in their own contexts. We first present the reflections of Mary Wanjiru Kang'ethe. A trained teacher of Christian religious education and KiSwahili (BA) and educational counsellor (MA), Mrs. Kang'ethe is currently the director of the Education Programme of the Kenya National Commission for UNESCO (2018 – present). In this role, she coordinates, among other activities, the Global Citizenship Education and Education for Sustainable Development. Before joining the National Commission as deputy director in 2016, she was the assistant director of Education of the Ministry of Education. As assistant director, she took up the role of coordinator of the Inter-country Quality Node on Peace education under the Association for Development of Education in Africa (ADEA). We then share the insights of Louis-Gervais Adomon Anoma, who, before he retired, had long served at the UNESCO offices in Abidjan, Dakar, and Accra (2009-2023), posts that included head of the National Education Program in Abidjan, and within the Ministry of National Education (2002-2009) as the head of the Pedagogy and Continuing Education Department (*Direction de la Pédagogie et de la Formation Continue*). Notably, he started his career as a chemistry and physics teacher in Côte d'Ivoire. Among the many teacher professional development (TPD) programmes on which he collaborated, he was involved in a project on youth civic engagement for violence-free elections in 2015, and on youth engagement in post-conflict reconstruction in Côte d'Ivoire. He also contributed to the guidelines of the Ministry for the inclusion of the module on Education for Peace and Tolerance, and Education in Humanitarian Law. In what follows, we share their contributions, which have been edited and paraphrased slightly with their consent.

7.1.1. Kenya: Mary Wanjiru Kang'ethe[31]

This book delves into post-conflict education creating an in-depth understanding of factors that influence its uptake and effective delivery. The authors explore the paradoxical position of history, sustaining conflicts if used selectively, is biased or distorted, while at the same time acting as a platform for lasting peace when objectivity and multiple perspectives are embraced. Recognizing the adverse effects of conflicts on the sub-Saharan region, the focus on the sub-Saharan Africa region is justifiable. The propensity of violence is related to disparities in education, relative deprivation regarding household assets, strong intraregional inequalities, and combined presence of natural resources and relative deprivation (Ostby et al., 2009). These factors have been further compounded by environmental degradation, and long-term climatic trends and short-term climatic triggers. This publication is, therefore, timely as similar studies focusing on the region and especially Kenya are scarce.

I am very grateful for the valuable insights gained into the key concepts related to historical narratives that emerge in post-conflict settings. The quote from Nguyen (2016) "all wars are fought twice, the first time on the battlefield, the second time in memory" makes the case for direct peace education to address the invisible war. While acknowledging the individual experiences of those affected by the conflict, it is important to emphasize the need to understand the shared meanings and narratives. A broader understanding of the concept creates momentum for exploring difficult histories and narratives through education in post-conflict settings. Since teachers in conflict-affected areas enjoy some autonomy and control over the implementation of post-conflict education at school, it is imperative that they are supported and empowered. Additionally, I found it reassuring that human rights education, citizenship and multicultural education are considered valuable alternatives when direct peace education meets strong resistance. It could be argued that the three approaches create a safe starting point for the direct peace education discourse. The proposed conflict-history education framework also creates perspectives for TPD, highlighting factors that determine uptake of direct peace education by teachers in their classrooms.

It was not surprising that, on the one hand, teachers can dispute the integration of their country's conflict history and resist its implementation, while on the other hand they can take personal initiatives to promote reconciliation and learn from the past, even when it is not officially included in the curriculum. Similarly, I was not surprised that the challenges of implementing conflict-history education include: building consensus around the multiple narratives of a conflict, lack of political and social support, fear of reviving repressed trauma among learners and lack of confidence among teachers in their ability to address sensitive issues in the classroom. Teachers are said to fear community reprisals either because of their identity or their perception that conflict-history education goes against the community-held narrative. This is consistent with my experiences in Kenya where despite teachers following a peace education course, some expressed safety concerns over implementing the programme in their classrooms. Considering teacher safety in relation to the provision of direct peace education is thus paramount. Finally, the findings from Kenya that stereotyping, partiality and low capacity for participatory and experiential pedagogies are the main drawbacks on teachers' competencies was also expected. This may be attributed to the nature of education delivery in secondary schools, which is primarily knowledge based, providing minimal opportunities for learning in the affective domain. This is expected to change as the ongoing curriculum reform to competency-based education reaches secondary schools.

Given the concerns about teacher safety, it was surprising that such a significant proportion of the teachers interviewed supported direct education, providing examples of how this could be implemented. In Kenya, this seems to be a significant change from the past. In a study to validate the 2014 child-friendly version of the Kenyan Truth, Justice and Reconciliation Report, we found that school administrators and teachers were reluctant to use the report in their schools. They expressed fear of arousing suppressed emotions and a lack of confidence in their ability to engage objectively, given their personal experiences of the conflicts. The consistent implementation of peace education initiatives by the Kenyan Ministry of Education and its partners, along with peacebuilding structures, may be bearing fruit.

Finally, the book emphasises the importance of engaging with and supporting key stakeholders, especially teachers affected by conflict, when designing and implementing direct peace education programmes.

However, most of the peace education programmes in the region are designed at a national level and rolled out to schools and communities with little or no consideration given to commensurate community-based interventions to minimize resistance. I therefore propose the following policy recommendations:

- Regionally, bodies such as ADEA and the Peace Education cluster within the African Union Commission should develop a regional framework on conflict-history education with the support of partners, and leverage their high-level platforms such as the ADEA Bureau of Ministers to facilitate uptake.
- Nationally, governments should
  - adopt a multisectoral and multistakeholder approach to the design and delivery of direct peace education. This will facilitate goodwill and promote synergy between school- and community-based interventions that balance bottom-up and top-down approaches in the conceptualization of programmes. Bottom-up voices should include local administrators, teachers and community leaders, and learners;
  - facilitate the integration of conflict-history education into formal and informal curricula across all subjects;
  - acknowledge teachers as the main carriers of the above-mentioned curricula and provide them with pre- and in-service TPD programmes that leverage remote learning opportunities. These programmes should equip teachers with the necessary personal and pedagogical skills to address student trauma and de-escalate tense situations in the classroom. Notably, they should provide teachers with the ability to engage with different perspectives on their country's history of conflict, and;
  - strengthen teachers' ability to implement positive discipline measures to prevent bullying, corporal punishment and gender-based violence in schools from hindering the effective delivery of direct peace education.

7.1.2. Côte d'Ivoire: Louis-Gervais Adomon Anoma[32]

In this book, the authors explore how violent conflicts could be introduced, explained, and discussed in teacher training institutions and schools; thus teaching about the contexts, causes, course, and acts of conflict, marked by atrocities, crimes against humanity, genocides, looting of tangible cultural property, and the desacralization of intangible property; as well as their consequences for people and communities and their repercussions, for the economy, governance and justice. The primary takeaway is that teaching history must, in addition to the subjects already covered in current programmes, integrate, as best as possible, the violent past, to ensure its memory, transmit facts, and foster civic skills to "capitalize positively on the violent past" so that its teaching can contribute to establishing or consolidating the processes of reconciliation and resilient society for an environment of peace.

That integrating conflict-history education is highly complex came as no surprise to me. After all, whether the conflict is defined as political, identity-based, or economically driven is highly politicized and risks masking the internal and external interests that drove the conflict. Nor was I surprised to discover that teachers had very different views on the causes of conflict and the events experienced, or to learn that many of them had suffered tremendously without receiving the necessary support and follow-up care in the aftermath of the conflict. Nevertheless, three aspects did stand out. First, I was surprised to learn that some teachers are not open to, or do not feel ready to teach about the violent past in school because of their experiences during the conflict. Second, I was equally surprised to discover that some take it upon themselves, even though it is not officially recommended/authorized, to find opportunities to address the subject. Third, I am astonished that, coming from periods of violent conflict, the rulers (the victors) do not show more interest in (conflict-history) education as part of their strategies for rebuilding the social fabric, and ultimately preventing such situations and ensuring cohesion on the basis of facts and truth, which they prefer to omit for unspeakable reasons.

Looking forward, we must no longer consider history as merely a discipline that relates distant facts about peoples and populations. Instead, we must view it as a subject that integrates contemporary facts about violence, even if they are painful. History should be taught without taboo, and it should "tell the facts" without omission or bias. If "the future is determined by the past", then we must learn from recent history. For such policies to emerge, there must be political will and consensus. Any policy change process must be embedded within a country's broader educational policies and political guidelines. Undoubtedly, securing the necessary political commitment is challenging. It requires policymakers to demonstrate good faith towards communities and to recognize that school curricula do not focus sufficiently on issues of tolerance, non-violence, conflict resolution, national integration, human rights, children's rights and international humanitarian law, violent extremism, and, notably, the violent past. It is then necessary to consult stakeholders, including communities affected by conflict, aggressors and victims alike, as well as experts in educational policy and programme design, contemporary history specialists, and teachers, whose involvement is crucial to the process. The following steps can be taken within this inclusive process:

- Integrate the teaching of the violent past into disciplines that are most appropriate, like history or 'Education for Human Rights and Citizenship (EDHC)' in Côte d'Ivoire, but also non-formal education (reaching out-of-school children); and ensure that content is validated and takes into account cultural, traditional and legal aspects, while being adapted to the learners' level;
- Prioritize continuous TPD for teachers or any group of resource persons/referents in the target conflict zones, followed by initial teacher training;
- Plan a pilot phase for teaching the violent past in the school curriculum, monitor and evaluate it, and deduce remedial measures, with a view to extending it.

Although complex, when stakeholders share vision and objectives, it is possible to complete these steps. The 'Program for Education for Peace and Tolerance (PEPT)', which I developed with my colleagues from the department of pedagogy and continuing professional development following the military-political crisis of September 2002, is a good example of this.

To conclude, I quote Karel Fracapane, Programme Specialist for Global Citizenship and Peace Education at UNESCO, during a workshop in the framework of the International Programme on Holocaust and Genocide Education:

> Learning from the past, honouring the memory of victims and survivors, and using the power of education to break the cycle of violence, today will contribute to informing [future generations] about the consequences of polarization, hate speech, discrimination and other dynamics that can lead to atrocity crimes and other human rights violations. (February 2023)

7.2. Policy recommendations

At the heart, and start, of this book were the insightful words of Bush and Saltarelli (2000), arguing that "if education is to have a sustainable peacebuilding impact, then it will have to be driven by those individuals and groups within war-torn, war-born, and war-threatened societies themselves" (p. 27). Accordingly, our main argument was that teachers within war-torn, war-born, and war-threatened societies themselves should be at the centre of any policy change aimed at integrating conflict-history education, or direct peace education, for which many scholars in the field of transitional justice and peace education advocate. By ensuring 'support from below' in addition to decisions 'from above' and 'support from outside', we can avoid teachers subverting or resisting new policies, and ensure that the final implementers are provided the support for an effective implementation of the curriculum in the classroom. Teachers, moreover, know best how a particular policy or programme will benefit learners (or not) and what is logistically feasible (i.e., time, material, etc.) (see also Harris & Morrison, 2003). Including teachers in the process can also trigger teachers' sense of responsibility to teach peace and create ownership. Their support therefore serves as an important indicator for what can be achieved in terms of confronting the history of conflict from multiple perspectives. More generally, it also provides an indicator for sociological time, or society's readiness to come to terms with its violent past. After all, teacher support is determined not only by personal beliefs and characteristics, but also by the responses they anticipate from students, other teachers, parents, school administrators, and society in general. The overall policy recommendation is therefore to **actively involve teachers from all sides of the conflict in educational decision-making processes to promote societal reconciliation and sustainable peacebuilding, and to respect their input**. In this process, we recommend the involved actors take the following recommendations to heart:

To international policymakers:
- Develop a strategy to help governments in post-conflict countries set up inclusive consultation processes to integrate direct peace education. This strategy should outline key objectives and stakeholders, as well as draw attention to dilemmas and challenges that participants need to consider during the process.

- Help to share knowledge by setting up a database of policy documents, curricula and teaching strategies that have been developed across Africa and the rest of the world to critically and constructively educate people about the perspectives of groups that have previously been in conflict. This database should be accessible to policymakers and teachers alike.

To national policymakers:
- Include forward-looking educational reforms in the transitional justice process. In addition to 'telling the truth about education', truth and reconciliation reports can recognize the potential of educational settings as places for conversations about 'telling the truth about the past' through revising existing such subjects as history, or introducing such new subjects as peace and/or human rights education. As was the case in South Africa, textbook content could incorporate testimonies provided during the work of the relevant commissions. In this respect, it is also recommended that teacher training and professional development be included to help teachers better understand and teach conflict (see below), something that no truth commission has done so far (Paulson & Bellino, 2017). Including at least one member of the commission with educational expertise can help to ensure that education is not overlooked.
- Prioritize investment in pre- and in-service teacher training. Since teachers actively influence policy initiatives, both consciously and unconsciously, investing in pre- and in-service teacher training could yield larger returns in terms of the peacebuilding process than printing new textbooks that might not be distributed or used. However, training is typically only provided by NGOs and is therefore short in duration (besides our case studies, this is also the case in other African settings, including Rwanda; Russell, 2019). While short teacher training programmes delivered by non-state actors can be effective, as demonstrated by our 'Uprooted' project and others (see Weldon, 2010 on a four- to five-day teacher development workshop delivered by the NGO Facing the Past – Transforming our Future in the Western Cape, South Africa), short-term teacher training sessions are not a panacea for changing the views and practices of the most vehement opponents (see Zembylas et al., 2016 on the outcomes of six teacher training workshops in Cyprus). Therefore,

it is recommended to avoid one-off training courses and to embed it in the official teacher training programmes at multiple stages.

To teacher trainers:
- Prepare teachers to deal with trauma. Both teachers and students have been affected by conflict in more or less direct ways. Therefore, the risk of direct peace education triggering trauma is substantial, in addition to the negative effects that post-traumatic stress can have on students' education or teachers' performance. It is therefore highly recommended that training is provided on how to address children's war traumas and how to deal with one's own traumatic experiences in the aftermath of conflict.
- Teach teachers how to manage heated classroom discussions and polarization. Engaging critically with multiple perspectives on the violent past can result in heated classroom discussions. In some cases, these discussions may further entrench ingroup beliefs and interpretations as students feel their sense of identity is threatened. If not managed well, students may become more polarized rather than less. It is therefore essential to integrate training modules for teachers on how to deal with controversy in the classroom and manage classroom discussions, taking into account the generally large classroom sizes.
- Use the conflict-history education framework for self-reflection in teacher training. Teachers who are unaware of their own stereotypes and biases, or who are naïve about their capacity to deal with trauma or polarization, will likely take great risks when engaging in conflict-history education even if they recognize its peacebuilding potential. Therefore, it is crucial that teachers ask themselves questions like: What is the role of education in promoting reconciliation? How does my identity affect my interpretation of the past? How would I deal with negative student reactions? Taking a stance within this framework can encourage self-reflection on one's own stereotypes, biases, narratives of conflict, and (potential) lack of pedagogical skills for teaching direct peace education in a critical and constructive manner. Teachers can then explore areas for further professional development. In this regard, we agree with Harris and Clarke (2011), who, in turn, paraphrase Korthagen et al. (2001) to note that shifting the attitudes of pre- and/or in-service teachers is only possible once their original positions are known (see also Fatah et al., 2023).

7.3. Teaching strategies

Since teachers are at the heart of direct peace education, we conclude this book by presenting actionable teaching strategies to help them critically and constructively explore the perspectives of different groups on the violent past. Because "we have classes sometimes up to 100 pupils per class, which is a big challenge making the delivery of a teacher quite ineffective" – quoting Kenyan teacher 'Jonathan' (see box 3.1.) – we suggest low-cost strategies that are feasible with large groups of students. Two strategies were inspired by the NGO Facing History and were incorporated into our project 'Uprooted'. The third strategy, 'forum theatre', is inspired by the Brazilian theatre practitioner Augusto Boal's 'Theatre of the Oppressed' (1979).

7.3.1. Silent conversations

Studies in transitional justice, peace education and social psychology have demonstrated that adopting the perspective of the 'other' as well as expressing one's own can contribute to intergroup forgiveness and help to create a more nuanced image of the 'other' in (post-) conflict settings (Bilali & Vollhardt, 2013; Bruneau & Saxe, 2012; Ron & Maoz, 2013). However, hearing divergent opinions in discussions can evoke strong emotional reactions that prevent us from truly understanding others, thereby entrenching our existing beliefs and attitudes. For example, this was the case for listeners of a talk show in eastern DR Congo, which encouraged discussion about intergroup conflict and cooperation (Paluck, 2010). By encouraging students to write down their thoughts, teachers can avoid emotional outbursts and help students to focus on the opinions of others, hereby ensuring that they give thoughtful and respectful responses. It also fosters inclusion, providing a safe space for all students (not only the vocal ones) to express their opinions.

In practice, a silent conversation involves several rounds of silent reflection on the causes, and course of, or the motivations of conflict (see Table 7.1. for a lesson plan). Prompts may include asking for a reaction to a conflict-related vignette, such as a testimonial from the Truth and Reconciliation Commission or a question aimed at the students, like 'What do you think are the most important causes of conflict in our country?'. After writing down their thoughts and/or feelings individually, the papers

Table 7.1. Lesson plan for silent conversation

Intended learning outcomes	The student ... • Gains insights into the perspectives of others with respect to the causes of past conflict and actors to blame; • Slows down his/her thinking before reacting to other perspectives, avoiding an emotional outburst; • Constructively engages with views other than his/her own; • Potentially reconsiders own perspective.
Didactic material	Paper and writing utensils Prepare prompt, e.g.: • Range of vignettes from Truth and Reconciliation report (testimony), book fragments, etc. that represent particular perspectives on conflict • Conflict-related question (e.g., who do you think is to blame for the conflict and why? Why do you think the conflict came about in [country]? ...)

Time	Teacher activity	Learner activity	Classroom assessment
10 min.	Instructions on Silent Conversation • Round 1: write down your response to the prompt • Round 2: read previous response and write down how you feel about the response, as well as what aspects you (dis)agree with and why • Round 3: respond in writing to previous responses Agree on a code of conduct, including at least: • Respectful language • Write in the first person: avoid making generalized statements (e.g., 'everybody knows this is true/false...') • Individual exercise, do not read what your neighbour is writing.	Listening	Check that the exercise is well understood.

Time	Teacher activity	Learner activity	Classroom assessment
20 min.	Carry out the exercise in three 5-minute rounds. Teacher's role: • Timing the round • Picking up the papers • Shuffling the papers • Redistributing the papers	Students formulate in writing their reaction to the prompt (round 1) or to the perspectives of the other(s) (rounds 2 & 3). Guiding questions when responding to other people's positions include: • How do you feel about the response? What emotions does it evoke? • What elements do you (dis)agree with and why?	To create a safe space to share, students sit apart as far as possible and teacher does not walk around. Before collecting the papers per round, the teacher checks whether everyone has been able to write what he/she wants.
10 min.	Teacher debriefs with a short oral discussion Guiding questions include: • Reading the contributions on your paper, do you think the different contributors have tried to understand each other? • Do you now understand better why some students have opinions that differ from yours? • How does this exercise make you feel? [use feeling thermometer]	Students share their responses to the questions. Make sure only one student is speaking at a time and that they are not interrupted while they are speaking. **Do not allow the discussion to derail into taking positions again;** this was limited to the written part.	Feeling thermometer: ask students to indicate how distressed they are by the exercise. You can use coloured flash cards (green = 'not distressed', yellow = 'somewhat distressed', red = 'very distressed'), or have them raise their hands (1 finger = 'not distressed at all', 5 = 'somewhat distressed', 10 = 'very distressed')

are collected, shuffled (to ensure anonymity) and redistributed to other students, who then respond to their peers' contributions. This process is repeated at least twice. The strategy typically ends with an open group discussion. So far, the method has only been evaluated qualitatively and with teachers (Weldon, 2015; Tibbitts & Weldon, 2017). However, it is used in relatively tranquil contexts to encourage students to discuss controversial topics (see the work by the NGO Facing History). On another level, silent conversations can help teachers to understand their students' knowledge, attitudes, and beliefs about conflict. This could enable them to adapt direct peace education lesson materials to the specific needs and challenges they are likely to face in their classrooms (Kuppens et al., forthcoming).

7.3.2. Exploring the unknown

Students who have grown up in societies affected by conflict have been educated at home, in their community and perhaps at school according to specific views about the causes and/or course of conflict. They may not question these views. Challenging their 'common knowledge about the past' can therefore threaten students' sense of identity, resulting in them rejecting the new information. The following three strategies start by giving students the opportunity to share what they already know, before inviting them to consider themselves what else they would like to know about a particular episode of violence or the conflict more broadly. Teachers can then encourage deeper reflection and challenge unfounded assumptions through questioning in a follow-up discussion, if necessary.

The '**Connect-extend-challenge**' strategy can be used alongside the analysis of texts, video clips, or other narrative formats.[33] It has three steps or questions, to which students can respond either individually or in pairs:
- *Connect:* How do the ideas and information in the *[text, video, testimonial, etc.]* connect to what you know already about [the particular episode of conflict, conflict dynamic, or the conflict as a whole]? In other words, what knowledge that you had does this contribution confirm?
- *Extend:* How does the *[text, video, testimonial, ...]* extend or broaden your knowledge about [particular episode of conflict, conflict dynamic, or the conflict overall]? In other words, did you learn anything new?

- *Challenge:* How does the *[text, video, testimonial, ...]* challenge or complicate what you know already about [particular episode of conflict, conflict dynamic, or the conflict overall]? What new questions does it raise?

Alternatively, the **K-W-L chart** similarly invites students to contemplate old and new knowledge using a table with three columns (see Table 7.2.):

Table 7.2. K-W-L Chart

K: What do you KNOW about the *[particular episode of conflict, conflict dynamic, or the conflict overall]*?	W: What do you WANT to know about the *[particular episode of conflict, conflict dynamic, or the conflict overall]*?	L: What did you LEARN about *[particular episode of conflict, conflict dynamic, or the conflict overall]*?

Facing History & Ourselves, "K-W-L Chart Template", last updated September 9, 2022.

Finally, the adaptation of the **3-2-1 strategy** focuses on students' curiosity as they explore new information, which can concern a narrative format, as well as visual materials, such as pictures, tables, or graphics.[34] This strategy also has three steps:
- Choose three takeaways that strike you about the *[table, picture, graph]* and explain why they surprise you.
- Articulate two questions that come to mind when you examine the *[table, picture, graph]*.
- Formulate one hypothesis, based on the *[table, picture, graph]*, that you would like to investigate further.

Teachers can modify the prompts of the 3-2-1 strategy to focus on particular content questions. For example, if students just read two opposing conflict narratives, the teacher can invite them to write down three differences between the narratives, two similarities, and one remaining question.

7.3.3. Forum theatre

Across the three case studies, curricula prescribe the use of role play in such courses as citizenship and human rights education, life skills education, but also language courses. Although the authors did not observe the implementation of such pedagogies in the classroom, teachers were generally very appreciative of role play to the extent that multiple teachers recommended its use to foster peace, within both the classroom and the broader school context:

> The school should organize plays for the children, we should not only take advantage of the teaching of dramatization in class but the school in general should organize plays where the children play the problems of conflicts, we show the consequences of conflicts, the advantages of peace in an environment and they can learn something from that. (French teacher, DR Congo, Goma, 2018)

One particularly interesting form of role play is forum theatre, also known as intervention or participatory theatre. Developed by the Brazilian theatre artist Augusto Boal in 1979, it is designed to encourage people to develop the skills needed to achieve social justice. It is currently widely used by a variety of NGOs in post-conflict settings in Africa and beyond to promote peaceful and non-violent attitudes and behaviours (Burns et al., 2015). Participatory theatre methodologies, like forum theatre, help address difficult topics, like in our case intergroup conflict, by clarifying misunderstandings and developing empathy for others (Feuchte et al., 2020). For example, in Kenya the Amani People's Theatre enacted scenes addressing the 2007-2008 post-election violence with youth from the Kalenjin and Kikuyu ethnic groups in Njoro, as well as with street children in Nairobi's Kibera slum (Burns et al., 2015); while NGO SAFE has been working with this methodology in and around Mombasa to encourage discussion about radicalization – the outcome being beautifully captured by the movie '*Watatu*'. In DR Congo and Rwanda, Search for Common Ground has been working with forum theatre since 2005. Importantly, a field experiment conducted in post-conflict Liberia showed that taking part in a forum theatre addressing intergroup conflict (using fictional groups) significantly improved intergroup trust and decreased social distance toward a disliked group, all the while strengthening participants' sense of community and collective action intentions (Feuchte et al., 2020).

Forum theatre performs as follows: rather than using a fixed script, spectators are invited to engage in the play by disrupting – or 'freezing' – a storyline that is being enacted on stage to imagine possible new endings – becoming 'spect-actors' (Burns et al., 2015; Feuchte et al., 2020). Facilitated by a 'joker', 'spect-actors' can either suggest potential solutions to be acted out by the actors on stage, or actually step into a scene to replace an actor and enact their solution themselves. This offers 'spect-actors' the opportunity to think, talk and ask questions about the staged situation, here a situation of conflict or process of reconciliation.

As a teaching strategy to implement direct peace education, we propose three steps. First, give the class the chance to develop a basic storyline that addresses particular conflict dynamics or a process of reconciliation. Since forum theatre is not scripted, this storyline does not require elaborate development – in addition, we advise keeping the theatre short (between 5 and 10 minutes). What is most important is that a beginning, moment of escalation ("hot" moment) and an end are identified. To facilitate this process, teachers could build upon students' own experiences or prepare didactic materials that students consult prior to creating the play. Second, the teacher selects a group of students who will enact the storyline. Again, since it is not scripted, there is no need to rehearse. Instead, students can improvise. Third, students act out the conflictual situation twice. The first time, they act from the beginning to the end, without interruption. The second time, the teacher takes up the role of 'joker', or facilitator. If the play turns "hot" at any moment, the teacher can either freeze the play and ask for possible interventions to cool down the situation, or moderate student responses as they occur. After acting out various potential solutions, the teacher ends the forum theatre and follows up with a classroom discussion. Note that the play can also be acted out in the broader school setting, such as during school assemblies, or be part of an extra-curricular activity through school peace clubs.

＊

It is our hope that these teaching strategies will inspire teachers who identify as critical design experts to implement direct peace education. And we invite teachers to share their experiences with us so that we can adapt or refine the strategies. We also welcome new ideas to bolster education's reconciliatory potential.

Dr. Line Kuppens, l.kuppens@uva.nl

Dr. Justin Sheria Nfundiko, justinsheria@uob.ac.cd

Appendix

Table A.1. Correlations between items of multicultural education and Kenyan teachers' background characteristics

	Kendall's τ				Cramer's V
	Gender	Age	Teaching exp.	National subjects	Ethnicity
The curriculum needs to include the study of the customs & traditions of the main ethnic & religious groups in Kenya.	-.064*	-.022	-.004	0.059*	0.101
Schools are the ideal place for pupils to learn how to respect other ethnic groups.	0.027	0.067*	0.066*	0.049	0.080
Diversity at school contributes to the debunking of stereotypes.	-.048	0.063**	0.064*	0.008	0.079
Pupils should be allowed to speak their ethnic language in the playground.	-.074*	0.015	0.014	-.061*	0.087
Pupils have the right to wear cultural or religious clothing and/or symbols at school.	-.107***	-.086***	-.085***	-.044	0.076

*significant at α<0.05; ** significant at α<0.01; *** significant at α<0.001

Table A.2. Correlations between items of EDHC and Ivorian teachers' background characteristics

	Kendall's τ			Cramer's V
	Gender	Age	Teaching exp.	Primary subject
EDHC contributes to students' knowledge of civic and moral values.	0.015	-.016	-.034	0.081
EDHC contributes to peaceful and tolerant student behavior.	-.018	-.053	-.028	0.077
The content of the EDHC is appropriate and meaningful.	0.012	-.124***	-.080**	0.070
The content, including civic and moral values, should be incorporated into all other courses.	-.033	-.030	0.034	0.118***
EDHC should be extended to the final year of secondary schooling.	0.006	-.091***	-.067**	0.097*

* significant at α<0.05; ** significant at α<0.01; *** significant at α<0.001

Table A.3. Associations (Cramer's V) between items on direct peace education activities and Ivorian teachers' background characteristics

	Gender	Age	Teaching exp.	Pol. Interest	Primary subject	Impact crisis
I taught my students about the causes and consequences of the Ivorian crises.	0.064	0.212	0.166	0.107***	0.128***	0.067
I organized a class discussion on the crises which allowed students to express themselves freely.	0.040	0.229	0.194	0.115***	0.125***	0.086
I have already used documents, texts, articles, or photos related to the crisis in the classroom.	0.055	0.200	0.201	0.131***	0.115***	0.078
I asked my students to read a book that speaks (in)directly about the crisis.	0.096*	0.210	0.221	0.085	0.165***	0.046

*significant at α<0.05; ** significant at α<0.01; *** significant at α<0.001*

Table A.4. Correlations (Kendall's τ) between items of ECM and Eastern Congolese teachers' background characteristics

	Gender	Teaching exp.	National subjects	City
ECM contributes to students' knowledge of civic and moral values.	-.080**	0.001	0.057*	0.055*
ECM contributes to peaceful and tolerant student behaviour.	-.031	0.101***	0.039	-.012
The content of the ECM is appropriate and meaningful.	0.031	0.033	0.091***	-.007
The civic and moral values included in ECM should be incorporated into all other courses.	-.006	0.082***	0.081***	-.041

*significant at α<0.05; ** significant at α<0.01;*** significant at α<0.001*

Notes

1. Keynes et al. (2021) define educationalization as "the process of rendering certain forms of knowledge (for example, knowledge of state crimes produced through inquiry commissions) into a new educational discourse" (p. 6).
2. Suffice to state that her other strategies include 'exit' (leaving the system) and 'voice' (speaking out publicly about what is perceived to be morally wrong).
3. Kenyatta and Ruto formed a coalition (Jubilee Alliance) after being indicted by the International Criminal Court, in contrast to key figures Odinga and Kibaki (Kagwanga, 2015).
4. Correlations between |0.059| and |0.107|.
5. $M_{\text{age women}}$ = 34.52, $SD_{\text{age women}}$ = 10.38; $M_{\text{age men}}$ = 31.68, $SD_{\text{age men}}$ = 9.38.
6. Correlations of $r_{\text{political history at primary - postelection violence at primary}}$ = 0,478, α <0.001; $r_{\text{political history at secondary - postelection violence at secondary}}$ = 0,569, α <0.001; $r_{\text{postelection violence at primary - postelection violence at secondary}}$ = 0,007, α = 0.837).
7. Expected age of 11-13.
8. Correlations of $r_{\text{sex-postelection violence at primary}}$ = 0,072, α < 0.05; $r_{\text{age-postelection violence at primary}}$ = 0,068, α < 0.05; $r_{\text{teaching experience-postelection violence at primary}}$ = 0,075, α < 0.05.
9. Original text: "*La Côte d'Ivoire [est] fragilisée par la guerre qui la ronge depuis septembre 2002 avec pour point culminant, la grave crise post-électorale de novembre 2010*". The text continues as follows: "*Il importe, dès lors, de trouver les ressources nécessaires pour opérer la transition vers une culture de la paix, en réussissant ensemble l'impératif de la réconciliation nationale. A cette fin, l'éducation aux droits de l'homme et à la citoyenneté (EDHC) constitue pour elle une véritable opportunité*" ["It is therefore important to find the resources needed to make the transition to a culture of peace, by working together to achieve the imperative of national reconciliation. To this end, education for human rights and citizenship (EDHC) offers a real opportunity"].
10. $r_{\text{primary-lower secondary}}$ = 0.516, α < 0.001; $r_{\text{primary-higher secondary}}$ = 0.256, α < 0.001; $r_{\text{lower-higher secondary}}$ = 0.525, α < 0.001.
11. Cramer's V = 0.097, α < 0.05.
12. Cramer's V ranging between 0.115 to 0.165, α<0.001.
13. Cramer's V ranging between 0.107 to 0.131, α<0.001.
14. Because of the ordinal nature of subjective impact of the crisis, we calculated Kendall's τ: 'It is appropriate and desirable to talk about the Ivorian crisis at lower secondary school', τ = -0.021, p>0.05; 'It is appropriate and desirable to talk about the Ivorian crisis at higher secondary school', τ = 0.030, p>0.05.
15. Because of violations of the assumptions of normality and homogeneity of variances, we calculated $\chi^2(df, N)$ tests of association. Inequality between groups: $\chi^2(4, 864)$ = 93.903, p<0.001; Exclusion of the North: $\chi^2 (4, 883)$=253.862, p<0.001; Ivoirité: $\chi^2 (4, 905)$ = 164.002, p<0.001; Inequitable justice: $\chi^2 (4, 876)$= 35.696, p<0.001; French interests: $\chi^2 (4, 924)$=140.980, p< 0.001; Foreign interests: $\chi^2 (4, 897)$= 72.473, p<0.001; Laurent Gbagbo: $\chi^2 (4, 905)$=116.512, p<0.001; and Alassane Ouattara: $\chi^2 (4, 927)$=83.038, p<0.001.
16. Inequality between groups: $\chi^2(4, 777)$=84.764, p<0.001; Exclusion of the North: $\chi^2(4, 792)$=210.308, p<0.001; Ivoirité: $\chi^2(4, 814)$ =139.491, p<0.001; Inequitable justice: $\chi^2(4, 788)$ = 31.136, p<0.001; French interests: $\chi^2(4, 826)$= 134.267, p<0.001; Foreign interests: $\chi^2(4, 804)$=87.586, p< 0.001; Laurent Gbagbo: $\chi^2(4, 812)$ =106.142, p<0.001; and Alassane Ouattara: $\chi^2(4, 820)$= 61.684, p< 0.001.

17. Correlation of r=0.738, which relates to the dichotomized variables of ethnicity (north/south) and religion (Muslim/Christian). The association between the original, nominal variables is weaker, yet significant (Cramer's V=0.573).
18. Fit indices: CFI=0.935, TLI=0.921, RMSEA=0.035.
19. Correlation of r=-0.308.
20. The June 2024 final UN experts report confirms that 3000 to 4000 Rwandans troops are fighting with the M23 in DR Congo.
21. Unlike the Banyarwanda, they are primarily living in the highlands of South Kivu province (Fizi, Uvira and Mwenga) and speak Kinyamulenge rather than Kinyarwanda.
22. Independent observers and the Catholic Church report that Martin Fayulu, a third candidate, would have won. According to Fayulu, a secret deal was made between Tshisekedi and Kabila, who could no longer vie for a third term, to grant the victory to the former.
23. Original text: *"Ce cours initie l'apprenant à pratiquer les bonnes habitudes que recommandent le civisme, le patriotism et le nationalisme. Bref, l'Education Civique et Morale développe le savoir et le savoir-être des apprenants pour un bon savoir-vivre dans la société, par le respect des lois et dans la mise en pratique des principes ou la mise en oeuvre des valeurs sociales."*
24. Correlations of $r_{primary\text{-}lower\ secondary} = 0{,}324$, $\alpha < 0.001$; $r_{primary\text{-}higher\ secondary} = 0{,}465$, $\alpha < 0.001$; $r_{lower\text{-}higher\ secondary} = 0{,}307$, $\alpha < 0.001$.
25. Correlations of $r_{experience\text{-}primary} = 0{,}075$, $\alpha < 0.01$; $r_{experience\text{-}lower\ secondary} = 0{,}111$, $\alpha < 0.001$; $r_{experience\text{-}higher\ secondary} = 0{,}056$, $\alpha < 0.05$.
26. Correlations of $r_{Bukavu\text{-}primary} = 0{,}133$, $\alpha < 0.01$; $r_{Bukavu\text{-}lower\ secondary} = 0{,}079$, $\alpha < 0.001$; $r_{Bukavu\text{-}higher\ secondary} = 0{,}052$, $\alpha < 0.05$.
27. Correlations of $\tau_{political\ interest\text{-}primary} = 0.086$, $p > 0.001$; $\tau_{political\ interest\text{-}higher\ secondary} = 0.075$, $p > 0.001$.
28. Correlations of $\tau_{impact\ conflict\text{-}teaching\ about\ the\ past} = 0.116$, $p > 0.001$; $\tau_{impact\ conflict\text{-}primary} = 0.111$, $p > 0.001$; $\tau_{impact\ conflict\text{-}lower\ secondary} = 0.077$, $p > 0.001$; $\tau_{impact\ conflict\text{-}lower\ secondary} = 0.048$, $p > 0.05$.
29. Organizations that provide teacher training include *Héritiers de la Justice* (Heirs of Justice) and *Ecole de la Paix* (School of Peace), but also local research institutes such as CEREP (*Centre de Recherche sur l'Education à la Paix*; Centre for Research on Peace Education). These trainings are usually rather short however, ranging from one to three days.
30. Visit the website: https://deracine.org/
31. Director of the Education Programme of the Kenya National Commission for UNESCO, Nairobi, Kenya.
32. Former head of Education at UNESCO office, Abidjan, Côte d'Ivoire.
33. To consult the original strategy, see: https://www.facinghistory.org/resource-library/connect-extend-challenge-chart
34. To consult the original strategy, see: https://www.facinghistory.org/resource-library/3-2-1

References

Abdi Ismael, J., & Deane, J. (2008). *The Kenyan 2007 Elections and their Aftermath: The Role of Media and Communication. Policy Briefing No. 1*. London: BBC World Service Trust.

Agirdag, O., Merry, M.S., & Van Houtte, M. (2016). Teachers' Understanding of multicultural Education and the Correlates of Multicultural Content Integration in Flanders. *Education and Urban Society, 48*(6), 556-582.

Aguilar, P., & Retamal, G. (2009). Protective environments and quality education in humanitarian contexts. *International Journal of Educational Development, 29*(1), 3-16.

Ahonen, S. (2013). Post-conflict history education in Finland, South Africa and Bosnia-Herzegovina. *Nordidactica: Journal of Humanities and Social Science Education*, (1), 90-103.

Aitken, A., & Radford, L. (2018). Learning to teach for reconciliation in Canada: Potential, resistance and stumbling forward. *Teaching and Teacher Education, 75*, 40-48.

Akindès, F. (2011). La Côte d'Ivoire depuis 1993: la réinvention risquée d'une nation. In F. Akindès (Ed.), *Côte d'Ivoire: la reinvention de soi dans la violence* (pp. 3-38). Dakar:Codesria.

Akindès, F. (2017). "On ne mange pas les ponts et le goudron": les sentiers sinueux d'une sortie de crise en Côte d'Ivoire. *Politique africaine, 4*(148), 5-26.

Akindès, F., Fofana, M., & Koné, G. (2010). Côte d'Ivoire: insurrection et contre-insurrection. *Alternatives Sud, 17*, 93-97.

Akulluezati, B., Ssempala, C., & Ssenkusu, P. (2011). Teachers' perceptions of the effects of young people's war experiences on teaching and learning in Northern Uganda. In J. Paulson (Ed.), *Education, conflict and development* (pp. 185-207). United Kingdom: Symposium books ltd.

Allport, G.W. (1954). *The nature of prejudice*. Cambridge: Addison-Wesley.

Almond, G.A., & Verba, S. (1963). *Civic Culture: Political Attitudes and Democracy in Five Nations*. USA: Sage.

Amnesty International (2013). *Côte d'Ivoire: The Victor's Law. The Human Rights situation two years after the post-electoral crisis*. London: Amnesty International Publications.

Amnesty International & Human Rights' Watch (2017). *"Kill Those Criminals": Security Forces Violations in Kenya's August 2017 Elections*. USA: Amnesty International & HRW.

André, G., & Poncelet, M. (2013). Héritage colonial et appropriation du «pouvoir 'éduquer». Approche socio-historique du champ de l'éducation primaire en RDC. *Cahiers de la recherche sur l'éducation et les savoirs*, (12), 271-295.

Arnaut, K. (2012). *Social Mobility in Times of Crisis: Militant Youth and the Politics of Impersonation in Côte d'Ivoire (2002-2011)*. MICROCON Research Working Paper 58. Brighton: MICROCON.

Autesserre, S. (2006). Local Violence, National Peace? Postwar "Settlement" in the Eastern D.R. Congo (2003-2006). *African Studies Review, 49*(3), 1-29.

Autesserre, S. (2012). Dangerous tales: Dominant narratives on the Congo and their unintended consequences. *African Affairs, 111*(443), pp 202-222.

Babo, A. (2017). Ivoirité and Citizenship in Ivory Coast: The Controversial Policy of Authenticity. In B. Lawrance & J. Stevens (Ed.), *Citizenship in Question: Evidentiary Birthright and Statelessness* (pp. 200-216). New York, USA: Duke University Press.

Ball, S. J., Maguire, M., Braun, A., & Hoskins, K. (2011). Policy subjects and policy actors in schools: Some necessary but insufficient analyses. *Discourse: studies in the cultural politics of education, 32*(4), 611-624.

Banégas, R. (2006). Côte d'Ivoire: Patriotism, Ethnonationalism and Other African Modes of Self-Writing. *African Affairs, 105*(421), 535-52.

Banégas, R., & Popineau, C. (2021). The 2020 Ivorian election and the 'third-term' debate: A crisis of "Korocracy"? *African Affairs, 120*(480), 461-477.

Banks, J. A. (1993). Chapter 1: Multicultural Education: Historical Development, Dimensions and Practices. *Review of Research in Education, 19*(1), 3-49.

Banks, J. A., & Banks, C.A. (Eds.) (2001). *Multicultural Education: Issues and Perspectives (4th Edition)*. New York: Wiley.

Barakat, S., Connolly, D., Hardman, F., & Sundaram, V. (2013). The role of basic education in post-conflict recovery. *Comparative Education, 49*(2), 124-142.

Barkan, E. (2015). Historical dialogue: beyond transitional justice and conflict resolution. In K. Neumann and J. Thompson (Eds.), Historical Justice and Memory (pp. 95-113). University of Wisconsin Press.

Bar-Tal, D. (2002). The Elusive Nature of Peace Education. In G. Salomon and B. Nevo (Eds.), *Peace Education: The Concept, Principles, and Practices Around the World* (pp. 27-36). New York: Psychology Press.

Bar-Tal, D., & Hameiri, B. (2020). Interventions to change well-anchored attitudes in the context of intergroup conflict. *Social and Personality Psychology Compass, 14*(7).

Bar-Tal, D., & Harel, A.S. (2002). Teachers as agents of political influence in the Israeli high schools. *Teaching and Teacher Education, 18*(1), 121-134.

Bar-Tal, D., Oren, N., & Nets-Zehngut, R. (2014). Sociopsychological analysis of conflict-supporting narratives: A general framework. *Journal of Peace Research, 51*(5), 662-675.

Bar-Tal, D., & Rosen, Y. (2009). Peace Education in Societies Involved in Intractable Conflicts: Direct and Indirect Models. *Review of Educational Research, 79*(2), 557-575.

Bar-Tal, D., & Rosen, Y., & Nets-Zehngut, R. (2010). Peace Education in Societies Involved in Intractable Conflicts: Goals, Conditions, and Directions. In N. Salomon and E. Cairns (Eds.), *Handbook on Peace Education* (pp. 21-43). USA: Psychology Press.

Bar-Tal, D., & Salomon, G. (2006). Israeli-Jewish narratives of the Israeli-Palestinian conflict: Evolution, contents, functions, and consequences. Israeli and Palestinian narratives of conflict: History's double helix, 19-46.

Barton, K.C., & Mccully, A.W. (2005). History, identity, and the school curriculum in Northern Ireland: an empirical study of secondary students' ideas and perspectives. *Journal of Curriculum Studies, 37*(1), 85-116.

Bassett, T.J. (2003). "Nord musulman et Sud chrétien": les moules médiatiques de la crise ivoirienne. *Afrique contemporaine, 206*(2), 13-27.

Battera, F. (2012). Ethnicity and Degree of Partisan Attachment in Kenyan Politics. *Journal of Asian and African Studies, 48*(1), 114-125.

Beelmann, A., & Heinemann, K.S. (2014). Preventing prejudice and improving intergroup attitudes: A meta-analysis of child and adolescent training programs. *Journal of Applied Developmental Psychology, 35*, 10-24.

Bekerman, Z. (2007). Developing Palestinian-Jewish Bilingual Integrated Education in Israel: Opportunities and Challenges for Peace Education in Conflict Societies. In Z. Bekerman & C. McGlynn (Eds.), *Addressing Ethnic Conflict Through Peace Education* (pp. 91-106).Hampshire, England: Palgrave MacMillan.

Bekerman, Z. (2009). "Yeah, It Is Important to Know Arabic – I just don't like Learning It:" Can Jews Become Bilingual in the Palestinian-Jewish Integrated Bilingual Schools? In C. McGlynn, M. Zembylas, Z. Bekerman and T. Gallagher (Eds.), *Peace Education in Conflict and Post-Conflict Societies: Comparative Perspectives* (pp. 231-246). New York: Palgrave Macmillan.

Bekerman, Z., & Zembylas, M. (2014). Some reflections on the links between teacher education and peace education: Interrogating the ontology of normative epistemological premises. *Teaching and Teacher Education, 41*, 52-59.

Bellino, M.J. (2014). Whose past, whose present?: Historical memory among the "postwar" generation in Guatemala. In J.H. Williams (Ed.), *(Re)building memory: School textbooks, identity, and the pedagogies and politics of imagining community* (pp. 131-152). Rotterdam: Sense Publishers.

Bellino, M. J., Paulson, J., & Anderson Worden, E. (2017). Working through difficult pasts: Toward thick democracy and transitional justice in education. *Comparative Education, 53*(3), 313-332.

Bellino, M. J., Ortiz-Guerrero, M., Paulson, J., Ariza Porras, A. P., Cortes, I. D., Ritschard, S., & Sánchez Meertens, A. (2022). 'Are we doing Cátedra de Paz?'Teacher perspectives on enacting peace education in Bogotá, Colombia. *Journal of Peace Education, 19*(3), 255-280.

Bennett, C. (2001). Genres of Research in Multicultural Education. *Review of Educational Research, 71*(2), 171-217.

Bentrovato, D. (2014). Accounting for violence in Eastern Congo: young people's narratives of war and peace in North and South Kivu. *African Journal on Conflict Resolution, 14*(1), 9-35.

Bentrovato, D. (2017). History textbook writing in post-conflict societies: From battlefield to site and means of conflict transformation. In: Psaltis C, Carretero M and Čehajić-Clancy S (eds.), *History Education and Conflict Transformation* (pp. 37-76). Cham: Springer International Publishing.

Bentrovato, D., Korostelina, K.V., & Schulze, M. (2016). *History Can Bite: History Education in Divided and Postwar Societies.* Gottingern, Germany: VandR Unipress.

Bentrovato, D., & Wassermann, J. (2018). Mediating transitional justice: South Africa's TRC in history textbooks and the implications for peace. *Global Change Peace & Security, 30*(3), 335-351.

Berghezan, G.(2018). Est du Congo: à qui profite la prolifération des groupes armés ? in *Eclairage du GRIP,* 3 janvier 2018.

Berman, B.J., Cottrell, J., & Ghai, Y. (2009). Patrons, Clients, and Constitutions: Ethnic Politics and Political Reform in Kenya. *Canadian Journal of African Studies, 43*(3), 462-506.

Biesta, G., Priestley, M., & Robinson, S. (2015). The role of beliefs in teacher agency. *Teachers and Teaching, 21*(6), 624-640.

Bilali, R., & Ross, M.A. (2012). 'Remembering intergroup conflict' in Linda Tropp (ed.), *The Oxford handbook of intergroup conflict* (pp. 123-135.5). Oxford University Press, UK, 2012.

Bilali, R., & Vollhardt, J.R. (2013). Priming effects of a reconciliation radio drama on historical perspective-taking in the aftermath of mass violence in Rwanda. *Journal of Experimental Social Psychology 49*(1), 144-151.

Bilali, R., & Vollhardt, J. R. (2019). Victim and perpetrator groups' divergent perspectives on collective violence: Implications for intergroup relations. *Political Psychology, 40*, 75-108.

Bloomfield, D., Barnes, T., & Huyse, L. (2003). *Reconciliation after violent conflict: A handbook.* Sweden: IDEA.

Boal, Augusto. 1979. *Theatre of the Oppressed.* New York: Urizen Books.

Bovcon, M. (2014). The progress in establishing the rule of law in Côte d'Ivoire under Ouattara's presidency. *Canadian Journal of African Studies, 48*(2), 185-202.

Bouquet, C. (2007). *Géopolitique de la Côte d'Ivoire: le désespoir de Kourouma.* Paris: Editions Colin.

Bouquet, C. (2011). *Côte d'Ivoire: le désespoir de Kourouma.* Paris: Editions Colin.

Branch, D. (2011). *Kenya: Between Hope and Despair, 1963-2011.* New Haven: Yale University Press.

Brandt, C. O. (2021). Reluctant representatives of the state: teachers' perceptions of experienced violence (DR Congo). *Compare: A Journal of Comparative and International Education, 51*(4), 546-563.

Bratton, M., & Kimenyi, M.S. (2008). Voting in Kenya: Putting Ethnicity in Perspective. *Journal of Eastern African Studies, 2*(2), 272-289.

Brett, R., & Malagón, L. (2022). Transitional justice and peacemaking/peacebuilding. *Contemporary Peacemaking: Peace Processes, Peacebuilding and Conflict*, 475-505.

Brown, C.S., & Bigler, R.S. (2002). Effects of minority status in the classroom on children's intergroup attitudes. *Journal of Experimental Child Psychology, 83*, 77-110.

Brown, G.K. (2011). The influence of education on violent conflict and peace: Inequality, opportunity and the management of diversity. *Prospects, 41*, 191-204.

Brown, G. K., & Langer, A. (2010). Conceptualizing and measuring ethnicity. *Oxford Development Studies, 38*(4), 411-436.

Bruneau, E.G., & Saxe, R. (2012). The power of being heard: The benefits of 'perspective-giving' in the context of intergroup conflict. *Journal of experimental social psychology, 48*(4), 855-866.

Bucyalimwe, S. (2006). L'est de la République démocratique du Congo: dix ans entre la guerre et la paix (1996-2006). Dans F. Reyntjens, *L'Afrique des Grands Lacs, annuaire 2005/2006: dix ans de transitions conflictuelles* (pp. 261-286). Paris: Harmattan.

Burde, D., Kapit, A., Wahl, R.L., Guven, O., & Skarpeteig, M.I. (2017). Education in Emergencies: A Review of Theory and Research. *Review of Educational Research, 87*(3), 619-658.

Burgess, R., Jedwab, R., Miguel, E., Morjaria, A., & Padró i Miquel, G. (2015). The Value of Democracy: Evidence from Road Building in Kenya. *American Economic Review, 105*(6), 1817-1851.

Burns, M. A., Beti, B. N., Okuto, M. E., Muwanguzi, D., & Sanyu, L. (2015). Forum theatre for conflict transformation in East Africa: The domain of the possible. *African Conflict and Peacebuilding Review, 5*(1), 136-151.

Büscher, K., & Vlassenroot, K. (2010). Humanitarian presence and urban development: new opportunities and contrasts in Goma, DRC. *Journal compilation, 34*(2), 256⬜S273.

Bush, K. D., & Saltarelli, D. (Eds.) (2000). *The Two Faces of Education in Ethnic Conflict*. Florence: UNICEF Innocenti Research Centre.

Castro, J. A. A., Miguélez, J. C., Alberto, L., Alves, M., & Maia, C. M. (2021). Learning to teach history in secondary education: Preservice teachers' attitudes when faced with emotional and controversial issues. *Handbook of Research on Teacher Education in History and Geography*, 259-282.

Cellule Technique pour les Statistiques de l'Education (2015). *Annuaire statistique de l'enseignement primaire, secondaire et professessionnel 2013-2014*. Kinshasa: CTSE.

Chandra, K. (2006). What is ethnic identity and does it matter?. *Annu. Rev. Polit. Sci., 9*(1), 397-424.

Chang, D.F., & Demyan, A. (2007). Teachers' Stereotypes of Asian, Black, and White Students. *School Psychology Quarterly, 22*(2), 91-114.

Chege, C., Bustrum, J.M., Caddell, T.M. (2022). Spoil the rod and spare the child: examining the colonial and missionary implications of corporal punishment in contemporary Kenya. *Afr. J. Clin. Psychol. 4*(3), 1-16.

Chelpi-den-Hamer, M. (2014). Quand la guerre s'invite à l'école. Impact de la crise ivoirienne en milieu scolaire. In F. Viti (Ed.), *La Côte d'Ivoire, d'une crise à l'autre* (pp. 185-210). Paris: L'Harmattan.

Chelpi-den Hamer, M. & ROCARE (2013). *Quand la guerre s'invite à l'école: Impact des crises ivoiriennes successives en milieu scolaire, Réponses gouvernementales, Stratégies pour accompagner le processus de réconciliation nationale*. UNICEF: Côte d'Ivoire.

Christie, P. (2009). Peace, Reconciliation, and Justice: Delivering the Miracle in Post-Apartheid Education. In C. McGlynn, M. Zembylas, Z. Bekerman and T. Gallagher (Eds.), *Peace Education in Conflict and Post-Conflict Societies: Comparative Perspectives* (pp. 75-92). New York: Palgrave Macmillan.

Christie, P. (2012). Beyond reconciliation: Reflections on South Africa's Truth and Reconciliation Commission and its implications for ethical pedagogy. In P. Ahluwalia, S. Atkinson, P. Bishop, P. Christie, R. Hattam and J. Matthews (Eds.), *Reconciliation and Pedagogy* (pp. 29-44). New York: Routledge.

Ciribuka, D.A. (2022). Construction de la paix par les compétences de vie courante en milieux scolaires de Bukavu/RDC. Regard sur les approches « Peace-campings et Clubs de paix scolaires ». *African Sociological Review / Revue Africaine de Sociologie, 26*(1), 73-93.

Cockrell, K. S., Placier, P. L., Cockrell, D. H., & Middleton, J. N. (1999). Coming to terms with "diversity" and "multiculturalism" in teacher education: Learning about our students, changing our practice. *Teaching and teacher education, 15*(4), 351-366.

Cole, E.A. (2007). Transitional Justice and the Reform of History Education. *The International Journal of Transitional Justice, 1*(x), 115-137.

Cole, E. A. (2012). Ourselves, others and the past that binds us: teaching history for peace and citizenship. In L. Davies (Ed.), *Education for global citizenship* (pp. 229-245). Doha: Education above all.

Cole, E.A., & Barsalou, J. (2006). *Unite or Divide? The Challenges of Teaching History in Societies Emerging from Violent Conflict.* Washington: United States Institute for Peace.

Collier, P. (2009). *Wars, guns & votes: democracy in dangerous places.* London: Vintage Books.

Cutolo, A. (2010). Modernity, autochthony and the Ivorian nation: the end of a century in Côte d'Ivoire. *Africa, 80*(4), 527-552.

Dabalen, A.L., & Paul, S. (2014). Estimating the effects of conflict on education in Côte d'Ivoire. *The Journal of Development Studies, 50*(12), 1631-1646.

Danesh, H.B. (2007). Education For Peace: The Pedagogy of Civilization. In Z. Bekerman & C. McGlynn (Eds.), *Addressing Ethnic Conflict Through Peace Education* (pp. 137-159). Hampshire, England: Palgrave MacMillan.

Danesh, H.B. (2010). Unity-Based Peace Education. Education for Peace Program in Bosnia and Herzegovina: A Chronological Case Study. In N. Salomon and E. Cairns (Eds.), *Handbook on Peace Education* (pp. 253-268). USA: Psychology Press.

Dassonneville, R., Quintelier, E., Hooghe, M., & Claes, E. (2012). The relation between civic education and political attitudes and behavior: A two-year panel study among Belgian late adolescents. *Applied Developmental Science, 16*(3), 140-150.

Davies, L. (2004). *Education and Conflict: Complexity and chaos.* London: Routledge Falmer.

Davies, L. (2010). The Different Faces of Education in Conflict. *Development, 53*(4), 491-497.

Davies, L. (2016). The politics of peace education in post-conflict countries. In A. Langer & G.K. Brown (Eds.), *Building Sustainable Peace: Timing and Sequencing of Post-Conflict Reconstruction and Peacebuilding* (pp. 181-199). Oxford: Oxford University Press.

Davies, L. (2017). Justice-sensitive education: the implications of transitional justice mechanisms for teaching and learning. *Comparative Education, 53*(3), 333-350.

De Baets, A. (2015). Post-conflict history education moratoria: A balance. *World Studies in Education 16*(1), 5-30.

De Herdt, T.,Marivoet, W., & Mugigirwa,F. (2015). *Analyse de la situation des enfants et des femmes en RDC: Vers la réalisation du droit à l'éducation de qualité pour tous.* UNICEF.

Demarest, L., & Langer, A. (2018). Understanding Violent Conflict in Africa: Trends, causes, and prospects. In C.P. Peterson (Ed.), *The Routledge History of World Peace since 1750* (pp. 344-354). UK: Taylor & Francis.

Dercon, S., & Guitérrez-Romero, R. (2012). Triggers and Characteristics of the 2007 Kenyan Electoral Violence. *World Development, 40*(4), 731-744.

Devine, P.G., & Sharp, L.B. (2009). Automaticity and control in stereotyping and prejudice. In T.D. Nelson (Ed.), *Handbook of prejudice, stereotyping and discrimination* (61-87). New York: Psychology Press.

Dinur, A. (2018). No future without a shared ethos: reconciling Palestinian and Israeli identities. *Reconciliation in Global Context Why It Is Needed and How It Works*, 151-78.

Direction de la Planification, de l'Evaluation et des Statistiques du Ministère de l'Education Nationale et l'Enseignement Technique (DPES-MEN) (2014). *Rapport d'analyse Statistique 2013-2014*. Abidjan: MENET.

Dryden-Peterson, S., & Robinson, N. (2023). Time, source, and responsibility: understanding changing uses of the past in 'post-conflict' South African history teaching, 1998 and 2019. *Compare: A Journal of Comparative and International Education*, 1-19.

Dunlop, E. (2024). Looking to the Past to Understand the Present: Legacies of Inequality, Status Changes, and Collective Memory in Burundi's Post-War Schooling. *Ethnopolitics*, 1-21.

Dunlop, E., & King, E. (2021). Education at the intersection of conflict and peace: The inclusion and framing of education provisions in African peace agreements from 1975-2017. *Compare: A Journal of Comparative and International Education*, *51*(3), 375-395.

Dy, K. (2013). Challenges of teaching genocide in Cambodian secondary schools. *Policy and practice: Pedagogy about the Holocaust and genocide papers*, 1-10.

Education Cluster (2011). *Attaques contre l'Education: Rapport sur l'impact de la crise sur le système éducatif ivoirien, Rapport numéro 2*. UNICEF: 2011.

Eifert, B., Miguel, E., & Posner, D.N. (2010). Political Competition and Ethnic Identification in Africa. *American Journal of Political Science*, *54*(2), 494-510.

Emerson, L. (2012). Conflict, transition and education for 'political generosity': learning from the experience of ex-combatants in Northern Ireland. *Journal of Peace Education*, *9*(3), 277-295.

Evrard, E., & Destrooper, T. (2024). Learning from the past? How the Khmer Rouge Tribunal, civil society initiatives and survivor stories shape young Cambodians' understanding of non-recurrence. *The International Journal of Human Rights*, 1-27.

Faden, L. Y. (2014). History teachers imagining the nation: World War II narratives in the United States and Canada. In J.H. Williams (Ed.), *(Re)building memory: School textbooks, identity, and the pedagogies and politics of imagining community* (pp. 191-220). Rotterdam: Sense Publishers.

Fatah, A. A., Kuppens, L., & Langer, A. (2023). Discerning risk-takers from avoiders: Which teachers are more likely to support teaching about the violent past in Ambon, Indonesia?. *Education, Citizenship and Social Justice*, 17461979231179142.

Fazio, R.H. (1990). Multiple processes by which attitudes guide behavior: The MODE model as an integrative framework. In M.P. Zanna (Ed.), *Advances in experimental social psychology Vol. 23* (pp. 75-109). New York: Academic Press.

Festinger, L. (1957). *A theory of cognitive dissonance*. USA: Stanford University Press.

Feuchte, F., Neufeld, K. H., Bilali, R., & Mazziotta, A. (2020). Forum theater can improve intergroup attitudes, sense of community, and collective action intentions: Evidence from Liberia. *Peace and Conflict: Journal of Peace Psychology*, *26*(3), 270.

Förster, T. (2013). Insurgent nationalism: Political imagination and rupture in Côte d'Ivoire. *Africa Spectrum*, *48*(3), 3-31.

Fountain, S. (1999). *Peace Education in UNICEF. Working Paper Education Section Programme Division*. New York: UNICEF.

Freedman, S.W., & Weinstein, H.M., & Murphy, K., & Longman, T. (2008). Teaching History after Identity-Based Conflicts: The Rwanda Experience. *Comparative Education Review*, *52*(4), 663-690.

Gallagher, T. (2010). Building a Shared Future from a Divided Past: Promoting Peace through Education in Northern Ireland. In In N. Salomon and E. Cairns (Eds.), *Handbook on Peace Education* (pp. 241-252). USA: Psychology Press.

Galston, W.A. (2001). Political Knowledge, Political Engagement, and Civic Education. *Annual Review of Political Science*, *4*, 217-234.

Gay, G. (2013). Teaching To and Through Cultural Diversity. *Curriculum Inquiry*, *43*(1), 48-70.

Gbagbo, L., & Mattei, F. (2014). *Pour la vérité et la justice*. Paris: Editions du Moment.

Gellman, M. (2015). Teaching silence in the schoolroom: whither national history in Sierra Leone and El Salvador? *Third World Quarterly, 36(1)*, 147-161.

Giroux, H.A. (1983). *Theory and Resistance in Education: A Pedagogy for the Opposition*. Massachusetts: Bergin & Garvey Publishers, Inc.

Glennerster, R., Kremer, M., Mbiti, I., & Takavarasha, K. (2011). *Access and Quality in the Kenyan Education System: A Review of the Progress, Challenges and Potential Solutions*. Nairobi: Office of the Prime Minister of Kenya.

Global Education Monitoring Report (2017). *Accountability in Education: Meeting Our Commitments*. Paris: UNESCO.

Gur-Ze'ev, I. (2001). Philosophy of Peace Education in a Postmodern Era. *Educational Theory, 51(3)*, 315-336.

Hadjivaplou, M. (2002). Cyprus: A Partnership between Conflict Resolution and Peace Education. In G. Salomon and B. Nevo, *Peace Education: The Concept, Principles, and Practices Around the World*, (pp. 193-208). New York: Psychology Press.

Hamilton, D.L., Sherman, S.J., Crump, S.A., & Spencer-Rodgers, J. (2009). The role of Entitativity in Stereotyping, Processes and Parameters. In T.D. Nelson (Ed.), *Handbook of prejudice, stereotyping and discrimination* (pp. 179-198). New York: Psychology Press.

Harber, C. (2019). *Schooling for Peaceful Development in Post-Conflict Societies: Education for Transformation?* Springer.

Harneit-Sievers, A., & Peters, R-M. (2008). Kenya's 2007 General Election and Its Aftershocks. *Africa Spectrum, 43(1)*, 133-144.

Harris, R., & Clarke, G. (2011). Embracing diversity in the history curriculum: A study of the challenges facing trainee teachers. *Cambridge Journal of Education, 41(2)*, 159-175.

Harris, I.M., & Morrison, M.L. (2003). *Peace Edcuation: Second Edition*. North Carolina: McFarland & Company, Inc.

Heyneman, S. P., & Todoric-Bebic, S. (2000). A renewed sense for the purposes of schooling: the challenges of education and social cohesion in Asia, Africa, Latin America, Europe and Central Asia. *Prospects, 30(2)*, 145-166.

Higgins, S., & Novelli, M. (2018). The potential and pitfalls of peace education: a cultural political economy analysis of the emerging issues teacher education curriculum in Sierra Leone. *Asian Journal of Peacebuilding, 6(1)*, 29-53.

Holbrook, A.L., & Krosnick, J.A. (2010). Social Desirability Bias in Voter Turnout Reports Tests Using the Item Count Technique. *Public Opinion Quarterly, 74(1)*, 37-67.

Horner, L., Kadiwal, L., Sayed, Y., Barrett, A., Durrani M., & Novelli, M. (2015). *Literature Review: The Role of Teachers in Peacebuilding*. [15.07.2025, INEE: https://inee.org/resources/literature-review-role-teachers-peacebuilding].

Hornsby, C. (2013). *Kenya: a history since independence*. London: I.B. Tauris.

Horowitz, J. (2016). The Ethnic Logic of Campaign Strategy in Diverse Societies: Theory and Evidence From Kenya. *Comparative Political Studies, 49(3)*, 324-356.

Hromadzic, A. (2009). "Smoking Doesn't Kill; It Unites!" Cultural Meanings and Practices of "Mixing" at the Gymnasium Mostar in Bosnia and Herzegovina. In C. McGlynn, M. Zembylas, Z. Bekerman and T. Gallagher (Eds.), *Peace Education in Conflict and Post-Conflict Societies: Comparative Perspectives* (pp. 109-125). New York: Palgrave Macmillan.

Human Rights Watch (2008). *Ballots to Bullets: Organized Political Violence and Kenya's Crisis of Governance*. New York: HRW.

Human Rights Watch (2015). *Notre école dvint un champ de bataille. L'utilisation des écoles comme lieux de recrutement et à des fins militaires dans l'Est de la République Démocratique du Congo.* Washington: HRW.

Ibrahim, S. (2021). *Unity Over Diversity: A Multi-cultural Education Perspective on Ethnicity, Social Cohesion and Secondary School Education in Kenya.* KU Leuven: PhD thesis.

Ichilov, O. (2003). Teaching Civics in a divided society: the case of Israel. *International Studies in Sociology of Education, 13*, 219-242.

International Crisis Group (2008). *Kenya in Crisis.* Brussels: ICG.

IPIS (2024). *Le M23 « version 2 »: Enjeux, motivations, perceptions et impacts locaux.* Goma / Anvers / Copenhague: International Peace Information Service (IPIS).

Jackson, S. (2006). Sons of Which Soil? The Language and Politics of Autochthony in Eastern D.R. Congo. *African Studies Review*, 97-123.

Johnson, L.S. (2007). Moving from Piecemeal to Systemic Approaches to Peace Education in Divided Societies: Comparative Efforts in Northern Ireland and Cyprus. In Z. Bekerman & C. McGlynn (Eds.), *Addressing Ethnic Conflict Through Peace Education* (pp. 21-34). Hampshire, England: Palgrave MacMillan.

Johnson, D.W., & Johnson, R.T. (2010). Peace Education in the Classroom: Creating Effective Peace Education Programs. In N. Salomon and E. Cairns (Eds.), *Handbook on Peace Education* (pp. 223-240). USA: Psychology Press.

Kaganda, P. (2013). *Mouvement Mai-Mai et participation politique au Sud-Kivu. Une contribution à la critique de la Sociologie de la paix en societé post-conflit.* Bukavu: Thèse de doctorat, Inédite, Université Officielle de Bukavu.

Kagwanga, P. (2015). The geopolitics of international criminal justice: ICC and Kenya's 2013 presidential elections. In K. Njogu & P. W. Wekesa, eds. *Kenya's 2013 general election: stakes, practices and outcomes.* Nairobi: Twaweza Communication, pp. 144-161.

Kalolo, J. F., & Kapinga, O. S. (2023). Towards ending corporal punishment in African countries: Experiences from Tanzania. *International Journal of Educational Development, 102*, 102839.

Kanon, G.L. (2012). Reconstruction de l'apprentissage à la paix et la citoyenneté dans le contexte post-conflit ivoirien. *African Education Development issues, 4*(x), 183-209.

Kello, K. (2016). Sensitive and controversial issues in the classroom: teaching history in a divided society. *Teachers and Teaching, 22*(1), 35-53.

Kello, K., & Wagner, W. (2017). History teaching as 'Propaganda'? Teachers' communication styles in posttransition societies. In: Psaltis C, Carretero M and Čehajić-Clancy S (eds) *History Education and Conflict Transformation.* Cham: Springer International Publishing, pp. 201-230.

Kelly, T. E. (1986). Discussing controversial issues: Four perspectives on the teacher's role. *Theory & research in social education, 14*(2), 113-138.

Kennes, E. (2000). *Le secteur minier au congo: «Déconnexion» et descente aux enfers.* Anvers: Annuaire Afrique des Grands-Lacs 1999-2000.

Kevers, R., Rober, P., Derluyn, I., & De Haene, L. (2016). Remembering collective violence: Broadening the notion of traumatic memory in post-conflict rehabilitation. *Culture, medicine, and psychiatry, 40*, 620-640.

Keynes, M. (2019). History education for transitional justice? Challenges, limitations and possibilities for settler colonial Australia. *International Journal of Transitional Justice, 13*(1), 113-133.

Keynes, M., Åström Elmersjö, H., Lindmark, D., & Norlin, B. (2021). *Introduction: Connecting historical justice and history education* (pp. 1-20). Springer International Publishing.

Kihangi, G. M. (2013). Enseigner l'Histoire, la Géographie et l'Education Civique et Morale aujourd'hui. Dans P. I. Mwapu, & B. Zigashane, *La didactique des disciplines et le droit de l'Homme dans les écoles secondaires de la ville de Bukavu* (pp. 139-158). Bukavu: Editions du Centre de Recherches Universitaire du Kivu.

Kitson, A., & McCully, A. (2005). 'You hear about it for real in school'. Avoiding, containing and risk-taking in the history classroom. *Teaching History, 120*, 32-37.

Korostelina, K. (2015). Reproduction of conflict in history teaching in Ukraine: a social identity theory analysis. *Identity, 15*(3), 221-240.

Korostelina, K.V., & Lässig, S. (2013). *History Education and Post-Conflict Reconciliation*. New York: Routledge.

Korthagen FAJ, Kessels J, Koster B, et al. (2001). *Linking Theory and Practice: The Pedagogy of Realistic Teacher Education*. Mahwah, NJ: Lawrence Erlbaum Associates.

Kramon, E., & Posner, D.N. (2016). Ethnic Favoritism in Education in Kenya. *Quarterly Journal of Political Science, 11*, 1-58.

Kucukaydin, I., & Cranton, P. (2012). Saying "No!" The Power of Transformative Learning. In P.R. Carr and B.J. Porfilio (Eds.), *Educating for Peace in a Time of "Permanent War": Are Schools Part of the Solution or the Problem?* (pp. 55-68). New York: Routledge.

Kuppens, L. (2018). *The role of education in building sustainable peace: an analysis of teachers' views and practices with regards to peace and conflict in Côte d'Ivoire and Kenya*. KU Leuven & University of Antwerp: PhD thesis.

Kuppens, L., Ibrahim, S., & Langer, A. (2020). Unity over diversity? Teachers' perceptions and practices of multicultural education in Kenya. *Compare: A Journal of Comparative and International Education, 50*(5), 693-712.

Kuppens, L., & Langer, A. (2016a). To address or not to address the violent past in the classroom? That is the question in Côte d'Ivoire. *Journal of peace education, 13*(2), 153-171.

Kuppens, L., & Langer, A. (2016b). Divided we teach? Teachers' perceptions of conflict and peace in Côte d'Ivoire. *Peace and Conflict: Journal of Peace Psychology, 22*(4), 329.

Kuppens, L., & Langer, A. (2018). Peut-on apprendre la paix à l'école? Une évaluation du cours «Éducation aux droits de l'homme et à la citoyenneté»(EDHC) en Côte d'Ivoire post-conflit. *International Review of Education, 64*(5), 633-650.

Kuppens, L., & Langer, A. (2019). Building Social Cohesion through Education in Africa? Lessons from Côte d'Ivoire and Kenya. In H. Hino, A. Langer, J. Lonsdale and F. Stewart (eds), *From Divided Pasts to Cohesive Futures. Reflections on Africa*, 322-45. Cambridge: Cambridge University Press.

Kuppens, L., & Langer, A. (2020). Reconciling before educating? Narratives of conflict and peace among teachers in Côte d'Ivoire. *International Journal of Intercultural Relations, 76*, 37-51.

Kuppens, L., & Langer, A. (2022). The role of secondary school teachers in shaping a political culture of ethnicity and ethnic favouritism: the case of Kenya. *The Journal of Modern African Studies, 60*(4), 547-569.

Kuppens, L., & Langer, A. (2023). Memory mobilization and Postconflict Stability in Côte d'Ivoire: Analysing the transmission of conflict narratives among Ivoirian Youth. *African Affairs, 122*(488), 403-427.

Langer, A. (2005) Horizontal Inequalities and Violent Group Mobilization in Côte d'Ivoire. *Oxford Development Studies, 33*(1), 25-45.

Langer, A. (2010). *Côte d'Ivoire's elusive quest for peace*. Centre for Development Studies, University of Bath Working Paper 11. Bath: CDS.

Langer, A., Stewart, F., Smedts, K., & Demarest, L. (2017). Conceptualising and measuring social cohesion in Africa: Towards a perceptions-based index. *Social Indicators Research, 131*, 321-343.

Lanoue, E. (2003). L'école à l'épreuve de la guerre. Vers une territorialisation des politiques d'éducation en Côte d'Ivoire ? *Politique africaine, 4*(92), 129-143.

Lanoue, E. (2007). Éducation, violences et conflits en Afrique subsaharienne. Sources, données d'enquête (Côte d'Ivoire, Burkina Faso) et hypothèse. *International Journal on Violence and Schools, 3*, 94-111.

Lasky, S. (2005). A sociocultural approach to understanding teacher identity, agency and professional vulnerability in a context of secondary school reform. *Teaching and Teacher Education, 21*, 899-916.

Lässig, S. (2013). Post-conflict reconciliation and joint history textbook projects. In K.V. Korostelina and S. Lässig (Eds.), *History Education and Post-Conflict Reconciliation* (pp. 1-18), New York: Routledge.

Lattimer, H., & Kelly, M. (2013). Engaging Kenyan secondary students in an oral history project: Education as emancipation. *International Journal of Educational Development, 33*(5), 476-486.

Lauritzen, S.M. (2016). Educational change following conflict: Challenges related to the implementation of a peace education programme in Kenya. *Journal of Educational Change, 17*, 319-336.

Levinson, M. (2015). Moral injury and the ethics of educational injustice. *Harvard Educational Review, 85*(2), 203-228.

Lewin, K.M., Wasanga, P., Wanderi, E., & Somerset, A. (2011). *Participation and Performance in Education in Sub-Saharan Africa with special reference to Kenya: Improving Policy and Practice.* Research Monograph No. 74. Sussex: University of Sussex.

Li, J. (2018). Ethnic favoritism in primary education in Kenya: the effects of coethnicity with the president. *Education Economics, 26*(2), 194-212.

Licata, L., Klein, O., & Gély, R. (2007). Mémoire des conflits, conflits de mémoires: Une approche psychosociale et philosophique du rôle de la mémoire collective dans les processus de réconciliation intergroupe. *Social science information, 46*(4), 563-589.

Lockwood, P. (2023). Hustler populism, anti-jubilee backlash and economic injustice in Kenya's 2022 elections. *African Affairs, 122*(487), 205-224.

Lonsdale, J. (2019). Kenya's four ages of ethnicity. In: H. Hino, A. Langer, J. Lonsdale, F. Stewart (Eds.), *From Divided Pasts to Cohesive Futures: African Reflections.* Cambridge: Cambridge University Press.

Lopes Cardozo, M., & Hoeks, C.M.Q. (2015). Losing ground: a critical analysis of teachers' agency for peacebuilding education in Sri Lanka. *Journal of Peace Education, 12*(1), 56-73.

Lynch, G. (2006). Negotiating ethnicity: Identity politics in contemporary Kenya. *Review of African political economy, 33*(107), 49-65.

Mac Ginty, R. (2016). Political versus sociological time: The fraught world of timelines and deadlines. Building Sustainable Peace: Timing and Sequencing of Post-Conflict Reconstruction and Peacebuilding, 15-31.

Mac Ginty, R. (2022). Temporality and contextualisation in Peace and Conflict Studies: The forgotten value of war memoirs and personal diaries. Cooperation and Conflict, 57(2), 191-209.

Makinen, M., & Kuira, M.W. (2008). Social Media and Post-Election Crisis in Kenya. *Information & Communication Technology Africa, 13*. Retrieved from: http://repository.upenn.edu/ictafrica/13.

Makoni, R. (2015). *Peace education in Zimbabwean pre-service teacher education: A critical reflection.* University of South Africa: PhD thesis.

Makori, A., & Onderi, H. (2014). Examining the teaching and learning resources related challenges facing small and medium-sized public secondary schools in Kenya: A comparative analysis. *African Educational Research Journal, 2*(2), 72-84.

Manning, P., & Paulson, J. (2024). Some contradictions of multiple perspectives approaches to peace and history education: lessons from Cambodia. *Ethics and Education*, 1-16.

Manning, P., Paulson, J., & Keo, D. (2024). Reparative remembering for just futures: History education, multiple perspectives and responsibility. *Futures, 155*, 103279.

Marchais, G., Falisse, J-B., Matabishi, S., & West, D. (2023). *Summary Report: BRiCE Project DRC and Niger. Teacher Wellbeing and Teaching Quality in Fragile and Conflict-Affected Contexts.* Brighton: Institute of Development Studies

Marshall-Fratani, R. (2006). The War of 'Who is Who': Autochthony, Nationalism, and Citizenship in the Ivoirian Crisis. *African Studies Review, 49*(2), 9-44.

McCauley, C. (2002). Head-first versus Feet-first in Peace Education. In G. Salomon and B. Nevo (Eds.), *Peace Education: The Concept, Principles, and Practices Around the World* (pp. 247-259). New York: Psychology Press.

McCully, A.W. (2012). History teaching, conflict and the legacy of the past. *Education, Citizenship and Social Justice, 7*(2), 145-159.

McGovern, M. (2011). *Making War in Côte d'Ivoire.* London: Hurst and Company.

Mendenhall, M., Chopra, V., & Bazlen, R. (Eds.) (2022). *Navigating Ethical Dilemmas in Education in Emergencies (EiE): A Compendium of Vignettes for Research and Practice.* Teachers College, Columbia University.

Miles, J. (2024). Guilt, complicity, and responsibility for historical injustice: towards a pedagogy of complex implication. *Pedagogy, Culture & Society, 32*(3), 619-635.

Miller-Lane, J., Denton, E., & May, A. (2006). Social studies teachers' views on committed impartiality and discussion. *Social Studies Research and Practice, 1*(1), 30-44.

Ministère de l'Education Nationale (MEN) (2012a). *Programmes Educatifs et guides d'Exécution. Education aux Droits de l'Homme et à la Citoyenneté (EDHC). Secondaire 5eme/6eme.* Abidjan: MEN.

Ministère de l'Education Nationale (MEN) (2012b). *Programmes Educatifs et guides d'Exécution. Education aux Droits de l'Homme et à la Citoyenneté (EDHC). Secondaire 4eme/3eme.* Abidjan: MEN.

Ministère de l'Enseignement Primaire, Secondaire et Professionnel (2002). *Programme National de Français au secondaire.* Kinshasa: MINESP.

Ministère de l'Enseignement Primaire, Secondaire et Professionnel (2007). *Programme National d'enseignement d'Education Civique et Morale.* Kinshasa: MINESP.

Ministère de l'Enseignement Primaire, Secondaire et Professionnel (2013). *Enquête nationale sur les enfants et les adolescents en dehors de l'école.* Kinshasa: MINESP.

Ministry of Education, Science and Technology (2014). *Education Sector Policy on Peace Education.* Nairobi: Ministry of Education, Science and Technology.

Mkangi, B., & Githaiga, N. (2012). *Kenya's new constitution and conflict transformation. Working Paper N°232 Institute for Security Studies.* Retrieved from (20/11/2016): https://issafrica.org/acpst/publications/papers/kenyas-new-constitution-and-conflict transformation

Mueller, S. D. (2020). High-stakes Ethnic Politics. *The Oxford handbook of Kenyan politics, 343.*

Mukwemulere, A.K. (2024). *Gouvernance politique et persistance des groupes armés au Nord-Kivu. Report.* Bukavu: Université Officielle de Bukavu.

Mulimbi, B. & Dryden-Peterson, S. (2018a). Response to cultural diversity in Bostwana's schools: links between national policy, school actions and students' civic equality. *Journal of Curriculum Studies, 50*(3), 364-386.

Mulimbi, B., & Dryden-Peterson, S. (2018b). "There is still peace. There are no wars.": Prioritizing unity over diversity in Botswana's social studies policies and practices and the implications for positive peace. *International Journal of Educational Development, 61,* 142-154.

Murphy, K. (2010). Examples of best practice 1. Teaching a Holocaust case study in a post-conflict environment: education as part of violence, reconstruction and repair. *Intercultural Education, 21*(S1), 71-77.

Murphy, K., Pettis, S., & Wray, D. (2016). Building Peace: The Opportunities and Limitations of Educational Interventions in Countries with Identity-Based Conflicts. In M. Bajaj and M. Hantzopoulos (Eds.). *Peace Education: International Perspectives* (pp. 35-50). New York: Bloomsbury Academic.

Musuasua, A. (2006). *Le Vocabulaire politique des leaders nationalistes congolais: de P. E. Lumumba à L. D. Kabila.* Metz: Université Paul Verlaine, Metz (UPVM).

Mwakikagile, G. (2007). *Kenya: Identity of a nation.* New Africa Press.

Mwambari, D. (2023). *Navigating Cultural Memory: Commemoration and Narrative in Postgenocide Rwanda.* Oxford University Press.

Ndahinda, F.M., & Mugabe, A.S. (2024). Streaming Hate: Exploring the Harm of Anti-Banyamulenge and Anti-Tutsi Hate Speech on Congolese Social Media. *Journal of Genocide Research, 26*(1), 48-72.

Ndonye, M. M., Yieke, F., & Onyango, J. O. (2015). Ethnicity as discursive construct in Kenyan televised comedy: humorous harm?. *The Journal of Pan African Studies, 8*(3), 44-60.

Ndugumbo, V. (2014). *La reconstruction de l'éducation en contexte « d'après-guerre » en République démocratique du Congo: visions et rôles des acteurs dans le développement du curriculum d'enseignement secondaire technique et professionnel au Sud-Kivu.* Laval: Université Laval.

Nfundiko, J.S. (2013). Dimension psychologique et sociale dans les programmes de réintégration des filles sorties des forces et groupes armés. Dans G. Odden, & M. Tohneim, *Filles ex-soldats du Congo. La route cahoteuse de la réintégration* (pp. 79-96). Paris: L'harmattan.

Nfundiko, J.S. (2015). Femmes du Sud-Kivu, victimes et actrices en situation de conflit et postconflit. *Hérodote* (158), 182-199.

Nfundiko, J.S. (2020). *The Role of Education in Building Durable Peace in eastern DR Congo.* KU Leuven: PhD Thesis.

Nfundiko, J. S., Kuppens, L., & Langer, A. (2025). The Congolese school as a driver of peace? An analysis of the attitudes of secondary school teachers in eastern Democratic Republic of the Congo. *McGill Journal of Education / Revue Des Sciences De l'éducation De McGill.*

Nguyen, V. T. (2016). *Nothing ever dies: Vietnam and the memory of war.* Harvard University Press.

Njoroge, G.K. (2007). The Reconstruction of the Teacher's Psyche in Rwanda: The Theory and Practice of Peace Education at Kigali Institute of Education. In Z. Bekerman & C. McGlynn (Eds.), *Addressing Ethnic Conflict Through Peace Education* (pp. 215-229). Hampshire, England: Palgrave MacMillan.

Niens, U. (2009). Toward the Development of a Theoretical Framework for Peace Education Using the Contact Hypothesis and Multiculturalism. In C. McGlynn, M. Zembylas, Z. Bekerman and T. Gallagher (Eds.), *Peace Education in Conflict and Post-Conflict Societies: Comparative Perspectives* (pp. 145-159). New York: Palgrave Macmillan.

Ntanyoma, R. D., & Hintjens, H. (2022). Expressive violence and the slow genocide of the Banyamulenge of South Kivu. *Ethnicities, 22*(3), 374-403.

Ntoto, F. P. (2013). Trajectoires, profils et insertion professionnelle des enseignants du secondaire à Kinshasa en République Démocratique du Congo. *Revue de l'Association Francophone Internationale de Recherche Scientifique en Éducation*, 16-32.

Nyairo, J (2015b). The circus comes to town: performance, religion and exchange in political party campaigns. In K. Njogu & P. W. Wekesa, eds. *Kenya's 2013 general elections: stakes, practices and outcomes* (pp. 124-143). Nairobi: Twaweza Communication.

Nyankanga, M.E., Joshua, B.N., Wekesa, W.N., Ongaga, E., & Orina, F. (2013). The changing trends in the development of teacher education in Kenya: The role of the Teacher's Service Commission. *Research on Humanities and Social Sciences, 3*(19), 82-85.

Nyatuka, B.O., & Bota, K.N. (2014). Equity in Access to Secondary Education in Kenya: A Historical Perspective. *Journal of Education and Practice, 5*(2), 48-54.

Oben, A. I., & Hui, X. (2025). Discipline or damage?: Students' experiences of corporal punishment in Cameroon secondary schools and implications for education. *International Journal of Educational Development, 113*, 103201.

Obura, A.P. (2002). *Peace Education Programme in Dadaab and Kakuma, Kenya: Evaluation Summary.* Nairobi: UNHCR.

Ocobock, P. (2012). Spare the Rod, Spoil the Colony: Corporal Punishment, Colonial Violence, and Generational Authority in Kenya, 1897-1952. *The International Journal of African Historical Studies, 45*(1), 29-56.

Odden, G., & Tohneim, M. (2013). *Filles ex-soldats du Congo. La Route cahoteuse de la réintégration.* Paris: L'Harmattan.

Office of the High Commissioner on Human Rights (2010). *Rapport d'Etapes du Programme Mondial en Faveur de l'Education aux Droits de l'Homme en Côte d'Ivoire.* Geneva: OHCHR. Retrieved from: http://www2.ohchr.org/english/issues/education/training/docs/replies/COTE_DIVOIRE_RAPPORT_DETAPES_9April2010.pdf

Oglesby, E. (2007). Educating citizens in postwar Guatemala: historical memory, genocide and the culture of peace. *Radical History Review, 97*, 77-98.

Olson, M.A., & Kendrick, R.V. (2008). Origins of Attitudes. In W.D. Crano & R. Prislin (Eds.), *Attitudes and Attitude Change* (pp. 111-130). New York: Psychology Press.

Østby, G., Nordås, R., and Rød, J.K. (2009). Regional Inequalities and Civil Conflict in Sub-Saharan Africa. *International Studies Quarterly, 53*(2), 301-324.

Paluck, E. L. (2010). Is it better not to talk? Group polarization, extended contact, and perspective taking in eastern Democratic Republic of Congo. *Personality and Social Psychology Bulletin, 36*(9), 1170-1185.

Paulson, J. (2006). The educational recommendations of truth and reconciliation commissions: Potential and practice in Sierra Leone. *Research in Comparative and International Education, 1*(4), 335-350.

Paulson, J. (2015). 'Whether and how?' History education about recent and ongoing conflict: A review of research. *Journal on Education in Emergencies, 1*(1), 115-141.

Paulson, J., & Bellino, M.J. (2017). Truth commissions, education, and positive peace: an analysis of truth commission final reports (1980-2015). *Comparative Education 53*(3), 351-378.

Pham, P. N., Balthazard, M., Gibbons, N., & Vinck, P. (2019). Perspectives on memory, forgiveness and reconciliation in Cambodia's post-Khmer Rouge society. *International Review of the Red Cross, 101*(910), 125-149.

Pherali, T. J. 2013. "Schooling in Violent Situations: The Politicization of Education in Nepal, before and after the 2006 Peace Agreement." *Prospects 43*(1), 49-67.

Piccolino, G. (2017). Rhétorique de la cohésion sociale et paradoxes de la "paix par le bas" en Côte d'Ivoire. *Politique africaine, 4*(148), 49-68.

Pingel, F. (2008). Can truth be negotiated? History textbook revision as a means to reconciliation. *The Annals of the American Academy of Political and Social Science, 617*(1), 181-198.

Poncelet, M., André, G., & De Herdt, T. (2010). La survie de l'école primaire congolaise (RDC): héritage colonial, hybridité et résilience. *Autrepart, Revue des Sciences Sociales du Sud,* 23-41.

Popineau, C. (2017). Prendre la craie. La mobilisation des enseignants rebelles dans le Nord de la Côte d'Ivoire (2002-2011). *Politique africaine, 4*(148), 27-48.

Quaynor, L., & Borkorm, B. (2020). Remapping citizenship: Relationships between education levels and ethnonational identities in Côte d'Ivoire, Ghana, and Liberia. *Education, Citizenship and Social Justice, 15*(1), 47-63.

Ramírez-Barat, C., & Duthie, R. (2015). *Education and Transitional Justice: Opportunities and Challenges for Peacebuilding*. UNICEF Learning for Peace. Retrieved from ICTJ (July 15 2025): https://www.ictj.org/publication/education-transitional-justice-opportunities-challenges-peacebuilding.

RDC. (2014b). *Rapport d'état du système éducatif: Pour une Éducation au Service de la Croissance et de la Paix*. Dakar: UNESCO IIPE Pôle de Dakar.

Reyna, C. (2000). Lazy, Dumb, or Industrious: When Stereotypes Convey Attribution Information in the Classroom. *Educational Psychology Review*, 12(1), 85-110.

Robinson, N. (2022). Conceptualising historical legacies for transitional justice history education in postcolonial societies. *History Education Research Journal*, 19(1), 10. DOI: https://doi.org/10.14324/HERJ.19.1.10.

Robiolle-Moul, T. (2013). *Promoting a culture of peace and non-violence in Africa through education for peace and conflict prevention Phase 1: Mapping – Final Report*. Paris: UNESCO.

Ron, Y., & Maoz, I. (2013). Dangerous stories: Encountering narratives of the other in the Israeli–Palestinian conflict. *Peace and Conflict: Journal of Peace Psychology*, 19(3), 281.

Rosoux, V. (2005). La gestion du passé au Rwanda: ambivalence et poids du silence. *Genèses*, (4), 28-046.

Rosoux, V. (2017). Reconciliation as a puzzle: Walking among definitions. Negotiating reconciliation in peacemaking: Quandaries of relationship building, 15-26.

Rosoux, V. (2018). Memory versus Reconciliation. *Reconciliation in Global Context*, 199.

Ross, M. H. (2001). Psychocultural interpretations and dramas: Identity dynamics in ethnic conflict. *Political psychology*, 22(1), 157-178.

Rwengabo, S. (2016). *Nation building in Africa: lessons from Tanzania for South Sudan*. Mandela Institute for Development Studies (MINDS) Youth Dialogue. Dar es Salaam, Tanzania.

Rubagiza, J., Umutoni, J., & Kaleeba, A. (2016). Teachers as Agents of Change: Promoting Peacebuilding and Social Cohesion in Schools in Rwanda. *Education as Change*, 20(3), 202-204.

Rudahindwa, N. (2020). *Etude qualitative sur la violence à l'école et sur le chemin de l'école en République Démocratique du Congo*. Washington: World Bank.

Russell, S. G. (2019). *Becoming Rwandan: Education, reconciliation, and the making of a post-genocide citizen*. Rutgers University Press.

Russell, S. G., & Tiplic, D. (2014). Rights-based education and conflict: A cross-national study of rights discourse in textbooks. *Compare: A Journal of Comparative and International Education*, 44(3), 314-334.

Sacanoud, K.B., Kanon, G.L., Kossi, K.F.J., Gogbeu, M., Yao, K.L., N'Guessan, S.Y., Archer, M., Kassi, A.L.D., Akre, S., Yapo, A.P., Bamba, M., Koffi, Z.B., Achi, K.A.V.O, & Soro, A. (2012). *Education aux Droits de l'Homme et à la Citoyenneté (EDHC): Manuel-guide à l'usage des formateurs de l'ENS, DE l'IPNETP, DE l'INSAAC, de l'infs et de l'infas*. Abidjan: MENET.

Salomon, G. (2002). The Nature of Peace Education: Not all Programs are Created Equal. In G. Salomon and B. Nevo (Eds.), *Peace Education: The Concept, Principles, and Practices Around the World* (pp. 3-14). New York: Psychology Press.

Salomon, G. (2004). Does peace education make a difference in the context of an intractable conflict? *Peace and Conflict: Journal of Peace Psychology*, 10, 257-274.

Salomon, G., & Nevo, B. (2005). *Peace education: The concept, principles, and practices around the world*. Psychology Press.

Salomon, G. (2006). Does Peace Education *Really* Make a Difference? *Peace and Conflict: Journal of Peace Psychology*, 12(1), 37-48.

Sanchez Meertens, A. (2013). Courses of Conflict: Transmission of Knowledge and War's History in Eastern Sri Lanka. *History and Anthropology*, 24(2), 253-273.

Sany, J. (2010). *Education and Conflict in Côte d'Ivoire*. Washington, D.C.: USIP.

Sapiro, V. (2004). Not Your Parents' Political Socialization. *Annual Review of Political Science*, 7, 1-3.

Sayed, Y., Badroodien, A., Omar, Y., Ndabaga, E., Novelli, M., Durrani, N., Barrett, A., Balie, L., Salmon, T., Bizimana, B., Ntahomvukiye, C., & Utomi, J. (2018). *The Role of Teachers in Peacebuilding and Social Cohesion in Rwanda and South Africa, ESRC/DFID Research Report*. UK: University of Sussex.

Search for Common Ground. (2012). *Education et Conflits » Une étude menée par Search For Common Ground dans 4 provinces de la RDC*. Kinshasa: UNICEF & Search For Common Ground.

Seixas, P. (2017). Teaching Rival Histories: In Search of Narrative Plausibility. In *International Perspectives on Teaching Rival Histories* (pp. 253-268). Palgrave Macmillan UK.

Shanks, K. (2018). The changing role of education in the Iraqi disputed territories: assimilation, segregation and indoctrination. *Education, Conflict, and Globalisation*, 14(3), 96-107.

Shepler, S., & Williams, J.H. (2017). Understanding Sierra Leonean and Liberian teachers' views on discussing past wars in their classrooms. *Comparative Education*, 53(3), 418-441.

Simson, R. & Green, E. (2022). 'Ethnic favouritism in Kenyan education reconsidered: when a picture is worth more than a thousand regressions'. *Journal of Modern African Studies*, 58(3), 425-460.

Skårås, M., & Breidlid, A. (2016). Teaching the violent past in secondary schools in newly independent South Sudan. *Education as change*, 20(3), 98-118.

Sleeter, C. E. (2011). An agenda to strengthen culturally responsive pedagogy. *English Teaching: Practice and Critique*, 10(2), 7-23.

Smith, A., & Vaux, T. (2003). Education, Conflict and International Development. Department for International Development. https://www.ulster.ac.uk/__data/assets/pdf_file/0010/228196/vaux-2003.pdf

Smith, A., Marks, C., Novelli, M., Valiente, O., & Scandurra, R. (2016). *Exploring the Linkages between Education Sector Governance, Inequity, Conflict, and Peacebuilding in Kenya: Research Report Prepared for UNICEF Eastern and Southern Regional Office (ESARO)*. Nairobi: UNICEF.

Solhjell, R. (2015). *Dimensions of statehood: A study of public goods in Bukavu, the Democratic Republic of Congo*. London: The London School of Economics and Political Science.

Soro, G. (2005). *Pourquoi je suis devenu rebelle: La Côte d'Ivoire au bord du gouffre*. Vanves Cedex: Hachette.

Staeheli, L.A., & Hammett, D. (2010). Educating the New National Citizen: Education, Political Subjectivity, and Divided Societies. *Citizenship Studies*, 14(6), 667-680.

Staub, E., Pearlman, L.A., & Bilali, R. (2010). Understanding the Roots and Impact of Violence and Psychological Recovery as Avenues to Reconciliation after Mass Violence and Intractable Conflict: Applications to National Leaders, Journalists, Community Groups, Public Education through Radio, and Children. In N. Salomon and E. Cairns (Eds.), *Handbook on Peace Education* (pp. 269-285). USA: Psychology Press.

Stearns, J. (2012). *Contexte historique des conflits dans la province du Nord-Kivu à l'Est du Congo*. London-Nairobi: Rift Valley Institute.

Stearns, J., & Botiveau, R. (2013). Repenser la crise au Kivu: mobilisation armée et logique du gouvernement de transition. *Politique Africaine*, 1(129), 23-48.

Steeves, J. (2015). Devolution in Kenya: derailed or on track? *Commonwealth & Comparative Politics*, 53(4), 457-474.

Stephan, W.G., & Stephan, C.W. (2001). *Improving Intergroup Relations*. Thousand Oaks: SAGE Publications.

Stewart, F. (2010). Horizontal inequalities in Kenya and the political disturbances of 2008: Some implications for aid policy. *Conflict, Security & Development*, 10(1), 133-159.

Tawil, S., & Harley, A. (2004). *Education, conflict and social cohesion* (Eds.). UNESCO International bureau of education: Paris.

Tenenbaum, H.R., & Ruck, M.D. (2007). Are Teachers' Expectations Different for Racial Minority Than for European American Students? A Meta-Analysis. *Journal of Educational Psychology*, 99(2), 253-273.

Thornton, S.J. (27.03.1989). *Aspiration and Practice: Teacher as Curricular-Instructional Gatekeeper in Social Studies*. Paper presented at the 70th Annual Meeting of the American Educational Research Association of 27-31 March 1989 in San Francisco.

Tibbitts, F. (2006). Learning from the past: supporting teaching through the Facing the Past history project in South Africa. *Prospects*, 36(3), 295-317.

Tibbitts, F.L., & Weldon, G. (2017). History curriculum and teacher training: Shaping a democratic future in post-apartheid South Africa? *Comparative Education*, 53(3): 442-461.

Tiemessen, A. (2014). The International Criminal Court and the politics of prosecutions. *The International Journal of Human Rights*, 18(4-5), 444-461.

Titeca, K., & De Herdt, T. (2011). Real governance beyond the 'failed state': Negotiating education in the Democratic Republic of the Congo. *African affairs*, 110(439), 213-231.

Torney-Purta, J. (2002). The School's Role in Developing Civic Engagement: A Study of Adolescents in Twenty-Eight Countries. *Applied Developmental Science*, 6(4), 203-212.

Trefon, T. (2013). *Congo, la mascarade de l'aide au développement*. Louvain-la-Neuve: Academia.

UNESCO. (2014). *République Démocratique du Congo Rapport d'Etat du Système éducatif Pour une éducation au service de la croissance et de la Paix*. Dakar: UNESCO/ IIEP.

Van Straaten, D., Wilschut, A., & Oostdam, R. (2016). Making history relevant to students by connecting past, present and future: A framework for research. *Journal of Curriculum Studies*, 48(4), 479-502.

Verweijen, J. (2013). Military business and the business of the military in the Kivus. *Review of African Political Economy*, 40(135), pp 67-82.

Verweijen, J. (2015). From Autochthony to Violence? Discursive and Coercive Social Practices of the Mai-Mai in Fizi, Eastern DR Congo. *African Studies Review*, 58(2), 157-180.

Verweijen, J., & Vlassenroot, K. (2015). Armed mobilisation and the nexus of territory, identity, and authority: the contested territorial aspirations of the Banyamulenge in eastern DR Congo. *Journal of Contemporary African Studies*, 33(2), 191-212.

Vinitzky-Seroussi, V., & Teeger, C. (2010). Unpacking the unspoken: Silence in collective memory and forgetting. *Social forces*, 88(3), 1103-1122.

Waiganjo, M. M., & Waiganjo, M. M. (2018). Relevance of life skills Education in preparing Kenyan Youth for National Development. *Journal of African Studies in Educational Management and Leadership* Vol: 10, 85-103.

Wainaina, P. K., Arnot, M. & Chege, F. (2011). Developing ethical and democratic citizens in a post-colonial context: citizenship education in Kenya. *Educational Research*, 53(2), 179-192.

Weinstein, H.M., Freedman, S.W., & Hughson, H. (2007). School voices: challenges facing education systems after identity-based conflicts. *Education, citizenship and social justice*, 2(1), 41-71.

Weldon, G. (2010). Post-conflict teacher development: facing the past in South Africa. *Journal of Moral Education*, 39(3), 353-364.

Weldon, G. (2015). South Africa and Rwanda: Remembering or Forgetting? In *Teaching History and the Changing Nation State: Transnational and Intranational Perspectives*, edited by Robert Guyver, 95-114. London: Bloomsbury Academic.

Wertsch, J. V., & Roediger III, H. L. (2008). Collective memory: Conceptual foundations and theoretical approaches. *Memory*, 16(3), 318-326.

Wessels, M. (2013). Cosmology, context and Peace Education. Dans P. Trifonos, & B. Wright, Crital Peace Education. Difficult Dialogues (pp. 90-99). Heidelberg; New-York: Springer.

Yieke, F.A. (2008). *The Discursive Construction of Ethnicity: The Case of the 2007 Kenyan General Election*. Paper presented at the 12th general assembly of Codesria. Yaoundé: 7-11 December 2008.

Yogev, E. (2012). The image of the 1967 war in Israeli history textbooks as test case: Studying an active past in a protracted regional conflict. *Oxford Review of Education, 38*(2): 171-188.

Zembylas, M. (2009). Inventing spaces for critical emotional praxis: The pedagogical challenges of reconciliation and peace. In *Peace education in conflict and post-conflict societies: comparative perspectives* (pp. 183-197). New York: Palgrave Macmillan US.

Zembylas, M. (2012). Suffering, memory and forgiveness: Derrida, Levinas and the pedagogical challenges of reconciliation in Cyprus. In P. Ahluwalia, S. Atkinson, P. Bishop, P. Christie, R. Hattam and J. Matthews (Eds.), *Reconciliation and Pedagogy* (pp. 45-64). New York: Routledge.

Zembylas, M. & Bekerman, Z. (2013). Peace education in the present: dismantling and reconstructing some fundamental theoretical premises. *Journal of Peace Education, 10*(2), 197-214.

Zembylas, M., Charalambous, C., & Charalambous, P. (2016). *Peace education in a conflict-affected society: an ethnographic journey*. Cambridge, Cambridge University Press, 2016.

Zuma, B. (2014). Contact theory and the concept of prejudice: Metaphysical and moral explorations and an epistemological question. *Theory & Psychology, 24*(1), 40-57

Index

3-2-1 strategy 205
additive approach 58
Africa's World War 21, 140
Akan 112
Alliance des Forces Démocratiques pour la Libération du Congo-Zaire, AFDL 140
Allied Democratic Forces – National Army of Liberation of Uganda, ADF-Nalu 141
antagonists 59
Apartheid 33, 36, 40, 48, 53
Babembe 141 141
Bafuliiru 141
Bantu 68, 141
Banyamulenge 141
Banyarwanda 140
Banyindu 141
Bédié, Henri Konan 104, 131
Blé Goudé, Charles 109
Botswana 43, 50, 52
champions 59
citizenship education 41, 56, 109
cognitive dissonance 44
collective memory of conflict 32
Commission de Dialogue, Vérité et Reconciliation, CDVR 106
committed impartiality 57
confident-uncertain-uncomfortable continuum 59
conflict history education 32, 61, 175, 198
conflict history education framework 60, 102, 137, 170, 176, 200
  avoider 61, 177
  container 62, 177
  critical design expert 62, 169, 177
  doing the job 61, 177
  risk-taker 62
conflict narratives 32, 130
Connect-extend-challenge 204
Constructive Controversy Theory 44
contributions approach 58
corporal punishment 36, 38, 162, 181, 195

Côte d'Ivoire 21, 103, 104, 178
  Ivoirité 133
Coulibaly, Amadou Gon 107
critical design expert 58
curricular-instructional gatekeeping 48, 120, 179, 183
Cyprus 48, 49, 53
doing the job 55
Eastern Democratic Republic of Congo 21, 139, 140, 178
education about peace 32, 38
Education aux Droits de l'Homme et à la Citoyenneté, EDHC 109, 116
education for peace 32, 38
Education Justice and Memory Network, EdJAM 165
enhancing heterogeneity 55
ethnic favouritism 94, 99, 180
ethno-empathy 38
exclusive neutrality 56
exclusive partiality 56
fatalists 59
forum theatre 206
Front populaire ivoirien, FPI 105, 131, 134
Gbagbo, Laurent Koudou 105, 131, 180
Genocide Against the Tutsi 59
Guéï, Robert 105
Gur 112
hiding, avoiding 56
historical perspective-taking 39, 175
Houphouët-Boigny, Félix 104, 130
human rights education 41, 109
hustler populism 71
Hutu 36, 40, 140
in-group bias 96
Ivoirité 104, 131
justice-sensitive education 37
Kabila, Joseph 142
Kabila, Laurent-Désiré 140
Kalenjin 68, 69
Kamba 68

Kenya 21, 67, 68, 178, 194
Kenyan African National Union, KANU 69
Kenyatta, Jomo 69
Kenyatta, Uhuru 71
Kibaki, Mwai E.S. 70
Kikuyu 68, 69, 71, 83, 94
Krou 112
leaving the truth open 56
liberation war 140
life skills education 75
Luhya 68, 100
Luo 68, 69, 73, 94
Mai Mai 141
majimbo, majimboism 69
Mandé Nord 112
Mandé Sud 112
March 23rd Movement, M23 141, 148
mediators 58
Mobutism 144
Mobutu, Sese Seko 140
Moi, Daniel arap 69
multicultural education 41, 58, 79, 81, 85, 209
multiperspectivity, multiple perspectives 38, 45, 129, 165, 175, 198, 200
Musyoka, Kalonzo 70
National Dialogue and Reconciliation Accord 70
National Rainbow Coalition, NARC 69
neutral partiality 57
Northern-Ireland 176
Odinga, Jaramogi Oginga 69
Odinga, Raila Amolo 70
Orange Democratic Movement, ODM 70
Ouagadougou Peace Agreement 106
Ouattara, Alassane Dramane 104, 131, 180
participatory pedagogies 42, 162, 181
Parti démocratique de Côte d'Ivoire, PDCI 104, 131, 132
peace education 17, 41, 74
    critical peace education 45
    direct peace education 32, 37, 43, 118, 175, 176
    indirect peace education 32, 38, 42, 114, 150

political generosity 39, 175
Rassemblement Congolais pour la Démocratie, RCD 140
Rassemblement des républicains, RDR 104, 131, 134
ripeness 27
risk-taking continuum 19, 50, 52, 176
    avoider 50, 176
    container 51, 176
    risk-taker 51, 177
Ruto, William K.S.A. 71
Rwanda 36, 39, 54, 59, 183
silent conversation 201
smoothing the edges 56
social action approach 58
sociological time 22, 40, 185, 198
Soro, Guillaume Kigbafori 109, 135
South Africa 33, 36, 37, 40, 48, 52, 199
South Sudan 49
stereotypes, stereotyping 33, 62, 83, 94
Sun City Peace Agreements 141
teacher professional development, TPD 184, 195, 197
transformative approach 58
transformative learning 44
transformers 58
transitional justice 34
transmitters 58
trauma 123
trauma, traumatization, retraumatization 53, 177, 179, 200
truth commission 35
Tshisekedi, Antoine Tshilombo 142
Tutsi 33, 36, 141, 147
Twa 140
Uganda 54
Uprooted 165, 184
Voltaïc 112

www.ingramcontent.com/pod-product-compliance
Ingram Content Group UK Ltd.
Pitfield, Milton Keynes, MK11 3LW, UK
UKHW021848140426
5217IPUK00022B/1656